ALASTAIR SAWDAY'S
SPECIAL PLACES TO STAY

BRITISH
BED & BREAKFAST FOR
GARDEN
LOVERS

Contents

Alastair Sawday Publishing

Our main aim is to publish beautiful guidebooks but, for us, the question of who we are is also important. For who we are shapes the books, the books shape your holidays, and thus are shaped the lives of people who own these 'special places'. So we are trying to be a little more than 'just a publishing company'.

New eco offices

In January 2006 we moved into our new eco offices. With super-insulation, underfloor heating, a wood-pellet boiler, solar panels and a rainwater tank, we have a working environment benign to ourselves and to the environment. Lighting is low-energy, dark corners are lit by sun-pipes and one building is of green oak. Carpet tiles are from Herdwick sheep in the Lake District.

Environmental & ethical policies

We make many other gestures: company cars run on gas or recycled cooking oil; kitchen waste is composted and other waste recycled; cycling and car-sharing are encouraged; the company only buys organic or local food; we don't accept web links with companies we consider unethical; we bank with the ethical Triodos Bank.

We have used recycled paper for some books but have settled on selecting paper and printing for their low energy use. Our printer is British and ISO14001-certified and together we will work to reduce our environmental impact.

In 2005 we won a Business Commitment to the Environment Award and in April 2006 we won a Queen's Award for Enterprise in the Sustainable Development category. All this has boosted our resolve to promote our green policies. Our flagship gesture, however, is carbon offsetting; we calculate our carbon emissions and plant trees to compensate. In future we will support projects overseas that plant trees or reduce carbon use.

Carbon offset

SCAD in South India, supports the poorest of the poor. The money we send to offset our carbon emissions will be used to encourage village tree planting and, eventurally, low-carbon technologies. Why India? Because the money goes a long way and admin costs are very low.
www.salt-of-the-earth.org.uk

Ethics

But why, you may ask, take these things so seriously? You are just a little publishing company, for heaven's sake! Well, is there any good argument for not taking them seriously? The world, by the admission of the vast majority of scientists, is in trouble. If we do not change our ways urgently we will

Who are we?

doom the planet and all its creatures – whether innocent or not – to a variety of possible catastrophes. To maintain the status quo is unacceptable. Business does much of the damage and should undo it, and provide new models.

Pressure on companies to produce Corporate Social Responsibility policies is mounting. We are trying to keep ahead of it all, yet still to be as informal and human as possible – the antithesis of 'corporate'.

The books – and a dilemma

So, we have created fine books that do good work. They promote authenticity, individuality and good local and organic food – a far cry from corporate culture. Rural economies, pubs, small farms, villages and hamlets all benefit. However, people use fossil fuel to get there. Should we aim to get our readers to offset their own carbon emissions, and the B&B and hotel owners too?

We are gradually introducing green ideas into the books: the Fine Breakfast scheme that highlights British and Irish B&B owners who use local and organic food; celebrating those who make an extra environmental effort; gently encouraging the use of public transport, cycling and walking. This year we published a *Green Places to Stay* focusing on responsible travel and eco-properties around the globe.

Our Fragile Earth series

The 'hard' side of our environmental publishing is the Fragile Earth series: *The Little Earth Book, The Little Food Book* and *The Little Money Book.* They consist of bite-sized essays, polemical, hard-hitting and well researched. They are a 'must have' for anyone who seeks clarity about some of the key issues of our time. This year we have also published *One Planet Living.*

Lastly – what is special?

The notion of 'special' is at the heart of what we do, and highly subjective. We discuss this in the introduction. We take huge pleasure from finding people and places that do their own thing – brilliantly; places that are unusual and follow no trends; places of peace and beauty; people who are kind and interesting – and genuine.

We seem to have touched a nerve with thousands of readers; they obviously want to stay in special places rather than the dull corporate monstrosities that have disfigured so many of our cities and towns. Life is too short to be wasted in the wrong places. A night in a special place can be a transforming experience.

Alastair Sawday

Acknowledgements

Nicola Crosse researched this book, did many of the inspections, wrote most of it and then put it all together. It is unfair to call her Editor; she is much more. She has done it all with unshakable good humour and determination.

Helping her have been Wendy Ogden and Jan Tomlinson, solidly supportive in their administrative roles. Inspiration has come from Tom Germain and Andreea Petre Goncalves who grow veg so well on our company allotment and have helped Nicola to get her hands dirty at critical moments of stress. Jo Boissevain has contributed the lovely article on gardening books and helped with literary tweaking.

Alastair Sawday

Series Editor Alastair Sawday

Editor Nicola Crosse

Assistants to Editor Wendy Ogden, Jan Tomlinson

Editorial Director Annie Shillito

Writing Nicola Crosse, Viv Cripps, Wendy Ogden

Inspections Jan Adam, David Ashby, Abigail Ballinger, Tom Bell, Neil Brown, Angie Collings, Nicola Crosse, Trish Dugmore, Becca Harris, Vicky Irving, Kim Mattia, Vickie McIver, Aideen Reid, Bea Shuttleworth, Jan Tomlinson, Bridget Truman

Accounts **Bridget Bishop,** Jessica Britton, Christine Buxton, Sandra Hasell, Sally Ranahan

Editorial **Jackie King,** Jo Boissevain, Florence Oldfield, Maria Serrano, Rebecca Stevens, Danielle Williams

Production **Julia Richardson,** Rachel Coe, Tom Germain, Rebecca Thomas, Allys Williams

Sales & Marketing & PR **Siobhán Flynn,** Andreea Petre Goncalves, Sarah Bolton

Web & IT **Russell Wilkinson,** Chris Banks, Isabelle Deakin, Joe Green, Brian Kimberling

Previous Editors James Belsey, Sue Colquhoun

And many thanks to those people who did the odd inspection or write-up

Interest in gardening seems to grow as dramatically as Japanese knotweed. No wonder, when it is such a powerful antidote to anxiety and stress. We are entitled to be envious of those whose gardens have a place in this book, for they must be at peace while at work.

This book brings you into the privileged circle of those who have put gardening at the heart of their lives – brilliantly – and combined this with a genuine willingness to receive visitors into their houses as guests. It is an extraordinary combination How could you otherwise invite yourselves to stay in beautiful houses surrounded by beautiful gardens?

Fourteen of these gardens are in the Good Gardens guide – quite an achievement. Thirty-three of them are open under the National Gardens Scheme. Many of them deserve to feature in our special Green Pages, though only six do. Nearly all of them go to great lengths to encourage wildlife; talk of badgers, buzzards, kestrels, sparrow-hawks, deer, hedgehogs and other beasts is common in their applications to us. (They rarely mention slugs, rabbits, crows and jays – but perhaps these are taken for granted.) It is clearly difficult to be a gardener and ignore nature

and its demands. So this book fits neatly with our growing interest in the environment.

The houses here are remarkable too. There are oak barns, cottages, manors, old rectories galore, seaside houses and townhouses, buildings ancient and modern – all in solid possession of the Special quality we look for in all our places. Most of these houses are lovely in their own right – gardens or no gardens.

This is an exceptional book – the only one of its kind in the world, I believe.

Alastair Sawday

Introduction

FROM HUGE ESTATES AND PARKLANDS TO COTTAGE GARDENS, TOWN GARDENS AND MODEST SUBURBAN PATCHES

What joy! We have an allotment at work. For years I have lived with a tiny shady town garden which seems inclined only to grow ferns, euphorbias and oodles of evergreen shrubs. All else (particularly flowers) is dispatched with ruthless efficiency by the battalions of slugs and snails that patrol my little tranche of Eden. I once put out, in a pot, some carefully grown-from-seed runner bean plants and scattered some slug pellets around before smugly retiring. Let them get through those, I thought, and slept the sort of sleep that Tom and Barbara in *The Good Life* must have slept.

In the morning: no slug pellets, no bodies, not even a stalk left of those carefully grown-from-seed runner beans. The pot had gum marks in it.

Finding and killing the culprits was out of the question; like Afghanistani guerrillas sneaking off to the hills my militant molluscs have a high wall with hidey-holes in it, and thickly brambled woods to bivouac down in. And, alarmingly, they have strategy. So they win – and under their vegetable-free thumb I well and truly am.

No such threat exists on the plot of land here at the Old Farmyard. While the builders were in, the space was used as a bit of a dumping ground and, when Alastair wistfully suggested it could be the perfect spot for an allotment, we couldn't picture it. We forgot, however, that a Sawday is not easily thwarted and found him a few days later furiously digging at the hard stony earth and then carefully planting some raspberry bushes. The boss had launched the project.

An allotment team was hastily scrambled. Early meetings were jolly affairs fuelled by smoking and posturing. Should we have Versailles-shaped diamonds for the beds? Perhaps some sculpture in the middle? Drawings and diagrams were pondered, books looked at and ideas discussed.

Photo left and bottom right Tom Germain
Photos top right Jo Boissevain

Introduction

By the fourth meeting, when we were loftily discussing Sartre and Kant and wondering whether vegetables could exist when you are not looking at them, somebody mentioned that the planting season would soon be over. Panic ensued. We had no tools, no seeds, no beds, no idea and a boulder-strewn grassy area that we had told *everybody* was going to be a productive vegetable patch this year.

The boss came to the rescue with a £50 donation to get us started. The Trust team (see back of book for details) had just donated some money to a city farm in Bristol and in return they were happy to send a young man and a rotivator to us for a few hours; he even gave us some strawberry plants. At last things were moving. Now we only had to make some beds – and handily the wooden picnic tables and benches from our old offices were wobbling and moulding and aching to be recyled.

There is only one man on the allotment team. His name is Tom and he has achieved almost iconic status (at least among the allotment team ladies). Within two lunch hours and with limited tools he had broken the wood into long planks. Then Andreea (the only one among us who has a clue about growing veg) and Julia dug trenches and created five beautiful oblong beds. When they were finished we got rid of the final

weeds, thoroughly composted the beds (with our own kitchen compost) and laid bark chippings in between them. They were ready.

Seeds were carefully planted and kept indoors to give them the best chance of success. Tomatoes, lettuce, carrots, leeks, cabbages, runner beans, courgettes and pumpkins lay dormant on the accounts department window in their cosy soil beds. The sun failed to shine for a few days. Nothing happened. We watered them frequently and sang to them a bit (well, that was only me actually) and still nothing happened. Imagine our excitement when, one Monday morning, we saw that they had not just sprouted but were aiming for the ceiling. As soon as they were thinned out the remaining plants grew well, and at last it was time to transplant them outdoors. They looked tiny in the bare beds but grew rapidly to fill the spaces in between (especially the courgettes and pumpkins which we realise we need to give more space to next year).

It hasn't all been plain sailing. The first and second lot of runner beans were lost to an unknown pest in spite of much protection from nets and environmentally friendly pellets. The third lot are thriving but it is so late in the season we are not sure whether we will have many beans from them. Carrots were a success story, as were all the salad leaves and lettuce, but cabbages both red and green have been systematically destroyed by caterpillars, and the strawberries nabbed by birds. We made the mistake of planting the tomatoes too closely together and so they will probably have to be used for chutney unless a miracle happens. But we can sell the chutney to add to our fund.

One thing it made us all feel is that we are glad we are not earning our living growing veg and fruit. There are so many pitfalls and it is hard work keeping an eye on things all the time, even with several of us to care for it. During a long and hot July we had to water as frequently as possible to keep things from being crisped, which involved many trips to the pond with watering cans.

It is September now, and things are beginning to calm down. Apart from pumpkins and leeks we will have nothing to harvest in the autumn (the lacy cabbages do not count) so we must start to think about what we could possibly grow for the winter, and about what we would like to plant for next year. With any luck we will make different mistakes instead of the same ones, and learn a tiny bit more.

Clever Andreea has made a profit of £34.75p by selling the veg and fruit

to colleagues at work and we think the patch looks attractive as you enter the drive – especially the runner-bean bamboo poles which add a rustic note. But the main joy has been being outdoors (especially on a sunny day) and working alongside others for a common purpose. We are grateful to Alastair for getting us started and to the Trust Team for enabling us to be rotivated free of charge and we hope to move on to bigger and better things next year.

Green entries

Many of the owners in this book will be providing you with things they have grown in their own gardens, whether they be just-picked vegetables at dinner or homemade jams at breakfast. In this edition, six owners who have made a particular effort to be kind to the environment have entries marked with a Special

Introduction

Green Entry stamp. That is not to say that others in the book are not making efforts, too; we plan to expand the green entries with each edition.

Choosing our special places

We visit them, sometimes stay overnight and sometimes eat, we chat to the owners and we take a good look around. The people in our books matter to us as much as the places. Unlike most other guide books – and tourist boards – who are more concerned with rules and regulations, we believe that a genuinely warm welcome, good (preferably organic or locally sourced) food, a really comfortable bed and a relaxed atmosphere are more important than the odd threadbare rug or dog hair on the sofa. There is great variety in our books, too; simple farmhouses, Palladian mansions, cottages, modern bungalows, townhouses and flats all put in an appearance. And they all reflect their owner's tastes, so you may expect everything from chintz and flowers to snazzy minimalism. You will see some fabulous art, sculptures and carvings from all over the world, gleaming antiques and family memorabilia. And, in this particular book, you will find the best gardens in the land.

A garden to explore is part of the package at these places, from huge estates and parklands to cottage gardens, town gardens and modest suburban patches. The owners are all garden lovers who love sharing their knowledge and experience with others. Anyone who has ever enjoyed growing something, whether it be a pot plant or a row of peas, can call themselves a garden lover. In these places you will meet owners with gardens at different stages of development: some will be finished masterpieces, others will be works in progress, all will be talking points. Our owners are experts on their own gardens and also can often organise private visits to other gardens, direct you to good local nurseries and give you the low-down on which public gardens to visit nearby. Armed with this book, *The Yellow Book* and *The Good Gardens Guide*, you have a vast choice of gardens and places to stay.

How we go about it

Our criteria are our own. We visit every place and choose only those places that we like, then write about them honestly so that you can take what you like and leave the rest. We don't all like the same things and this book celebrates diversity. Writing each entry can be challenging; we try to avoid brochure-speak and cliché and we try to be honest, and this can lead to the odd clash with an owner. So, while we are happy to correct factual errors or include important facts we have missed, the descriptions are written by us. As a result, our readers trust us.

Introduction

Subscriptions

Owners pay to appear in this guide. Their fee goes towards the high costs of inspecting and producing an all-colour book and maintaining a sophisticated web site. We only include places that we like and find special for one reason or another. It is not possible for anyone to buy their way onto these pages.

What to expect

Not a hotel! These are people's homes. Most of our owners say they love having 'Sawday people' to stay because, among other things, they understand the rules of B&B. And what are these rules? It would be impolite to arrive too early (generally arrival is after 4pm) and rude to over-stay (departure by 11am). You shouldn't expect room service, your bags to be carried or your shoes to be polished, breakfast will be most likely at a shared table and you are unlikely to have a key to your bedroom door. From time to time the best-laid plans will come unstuck so, if you know you are going to arrive late, do telephone and warn the owners, especially if you have booked dinner. Some hosts are happy for guests to roam the garden alone, others want to be there with you. Some may be generous with cuttings, others charge or prefer not to. Good manners and humour will go a long way in the house and the garden.

Finding the right place for you

In our Quick Reference indices at the back of the book we list those owners:
● who have wheelchair access
● who let you stay all day
● whose houses are within ten miles of a coach or train station and who can arrange collection so you don't have to drive
● from whom you can buy cuttings
● who have double rooms for £70 or under
● who can stable your horse

How to use this book

Look at the map in the front of the book, find the area you wish to visit and find the nearest houses by number. In cities, check individual entries for their position. Don't use the maps as anything other than a rough guide or you will get lost.

Rooms

Usually double, twin, family or single. Sometimes these can be juggled, or extra beds added (for three or more people). Do ask.

Bathrooms

Bathroom details are only mentioned if they are *not* en suite or if they are shared between rooms (usually to members of the same party only).

Prices

We give the per room price not the per person price. The 'singles' rate shows what is charged if you take a double room for yourself. Do remember that this book will last for two years so prices may change.

Some of our houses offer a discount for stays of more than two or three nights. Others may charge supplements at certain times of the year or during certain events (like Glyndebourne or the Edinburgh Festival). Book early for popular holidays or if you know you want a particular room.

Breakfast

Unless we say otherwise, breakfast will be included in the room price. In many cases this will be a feast of fresh fruit, homemade muesli, cereals, freshly baked bread and a choice of something cooked, from kedgeree to local bacon and sausages. Many of our owners either have their own hens or buy locally so eggs will be fresh and delicious, and jams and marmalades are nearly always homemade. Often you will have breakfast at the same table as other guests, and sometimes you can have it in your room or in the garden. If these things are important, then check before booking.

Symbols

At the back of the book we explain the symbols at the bottom of the pages for each entry. Remember that they are just a guide and owners

Photo The Wagon House, entry 12

may be prepared to bend their own rules from time to time.

Children

The ♟ symbol is given to those properties that accept children of any age. Don't assume, though, that these places have all the equipment your child may need.

Dogs

The ☚ symbol is given to those properties that allow pets to sleep in the room with you, but not on the bed. Places that do not have the pet symbol are sometimes happy for your pet to come with you, but they may have to sleep outside in a kennel or in your car. Ask when you book, and do be honest about the size and nature of your dog.

Smoking

A ✗ symbol means you cannot smoke anywhere in the house. If you are a smoker, you may get to know the garden a little better, but take a small tin for your ends; don't hurl them into a border and hope they won't be seen.

Introduction

Dinner

Apart from breakfast, don't expect to be provided with any other meals unless you arrange them; even owners who regularly do dinner or packed lunches require notice. Prices for dinner are quoted per person. Very few of our houses are licensed but many of our owners will offer a drink before, and wine during, dinner. Some places are happy for you to bring your own wine, but do ask.

Booking

Bookings are usually made by phone. This gives you the chance to discuss any particular requirements and to get the feel of the people and place. It's a good idea to get written confirmation of the room booked, the price for B&B and for meals. State roughly what time you think you will arrive, especially if you have booked dinner. You may be asked to pay a deposit which may be non-refundable. Be sure you know what their policy is – the contract is between you and the owner.

Cancellations

If you have to cancel your booking, telephone as soon as possible. You may lose part or all of your deposit and, depending on how late the cancellation is made, may have to pay part of the cost of your booking. Again, the contract is between you and the owner, so do check.

Payment

All our owners take cash and cheques with a cheque card. Those owners who accept credit cards have been given the appropriate symbol. Check that yours is acceptable.

Tipping

Owners do not expect tips. If you are overwhelmed with gratitude then a thank you letter or a small gift is always a delight.

Internet

www.specialplacestostay.com has online pages for all the special places featured here and from all our other books – around 5,000 in total. There's a searchable database, a taster of the write-ups and colour photos. And look out for our dedicated web site on self-catering in England, Scotland and Wales, www.special-escapes.co.uk. For more details, see the back of the book.

Disclaimer

We make no claims to pure objectivity in choosing our Special Places. They are here because we like them. Our opinions and tastes are ours alone and this book is a statement of them; we hope that you will share them. We have done our utmost to get our facts right and

Introduction

we apologise unreservedly for any errors that may have crept in.

We do not check such things as fire alarms, swimming pool security or any other regulation with which owners of properties receiving paying guests should comply. This is the responsibility of the owners.

Feedback

Feedback from you is invaluable and we always act upon comments, which may be sent by letter or email to info@sawdays.co.uk. Or you can visit our web site and write to us from there. With your help and our own inspections we can maintain our reputation for dependability.

Poor reports are followed up with the owners in question: we need to hear both sides of the story.

Really worrying reports lead to incognito visits, after which we may exclude a place. As a general rule, do mention any problems that arise to the relevant people during your stay; they are the only ones who can do anything about such things and may be able to resolve them on the spot.

Owners are informed when we receive substantially positive reports about them and recommendations are followed up with inspection visits where appropriate. If your recommendation leads us to include a place, you receive a free copy of the edition in which it first appears.

So tell us if your stay has been a joy or not, if the atmosphere was great or stuffy, whether the owners or staff were cheery or bored. We aim to celebrate human kindness, fine architecture, real food, history and landscape, and hope that these books may be a passport to memorable experiences.

I very much hope you enjoy staying at these special places and meeting the owners. Remember that they are usually hugely knowledgeable about gardens to visit, too, and can sometimes organise visits to gardens that are not usually open to the public. So do ask! Happy travels.

Nicola Crosse

Photo South Newington House, entry 82

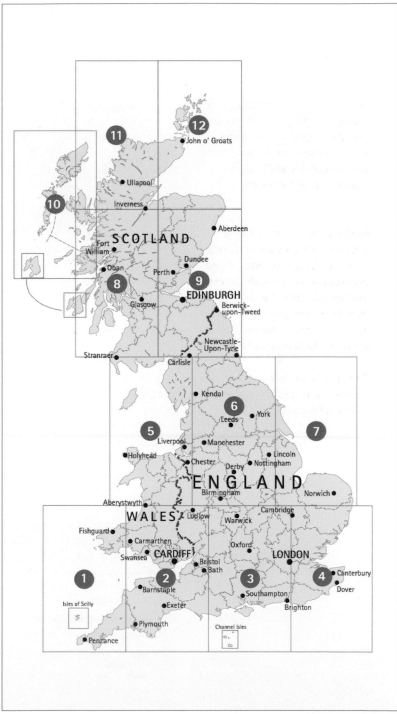

Map 1

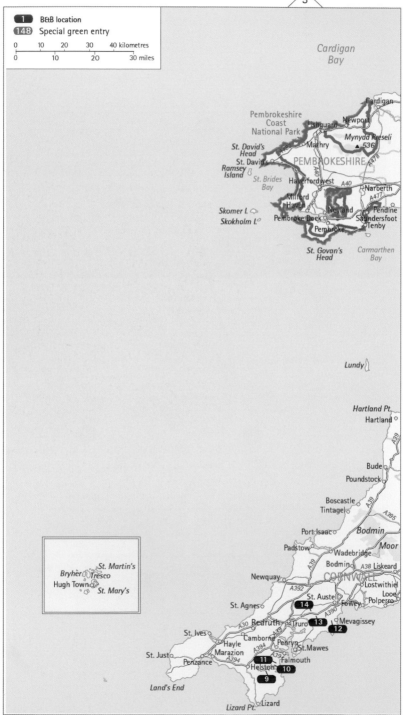

1 B&B location
148 Special green entry

0   10   20   30   40 kilometres
0   10   20   30 miles

Cardigan
Bay

Pembrokeshire
Coast
National Park

Cardigan
Fishguard   Newport
Mathry   Mynydd Preseli
▲ 536
St. David's
Head
St. David's   PEMBROKESHIRE
Ramsey
Island   St. Brides
Bay   Haverfordwest   A40   Narberth
A477
Milford   Pendine
Haven   Neyland   Saundersfoot
Skomer I.   Pembroke Dock   Tenby
Skokholm I.   Pembroke
St. Govan's   Carmarthen
Head   Bay

Lundy

Hartland Pt.
Hartland

A39

Bude
Poundstock

Boscastle   A39
Tintagel   A395

Port Isaac   Bodmin
Padstow   Moor
Wadebridge
Bodmin   A38 Liskeard
Newquay   CORNWALL
A392   Lostwithiel
St. Austell   Looe
St. Agnes   **14**   Fowey   Polperro
A390
A30 Redruth   Truro   **13**   Mevagissey
St. Ives   **12**
Camborne   Penryn
St. Just   Hayle   A394   St. Mawes
Marazion   A39
Penzance   A394   Falmouth
Helston   **10**
11
9
Land's End

St. Martin's
Bryher   Tresco
Hugh Town   St. Mary's

Lizard Pt.   Lizard

Map 2

23

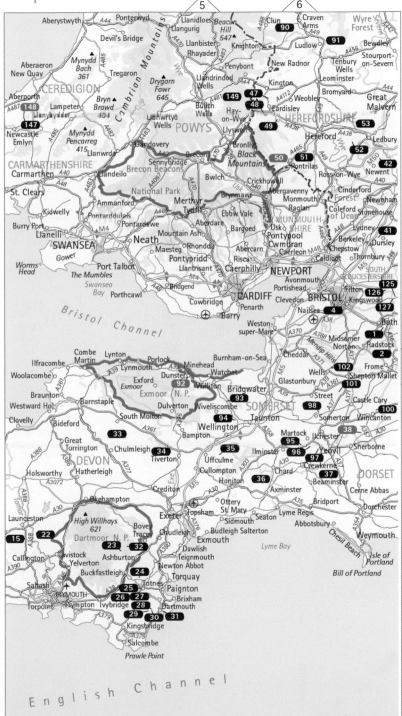

©Maidenhead Cartographic, 2006

Map 3

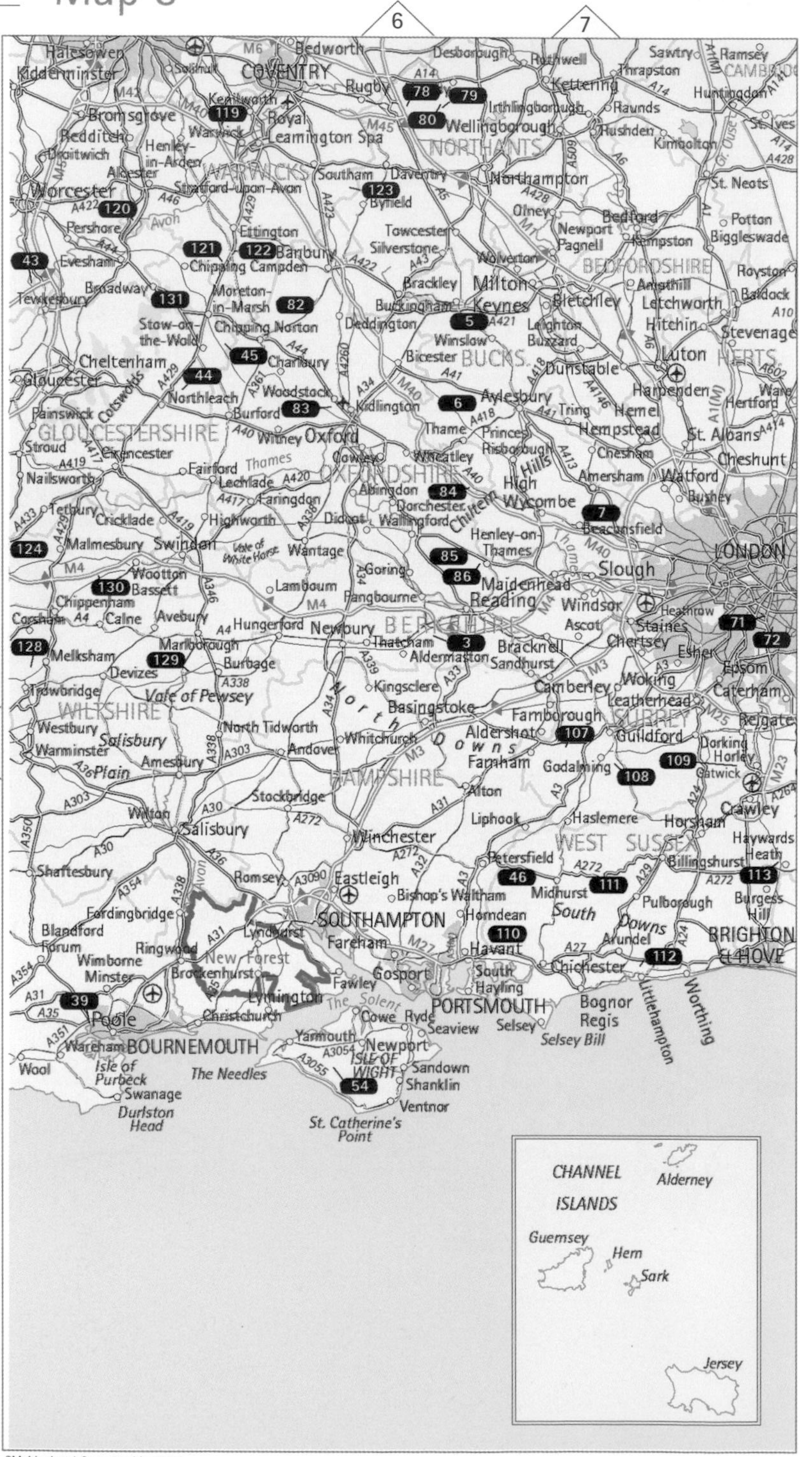

6 7

Halesowen
Kidderminster
Bromsgrove
Redditch
Droitwich
Henley-in-Arden
Alcester
Worcester
Pershore
Evesham 43
Broadway
Tewkesbury
Stow-on-the-Wold
Cheltenham
Gloucester
Painswick
Northleach
Stroud
Cirencester
Nailsworth
Fairford
Lechlade
Tetbury
Cricklade
Malmesbury 124
Highworth
Swindon
Wootton Bassett 130
Chippenham
Corsham
Calne
128
Melksham
Devizes
Trowbridge
Westbury
Warminster
Salisbury
Wilton
Shaftesbury
Fordingbridge
Blandford Forum
Wimborne Minster 39
Ringwood
Poole
Wool
Isle of Purbeck
Swanage
Durlston Head

COVENTRY
Kenilworth 119
Royal Leamington Spa
Warwick
Southam
Stratford-upon-Avon
WARWICKS
120
121
Chipping Campden 122
Moreton-in-Marsh 131
Chipping Norton 82
Stow
45
Charlbury
Woodstock 83
Witney
Oxford
OXFORDSHIRE
Abingdon 84
Dorchester
Wallingford
Goring 85
Pangbourne 86
Reading
BERKSHIRE
Newbury
Thatcham 3
Aldermaston
Kingsclere
Basingstoke
Whitchurch
Andover
North Tidworth
HAMPSHIRE
Stockbridge
Winchester
Eastleigh
Romsey
Bishop's Waltham
SOUTHAMPTON
Fareham
Gosport
Lymington
Brockenhurst
New Forest
Lyndhurst
Christchurch
BOURNEMOUTH
Wareham
Yarmouth
Cowes
Newport
ISLE OF WIGHT 54
Sandown
Shanklin
Ventnor
St. Catherine's Point
The Needles

Bedworth
Rugby
78 79
80 Wellingborough
Irthlingborough
NORTHANTS
Northampton
Olney
Towcester
Silverstone
Brackley
Buckingham
Deddington
Bicester
5
Winslow
BUCKS
Aylesbury 6
Thame
Princes Risborough
High Wycombe
Henley-on-Thames
Maidenhead
Windsor
Ascot
Bracknell
Sandhurst
Camberley
Farnborough
Aldershot 107
Farnham
Godalming 108
Alton
Liphook
Haslemere
Petersfield
46
Midhurst
111
Horndean
110
Havant
South Hayling
PORTSMOUTH
Seaview
Selsey
Selsey Bill

Desborough
Rothwell
Kettering
Thrapston
NORTHANTS
Rushden
Higham Ferrers
Bedford
Newport Pagnell
Milton Keynes
Bletchley
BEDFORDSHIRE
Leighton Buzzard
Dunstable
Luton
HERTS
Harpenden
Hemel Hempstead
St. Albans
Chesham
Amersham
Watford
Beaconsfield
Slough
LONDON
Staines
Heathrow
Chertsey
Esher
Woking
SURREY
Guildford
109
Gatwick
WEST SUSSEX
Pulborough
Arundel
Chichester 112
Bognor Regis
Littlehampton
Worthing
BRIGHTON & HOVE

Sawtry
Ramsey
CAMBS
Huntingdon
St. Ives
St. Neots
Potton
Biggleswade
Royston
Baldock
Hitchin
Stevenage
Ware
Hertford
Cheshunt
Bushey
71
72
Epsom
Caterham
Leatherhead
Dorking
Horley
Reigate
Crawley
Haywards Heath
Billingshurst 113
Burgess Hill

CHANNEL ISLANDS
Alderney
Guernsey
Herm
Sark
Jersey

©Maidenhead Cartographic, 2006

Map 4

25

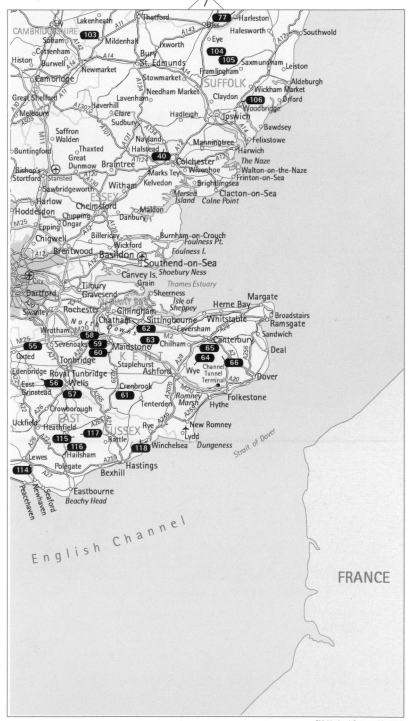

Map 5

8   9

Stranraer
Portpatrick
Glenluce
A75
Wigtown
Gatehouse of Fleet
Dalbeattie
Kirkcudbright
Carlisle

The Rhins
Luce Bay
The Machars
Port William
Whithorn
Wigtown Bay
Wigton
A596
Wigton

Solway Firth

Drummore
Burrow Head
Aspatria

Mull of Galloway
Maryport
Cockermouth
CUMBRIA
Penrith

Workington
A66
A595
Keswick
Ullswater
Helvellyn
949
A592

Whitehaven
St. Bees Head
St. Bees
Egremont
Cleator Moor
Scafell Pike
978
Lake
Cumbrian Mountains
Grasmere
Ambleside
Lake District
National Park

Point of Ayre
Ravenglass
District
Windermere
Newby Bridge

Isle of Man
Ramsey
A3
A2
Laxey
Broughton-in-Furness
16
17
Milnthorpe
18

Peel
A4
A1
Millom
Dalton-in-Furness
Ulverston
A590

Port Erin
A3
A5
Douglas
Barrow-in-Furness
Morecambe Bay
Carnforth

Castletown
Isle of Walney
Morecambe
Heysham

Irish Sea
Fleetwood
Cleveleys
Garstang
Thornton

Poulton-le-Fylde
M55
BLACKPOOL
Kirkham

Lytham St. Anne's
A59

Southport
Formby
Ormskirk
Skelmersdale

Liverpool Bay
Crosby
Wallasey
Kirkby
St. Helens

Amlwch
Great Ormes Head
Hoylake
Birkenhead
LIVERPOOL
Widnes
Runcorn

Holyhead
Holy Island
ANGLESEY ISLE
Benllech
Llandudno
Colwyn Bay
Rhyl
Prestatyn
Heswall
Neston
Helsby

Valley
Menai Beaumaris
Conwy
Abergele
Rhuddlan
Holywell
Flint
Chester

Rhosneigr
Llangefni
Bridge
Bangor
Llanfairfechan
St. Asaph
Denbigh
FLINTSHIRE
Mold
Buckley
A51

Bethesda
Capel Curig
CONWY
Llanrwst
Bylchau
Ruthin
8
Llay
Holt

Caernarfon
Snowdon
1085
Betws-y-Coed
Pentrefoelas
DENBIGHSHIRE
Wrexham
Malpas

Nefyn
Lleyn Peninsula
Blaenau Ffestiniog
Bala
A5
Llangollen
Ruabon
Overton

Criccieth
Ffestiniog
Snowdonia
National
Park
Bala Lake
A494
Corwen
Chirk
Ellesmere
Whittington
Wem

Caernarfon Bay
Menai Strait
A487
Pwllheli
Porthmadog
Trawsfynydd
Lake Vyrnwy
Oswestry

Aberdaron
Abersoch
Harlech
GWYNEDD
Dolgellau
Llanfyllin
Shrewsbury

Bardsey Island
Tremadog Bay
Barmouth
Cader Idris
892
Welshpool
Minsterley
88

Barmouth Bay
Mallwyd
Llanfair Caereinion
Montgomery
SHROPSHIRE

Tywyn
Aberdovey
A493
Machynlleth
Moelfre
468
Caersws
Bishop's Castle
Church Stretton

Borth
Talybont
Cambrian Mountains
Newtown

Map 6

27

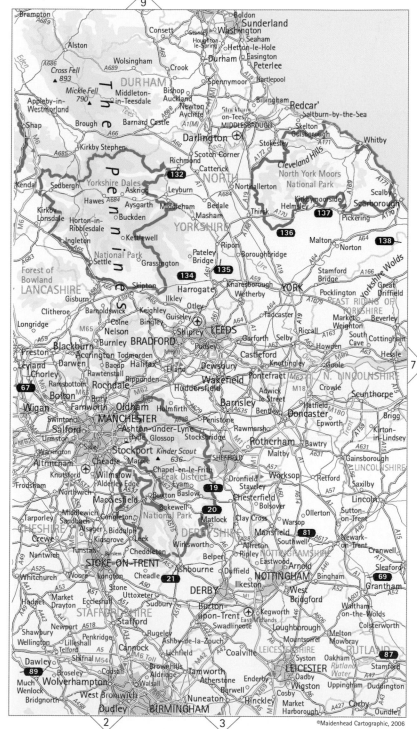

©Maidenhead Cartographic, 2006

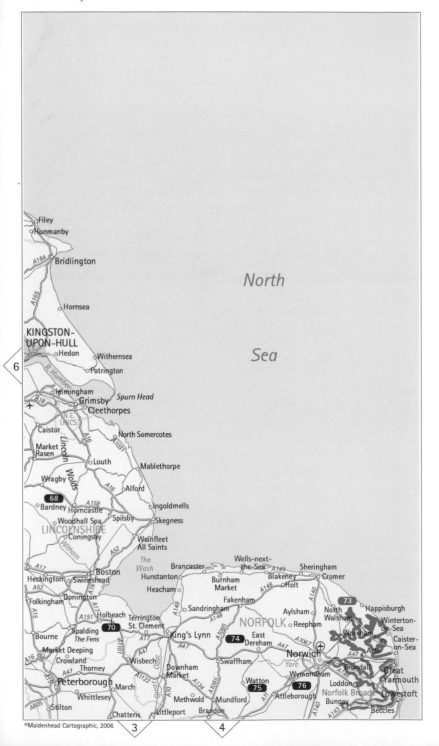

Map 8

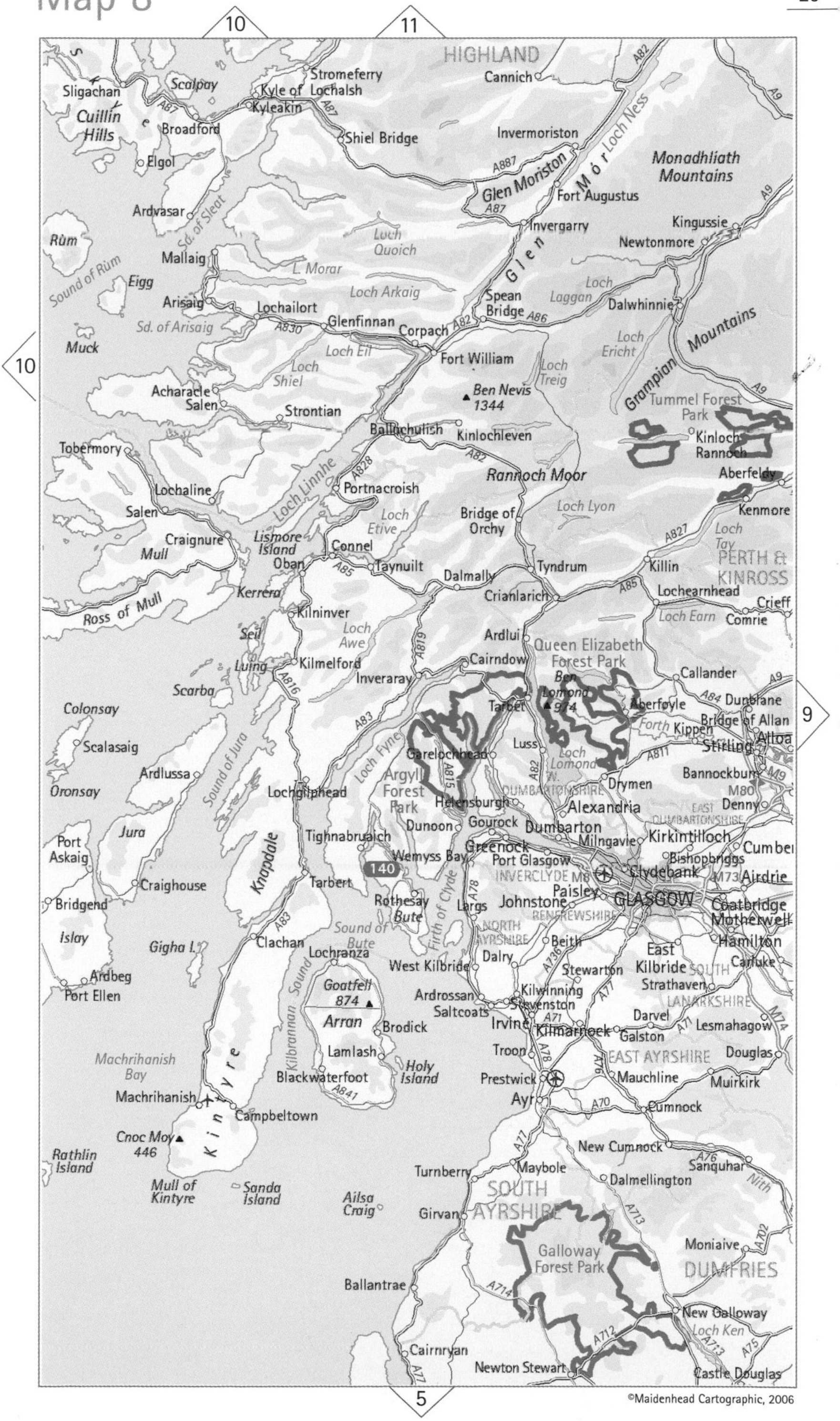
10
11
HIGHLAND
Cannich
A82
A9
Sligachan
Scalpay
Stromeferry
Kyle of Lochalsh
Kyleakin
Cuillin Hills
A87
Broadford
Shiel Bridge
Invermoriston
Loch Ness
Monadhliath Mountains
Elgol
A887
Glen Moriston
Fort Augustus
Ardvasar
Sd. of Sleat
Glen Mòr
Invergarry
Kingussie
Rùm
Loch Quoich
Newtonmore
Mallaig
L. Morar
Sound of Rùm
Eigg
Loch Arkaig
Spean Bridge
Loch Laggan
Arisaig
Lochailort
A86
Dalwhinnie
Sd. of Arisaig
A830
Glenfinnan
Corpach
Grampian Mountains
Muck
Loch Eil
Loch Ericht
10
Fort William
Loch Shiel
Loch Treig
Acharacle
Ben Nevis
1344
Salen
Strontian
Tummel Forest Park
Ballachulish
Kinlochleven
Kinloch Rannoch
Tobermory
A828
A82
Rannoch Moor
Aberfeldy
Loch Linnhe
Lochaline
Portnacroish
Salen
Loch Etive
Bridge of Orchy
Loch Lyon
Kenmore
Craignure
Lismore Island
Mull
Connel
A827
Loch Tay
Oban
A85
Taynuilt
Tyndrum
Killin
PERTH & KINROSS
Dalmally
Kerrera
Crianlarich
Lochearnhead
Ross of Mull
Crieff
Kilninver
Loch Earn
Comrie
Seil
Loch Awe
A819
Ardlui
Queen Elizabeth Forest Park
Luing
Kilmelford
Cairndow
Scarba
Inveraray
Ben Lomond
974
Callander
A816
Tarbet
Aberfoyle
A84
Dunblane
9
Colonsay
A83
Forth
Kippen
Bridge of Allan
Alloa
Scalasaig
Garelochhead
Luss
Loch Lomond
Stirling
Sound of Jura
Loch Fyne
A811
Ardlussa
A815
A82
Bannockburn
M9
Oronsay
Argyll Forest Park
Drymen
M80
Lochgilphead
Helensburgh
DUMBARTONSHIRE
Alexandria
EAST DUNBARTONSHIRE
Denny
Jura
Dunoon
Gourock
Dumbarton
Port Askaig
Tighnabruaich
Greenock
Milngavie
Kirkintilloch
Cumbe
Knapdale
140
Wemyss Bay
Port Glasgow
Bishopbriggs
Craighouse
Tarbert
INVERCLYDE
M8
Clydebank
M73
Airdrie
Bridgend
Paisley
Rothesay
Bute
A78
Largs
Johnstone
GLASGOW
Coatbridge
RENFREWSHIRE
Motherwell
Islay
Gigha I.
A83
Sound of Bute
Firth of Clyde
NORTH AYRSHIRE
Beith
Hamilton
Clachan
Lochranza
East Kilbride
West Kilbride
Dalry
A736
Stewarton
Carluke
Ardbeg
SOUTH LANARKSHIRE
Port Ellen
Goatfell
874
Kilwinning
Strathaven
Ardrossan
Stevenston
A77
Kilbrannan Sound
Arran
Saltcoats
A71
Darvel
M74
Brodick
Irvine
Kilmarnock
Galston
Lesmahagow
Machrihanish Bay
Kintyre
Lamlash
Troon
A78
EAST AYRSHIRE
Douglas
Holy Island
A76
Blackwaterfoot
Prestwick
Mauchline
Muirkirk
Machrihanish
A841
Ayr
A70
Cumnock
Campbeltown
Cnoc Moy
446
A77
New Cumnock
Rathlin Island
Turnberry
Maybole
A76
Sanquhar
Dalmellington
Nith
Mull of Kintyre
Sanda Island
SOUTH AYRSHIRE
Ailsa Craig
Girvan
A713
Moniaive
A702
Galloway Forest Park
DUMFRIES
Ballantrae
A714
New Galloway
Loch Ken
A712
A713
A75
Cairnryan
A77
Newton Stewart
Castle Douglas
5

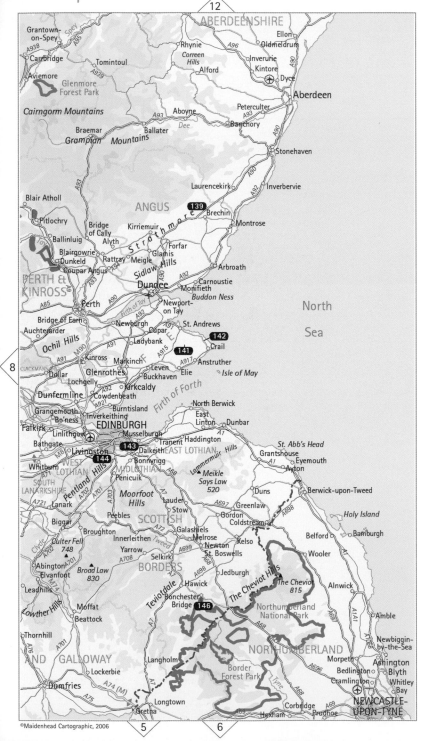

©Maidenhead Cartographic, 2006

Map 10

31

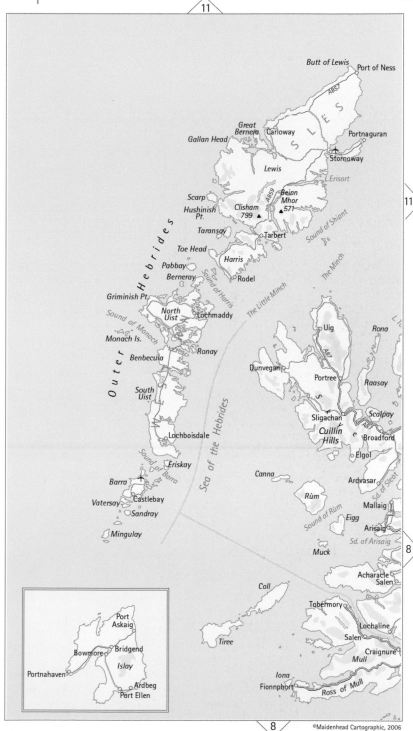

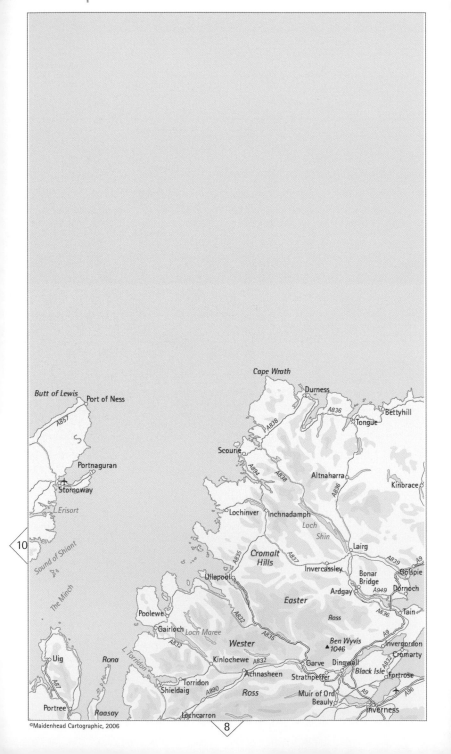

Map 12

33

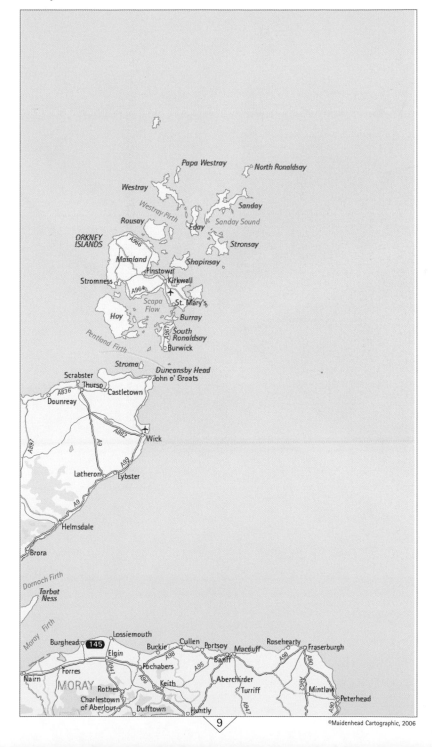

©Maidenhead Cartographic, 2006

England

Grey Lodge

Jane & Anthony Stickland
Grey Lodge,
Summer Lane,
Combe Down,
Bath, Bath & N.E. Somerset BA2 7EU

tel   01225 832069
fax   01225 830161
email   greylodge@freenet.co.uk
web   www.greylodge.co.uk

An encyclopaedic knowledge of plants and a collector's delight in finding new treasures have inspired Jane and Anthony's south-west-facing terraced garden. The structure was laid out when the house was built in the 1860s, and their most cherished inheritance, a magnificent *Robinia pseudacia*, was probably planted then. For 39 years they have been adding to the garden's attractions, planting the series of borders with labour-saving in mind, since they do most of the work themselves. It's a garden that's great fun to explore because of its sloping layout and secret paths. The large lawn at the upper level leads to another — and another. A vine planted on the main terrace wall in 1973 now covers 14 yards of wall in three tiers and a fan-trained apricot nestles beside it. Jane caught the climbing rose bug some years ago, hence the very large 'Paul's Himalayan Musk'. There are more than 70 old roses; plants with scented leaves and flowers are much loved. The soil is free-draining alkaline, so sun lovers like cistus, hebe, euphorbia and phormium have been chosen for the more open areas. Play boules or soak up the sun and scents on the main lawn, chat to your hosts about special plants, discover botanical treasures. A garden lover's garden with interesting plants to enjoy in every season.

rooms	3: 2 twins/doubles, 1 family room.
price	£75–£85. Singles £45–£50.
meals	Pub/restaurant 2 miles.
closed	Rarely.
directions	From A36, 3 miles out of Bath on Warminster road, take uphill road by lights & Viaduct Inn. 1st left, 100 yds, signed Monkton Combe. After village, house 1st on left; 0.5 miles on.

Map 2 Entry 1

You are in a conservation area, yet just five minutes from the centre of Bath. And the views: breathtaking from wherever you stand. The steep valley rolls out ahead of you from most of the rooms and from the garden comes a confusion and a profusion of scents and colours. The friendly and likeable Sticklands are conservationists too and have a Green Certificate to prove it. Breakfasts are a feast: bacon and eggs, cereals, home-grown jam, fresh fruit. Jane will tell you all about excellent local gardens to visit. *Family room has adjoining room with space for cot. Minimum stay two nights at weekends.*

Hollytree Cottage

Mrs Julia Naismith
Hollytree Cottage,
Laverton,
Bath,
Bath & N.E. Somerset BA2 7QZ

tel   01373 830786
fax   01373 830786
email   julia@naismith.fsbusiness.co.uk
web   www.hollytreecottagebath.co.uk

Meandering lanes lead to this 17th-century cottage –
quintessentially English with roses round the door,
a grandfather clock in the hall and an air of genteel
tranquillity. Julia has updated the cottage charm with
Regency mahogany in the inglenook dining room and
sumptuous sofas in the sitting room. Bedrooms have
long views over farmland and undulating countryside;
behind is a conservatory and the sloping, south-facing
garden. Ask your hostess about Bath (20 minutes away) –
she worked in the Holburne Museum and knows the
city well.

rooms	4: 2 doubles, 1 twin, 1 four-poster.
price	£70-£80. Singles £40.
meals	Pubs/restaurants 2-3 miles.
closed	Rarely.
directions	From Bath, A36 to Wolverton. Just past Red Lion, turn for Laverton. 1 mile to x-roads; towards Faukland; downhill for 80 yds. On left, just above farm entrance on right.

Map 2 Entry 2

Twenty years of trial and error have gone into creating this cottage garden which slopes gently down from the house to fields below and which complements the house perfectly. It has everything you could want in an open, informal country garden. Very good trees and shrubs including a tamarisk, a white-flowering amelanchier and a soft pink *Magnolia stellata* have been introduced over the years. A tall laburnum flowers profusely in season and Julia's collection of prunus have been carefully planted so that they flower in succession in spring time. A series of irregular beds have been planted with skill and flair. Julia is a keen member of her local horticultural society and buys many treasures at their plant sales, including clematis from the late Betty Risdon who ran the famous Rode Bird Gardens nearby and who was a leading member of the Clematis Society. Fish swim in the little pond, surrounded by water-loving plants, and for fresh vegetables and fruit, there is an immaculate kitchen garden edged with railway sleepers. The small conservatory is packed with the more tender plants, a perfect spot to sit and enjoy the colour and interest outside. The position is delightful and the garden has been designed to make the most of its glorious views. *Royal Horticultural Society.*

The Old Manor

Mrs R A G Sanders-Rose
The Old Manor,
Whitehouse Green,
Sulhamstead,
Reading,
Berkshire RG7 4EA

tel   0118 983 2423
fax   0118 983 6262
email   rags-r@theoldmanor.fsbusiness.co.uk

A young, developing garden with 10 acres which are being transformed into a mix of the formal and informal, and views across open farmland in a deeply rural corner of Berkshire. One gorgeous feature is already in place: a beautifully worked, elaborate knot garden in the form of two roses, its little box hedges set among pristine gravel. Another is a long pergola heavy with roses and honeysuckle. There are as many family associations in the garden as there are inside Peter and Rosemary's home. One is the eye-catching stately sorbus avenue which was planted to celebrate their daughter's wedding; edged by tall, waving, uncut grasses, it leads you to a shady, creeper-covered bower with countryside beyond. Roses clamber up the façade of the house and the wide, open, sunny patio guarded by two bay sentinels in containers is a lovely place to sit and enjoy the view while a fountain splashes. An intimate side patio is bounded by flowers and hedges, with an arch covered in golden hop and honeysuckle. Deer abound, so Rosemary chooses plants which they dislike! Specimen trees are being planted across the 10 acres and, beyond the tall enclosing hedge sheltering the large croquet lawn, an avenue of ancient oaks bears witness to the centuries-old history of the manor. A handsome and increasingly interesting garden.

rooms	3: 1 double, 1 four-poster, 1 single.
price	£80. Singles £40-£60.
meals	Dinner with wine, £15. Pub/restaurant 1-2 miles.
closed	Christmas & New Year.
directions	M4 junc. 12 for Newbury. Follow signs to Theale station, over r'way to lights. After 500 yds, right at r'bout. Keep on country road for 0.75 miles, then left at x-roads. Entrance ahead.

Map 3 Entry 3

Time-travel through Rosemary and Peter's luxurious house, part 1600s manor, part 1950s, part 1990s. The drawing room, with deep sofas, is modern and the cosy breakfast room is beamed. Bedrooms, one with a four-poster, are in the old part of the manor, with beamed ceilings and every comfort – one has a whirlpool bath. Family pictures give a homely touch and guests are treated as friends. Delicious dinners – both Rosemary and Peter are excellent cooks – are served at the long dining table sparkling with silver. Prepare to be thoroughly pampered.

21 Royal York Crescent

Mrs Susan Moore
21 Royal York Crescent,
Clifton,
Bristol BS8 4JX

tel   0117 973 4405

A large, airy and comfortable flat on the promenade level
of this gracious Georgian terrace, reputed to be the longest
in Europe – a perfect launch pad for all that the city has
to offer. Susan is a relaxed and generous hostess, whose
big, terracotta-coloured sitting room with huge views to
the Somerset hills is crammed with books, pictures and
good furniture; meals are taken at a long table. The guest
bedroom, with elegant new bathroom, is down the corridor
at the back; wonderfully private, painted in creams and
greens with pretty curtains of sprigged arbutus, it has
doors to the delightful, young garden. *Minimum stay two
nights at weekends.*

rooms	1 double.
price	£75.
meals	Dinner £20.
	Restaurants 5-minute walk.
closed	Occasionally.
directions	Follow Suspension Bridge signs from city centre to T-junc. opp. Clifton Village's Pizza Provencale. Left down Regent St, then immediately right. House on right, in centre of terrace on upper level.

Map 2 Entry 4

Susan's former town garden was regularly open to the public under the National Gardens Scheme; several years ago, armed only with her beautiful sculptures and one or two other things she couldn't bear to leave behind, she embarked on a new venture. Her exotic oasis is now flourishing: brick-edged beds on either side around a central courtyard theme, backed by a high wall with plenty of colourful climbers such as *R.banksiae* 'Lutea' and *Campsis grandiflora*. Large stepping stones set into gravel, with plenty of seating, lend interest, and a wooden, climber-entwined pergola gives height. This is a south-west facing garden and the huge beds contain a mix of architectural plants, some scented shrubs and a quince. The sculptures fit in well with this design-led space; a cube of floating stones with box edging, a ceramic pod surrounded by choysia and a large raised water tank set against a wall of clambering roses; yet another place to sit and breathe in the peaceful serenity. (And who would guess you were a short walk from the city centre?). It is worth coming back from time to time to admire the developments of this peaceful and secluded retreat.

The Old Vicarage

Mrs Belinda Morley-Fletcher
The Old Vicarage,
Padbury,
Buckinghamshire MK18 2AH

tel   01280 813045
fax   01280 824476
email   belindamf@freenet.co.uk

Belinda says it's Hugo who's the gardener: he has the passion and knowledge while she harvests and cooks. The garden's design is part inherited and part created by Hugo over 35 years. It's on several levels, with an unusual shape – the result of bits being added over the years. As well as a rose garden, terraces, a sunken garden, arcades and the charmingly named Phoebe's Garden, there's a romantically overgrown pond presided over by a pair of elegant metal cranes. Hugo plants mainly for leaf-colour combinations: he has more than 50 types of hebe and quite a few rare trilliums and epimediums. The trees (over 40 varieties) provide a protective barrier; some are over a century old. In the big organic kitchen garden, Hugo grows potatoes and asparagus, peas and beans, and – pigeons permitting – brassicas. There's soft fruit, too, and apples, pears, quinces and stone fruit. Any surplus is sold, along with his plants, at the Buckingham Country Market. The garden is opened for the public on some days each year, but it is also visited by a variety of wildlife, including the occasional barking deer, and a goodly array of birds, from owls and woodpeckers to house martins and finches. *NGS*

rooms	2: 1 double, 1 twin each with separate bath/shower.
price	£45-£50. Singles £30.
meals	Pub 1-2 miles.
closed	Usually Christmas.
directions	Padbury is 2 miles south of Buckingham on A413. Head to Thornborough Rd (north of village, west of A413), 1st house on right, behind white fence.

Map 3 Entry 5

A reeling five-bar gate and rampantly overgrown fence set the tone. This interesting, eccentric Victorian house is not for you if you're fanatically tidy! A porch overflowing with odd shoes, books and gardening clutter leads to a spacious hall with a huge old tapestry and an air of shabby grandeur. The sitting room, dominated by fireplaces at either end, is full of ancestral oils and faded family furniture; the bedrooms are big, old-fashioned and have comfortable beds. Belinda and Hugo are child- and dog-friendly hosts — and you'll get an exuberant welcome from Boris the cocker spaniel.

The Bunch

Francis & Panna Newall
The Bunch,
Wotton Underwood,
Aylesbury,
Buckinghamshire HP18 ORZ

tel   01844 238376
fax   01844 237153
email   newallf@btconnect.com

Built in the 18th century for the Duke of Buckingham as
staff cottages for the estate, these five have been knocked
into one long, low, cosy home. Francis and Panna are
much-travelled and have a great interest in people,
education and development; you will be beautifully looked
after. The drawing room is hugely comfortable and stylish,
with a dark polished floor, old rugs and plenty of squashy-
sofa seating. Dinner is eaten in the warm red dining room
and breakfast in the slate-floored conservatory. The
downstairs bedroom is beamed and large with lovely
garden views; the other twin is smaller but equally
comfortable.

rooms	2: 1 twin; 1 twin with separate bath.
price	£70–£80. Singles from £40.
meals	Dinner £30. Pub/restaurant 0.75 miles.
closed	Easter, Christmas & New Year.
directions	From Kingswood, A41 for Wotton & Brill. At next 2 T-juncs. left, & left again at sign Wotton only. 1st house on right with mushrooms at gate, which opens automatically.

Map 3 Entry 6

Mixed borders around an immaculate lawn and a series of rooms divided by neat hedging – about three acres in all. Mature trees stud the lawn, including a mulberry and a weeping pear; roses 'Rambling Rector' and 'Bobby James' romp up frames. The bird theme is strong: woven willow ducks and peacocks and a tennis hut whose back wall has been painted with pheasants; from here, a gorgeous view across to distant hills. Pots, urns and statues abound, there's a Whichford Pottery greyhound on a brick plinth with a blue wooden bench curving around it, looking down a mown path with an avenue of photinias towards the house. The tennis court has roses growing up the outside wire (mostly 'Canary Bird' – of course!) and lawsoniana bushes cut into pear-drop shapes. A little formal garden has low lonicera hedges, there's a wild pond shaded by mature trees with a waterfall trickling down old stones and a seat where you can admire more willow birds. The vegetable garden is immaculate and productive and the cutting garden always yields something colourful for Panna's perfect arrangements. Seeds and cuttings are grown in the hot and cold greenhouses; they buy in very little. Last, but not least, are the aviary and pens: canaries, bantams, guinea fowl and golden pheasants are much loved and highly vocal. Waddesdon Manor and Claydon House are nearby. *NGS.*

Spindrift

Norma Desmond-Mawby
Spindrift,
Jordans,
Buckinghamshire HP9 2TE

tel   01494 873172
fax   01494 876442
email   johnmawby@hotmail.com

A 1933 Quaker house in a very quiet village. Here are still the Meeting House and barn made with timbers from the Mayflower. It is a long house in a secluded garden on a site where Stone Age axes were made, some of which are in the British Museum. Much of the house is open to guests and Norma is Winkfield-trained so food is superb. Bedrooms are luxurious with new beds, powerful showers and lovely coral pink and jade green curtains at windows that overlook the garden. A heated pool awaits, as do stunning walks — or just slump in a comfortable chair in the guest sitting room, its French windows opening to the garden.

rooms	2: 1 double, 1 twin.
price	£100. Singles £60.
meals	Lunch £25. Dinner, 4 courses, £30. Packed lunch £12.50. Pub 2 miles.
closed	Rarely.
directions	M40 exit 2 for Beaconsfield. A40 for Gerrards Cross. Left at first junction into Pot Kiln Lane; 2nd left for Jordans village. Right at corner of Green, keeping it on your right; continue, house is in cul de sac left of school.

Map 3 Entry 7

Norma – "chlorophyll gives me a kick!" – has loved plants since her grandmother took her to Kew when she was very young. As soon as she realised that the garden at Spindrift was a similar shape to Monet's, off she went into arches, walkways, a heavenly series of 'rooms', beautiful herbaceous borders and fountains. It is all on different levels with a landscaped gravel pit and a pond in one corner, fine lawns to the front flanked by colourful borders and, to one side, a heated, kidney-shaped pool in a sunny raised area with lots of pretty pots. The fruit and vegetable gardens are terraced down a hill and produce 29 different varieties of vegetables and 13 of fruit, all for the table. There is a large garden room where meals can be served in fine weather, a circular theme for the arched doorways and walkways, a pristine hosta corner showing off different vareties (not a sign of lace: snails and slugs are somehow deterred) surrounding a raised fountain, and The Dell, which contains a second pond with newts, toads and frogs. Norma is very 'hands on' and often takes children from the school next door around the garden for nature and art. Colours are muted, the softest pinks, blues and mauves backed up by every conceivable green, silver and grey from her beloved hostas. The house is filled with flowers from the garden at every time of year – perfectly arranged.

The Mount

Jonathan & Rachel Major
The Mount,
Higher Kinnerton,
Chester,
Cheshire CH4 9BQ

tel   01244 660275
fax   01244 660275
email   major@mountkinnerton.freeserve.co.uk
web   www.bandbchester.com

Peaceful indeed. ("Our guests seem to oversleep", says
Rachel.) Britain at its best with a fruitful kitchen garden,
scented conservatory, a tennis court, croquet lawn and a
genuine welcome. The Victorian house, built for a Chester
corn merchant, is furnished in elegant and traditional style,
with garden views from every angle. You get a light-filled
drawing room, a high-ceilinged dining room, and bedrooms
that are most inviting – bright, big, with attractive fabrics,
art and lovely furniture. Heaven for garden buffs, walkers,
bookworms and birdwatchers (with easy access to Chester
and North Wales). *Arrivals from 5pm.*

rooms	3: 1 double, 2 twins/doubles.
price	£60. Singles £38.
meals	Pubs in village.
closed	Christmas & New Year.
directions	A5104 to Broughton; left at 2nd r'bout to A5104 Pennyfordd; through Broughton, cross over A55; 1st left to Higher Kinnerton down Lesters Lane. On right, on bend, 0.75 miles down.

Map 5 Entry 8

Look up — you might catch sight of careering young sparrowhawks testing their wings overhead. Some old and very beautiful trees date back to the building of the house in 1860 while the front garden's acre outline was set out in the early 1950s. Rachel has worked wonders with grounds which were once simply open lawns and trees, developing them gradually over the years, reflecting her, and Jonathan's, growing interest and commitment to gardening. The formality of the new beech-hedged kitchen garden contrasts happily with the more informal mood elsewhere. The front garden's croquet lawn, overlooked by trees, takes you down steps past stone pineapples into the cool seclusion of woodland, with the pink-flushed 'Francis E Lester' rose soaring dizzily up a tall conifer. Roses, clematis and hydrangea sparkle on The Mount's façade as housemartins flit in and out of nests beneath the eaves. Another recent addition is a pond to one side of the house — a mass of bullrushes, foxgloves and iris which is perfect for wildlife. Behind the house the planting is more open and free, decorated with new beech hedges to give shape and form. The handsome pergola is wrapped in wisteria, and a young arbour of willows is settling in nicely. A lovely garden in perfect harmony with the handsome Victorian house. *NGS.*

Tremayne House

Anthony & Juliet Hardman
Tremayne House,
St Martin-in-Meneage,
Helston,
Cornwall TR12 6DA

tel   01326 231618
fax   01326 231080
email   staying@tremaynehouse.com
web   www.tremaynehouse.com

A fine late Regency country house with a sweeping cantilevered staircase, intricate door surrounds, flagstone floors, shuttered windows and beautiful proportions which hides in the Helford River woods close to Tremayne Quay and Frenchman's Creek. Juliet is an interior designer and her skills are evident: the double and twin rooms are furnished in lavish country house style mixing textured chenilles with silks and checks, florals and chintzes. The garden suite is more contemporary but no less plush. Top quality beds, fabulous flowers, lobster dinners and friendly, interesting hosts.

rooms	3: 1 suite & kitchen; 1 double, 1 twin, each with separate bath/shower.
price	From £110. Singles from £80. Suite £120.
meals	Dinner £30.
closed	Christmas & New Year.
directions	A3083 from Helston. B3293 for St Keverne. After 1.5 miles turn left through Mawgan to St Martin. Just past school left for Mudgeon, on to x-roads. Left & after 200 yds, right. House at end of lane through large granite gate piers.

Map 1 Entry 9

The Hardmans took on an unstructured garden and have slowly turned it around, although there is still much to do. The entrance, through granite piers, leads up a sweeping drive beneath large deciduous trees. Here a shaded border has been created with ferns, tree ferns and shade-tolerant perennials. A circular grass island is cut into a maze pattern and the formal parterre and box topiary balances the front elevation of the house creating a dramatic entrance. There are two acres in total with the garden on three sides, the front overlooking a truly rural landscape. The main themes are based on geometric forms of different types, the colour schemes range from whites through to silvers, blues and greys and, further out, mixed colours. The plants themselves may not be rare but they have been put together in an unusual way. The once kitchen garden is the latest project: to be called The Life Garden, it will consist of planting around a swimming pool, a pavilion and an outdoor eating area complete with fire. Through gates in the wall, granite steps lead to the long borders and individual rooms walled by beech hedges. The planting is informal herbaceous, mostly whites, blues and silvers, progressing in the autumn to bold purples, pinks and reds. This is a garden to watch: when the plans are complete the ensemble will be stunning.

Glendurgan

Charles & Caroline Fox
Glendurgan,
Falmouth,
Cornwall TR11 5JZ

tel   01326 250326

In 1827 a thatched cottage stood where the light-filled
family house now surveys the glen. The sixth generation –
as accustomed as their ancestors to receiving guests – has
mixed family furniture, books and paintings with modern
touches (such as the pristine, Aga-driven kitchen). Caroline
trained as a cook and her breakfasts draw on the best of
local and homemade. Bedrooms have sensational south-
facing views; Violet, next to the bathroom, and Magenta,
a few yards down the corridor, are as your Edwardian aunt
would have liked. No TV but a grand piano, and garden
heaven on the doorstep.

rooms	2 twins sharing bathroom.
price	From £80. Singles £60.
meals	Pubs/restaurants within four miles.
closed	Occasionally.
directions	Brown sign to Glendurgan from Mawnan Smith. Ignore signed entrance to garden. Continue on for 200 yards. Take private entrance through white gate on left hand side.

Map 1 Entry 10

Three Fox brothers created glen gardens near Falmouth in the 1820s: Robert: Penjerrick; Charles: Trebah; Alfred: Glendurgan – which, in 1962, was donated to the National Trust. It's a magical, exotic, heavily shrubbed and wooded place, the tulip trees are some of the largest and oldest in Europe, and there's a sense of fun and discovery as you wend down on steep, superbly maintained paths (pebble-cobbled, bamboo-balustraded) to take a breather on Durgan beach – before climbing back up the other side. It is splendidly scented in spring with camellias, bluebells, primroses and lime-tree flowers. Summer, to quote Charles's excellent book, "breaks in a wave of whiteness, with eucryphia, hoheria, myrtus and that 'bombe Alaska' of rhododendrons, 'Polar Bear', while autumn is awash with bulbs such as amaryllis, colchicum, crinum and nerine." In the winter this is still an important garden in terms of its collection of fine trees, and, even in the wildest weather, a deeply romantic place to be. There is much to explore and Charles will tell you all you want to know; he is an artist as well as a garden designer, trained at Kew and the Inchbald School of Garden Design, and leads garden tours.

Carwinion

Mr & Mrs Anthony Rogers
Carwinion,
Mawnam Smith,
Falmouth,
Cornwall TR11 5JA

tel   01326 250258
fax   01326 250903
email   jane@carwinion.co.uk
web   www.carwinion.co.uk

This rambling manor began life in 1790 as a small farmhouse, and was enlarged in the 1840s shortly after the garden was originally designed and planted. The manor has the faded grandeur and collections of oddities (corkscrews, penknives, magnifying glasses) that successive generations hand on. Your charmingly eccentric host will introduce you to his ancestors, his antiques, his fine big old bedrooms — and he and the tireless Jane serve "a breakfast to be reckoned with". The self-catering wing has a fenced garden to keep your children in and Carwinion dogs out.

rooms	3: 1 double, 2 twins/doubles.
price	£80. Singles £45.
meals	Occasional dinner. Pub 400 yds.
closed	Rarely.
directions	Left road in Mawnam Smith at Red Lion pub, onto Carwinion Road. 400 yds up hill on right, sign for Carwinion Garden.

Map 1 Entry 11

If an inquisitive, errant dinosaur were to come rustling out of the great stands of bamboo or soaring gunnera, you might not be that surprised. These 14 acres are a ravishing homage to leaf, foliage, wildness… a heavenly place of trees, ponds, streams. No wonder that Jane, who has done so much for these grounds in recent years, calls it an "unmanicured garden". At the end of the 19th century, Anthony's grandfather planted the first bamboos in this gorgeous valley garden leading down to the Helford River. Today Carwinion has one of the finest collections in Europe, more than 200 species with wonderful leaf and stem forms… members of the Bamboo Society of Great Britain flock here for annual get-togethers. The lushness soars impressively to the sky – don't miss the 20-foot pieris. Jane has made a series of paths to lead you through one breathtakingly romantic area after another, a palm sheltering under a tall beech tree, a banana tree thriving in the mild atmosphere. Tree ferns soar and, in a final flourish at the foot of the garden, she has transformed an old quarry into an enchanting fern garden. Springtime's azaleas and rhododendrons are a joy. Magic everywhere. *NGS, Good Gardens Guide.*

The Wagon House

Charles & Mally Francis
The Wagon House,
Heligan Manor,
St Ewe,
St Austell,
Cornwall PL26 6EW

tel   01726 844505
email   thewagonhouse@mac.com
web   www.thewagonhouse.com

The 18th-century wagoners would be amazed if they could see the house today. Spotless bedrooms upstairs in what used to be the joiner's workshop, and, where the wagons rolled in, five huge windows through which the morning light streams (along with the dawn chorus). There's tea in the cheerful sitting room on arrival; breakfast consists of Aga-cooked local farm produce to keep up the energy levels for Heligan, the Eden Project and many other Cornish gardens. Across the drive, courses in botanical art are held in the Saw-Pit Studio where, as you would imagine, the walls are lined with fascinating paintings and photographs.

rooms	2: 1 twin with separate bath; 1 twin sharing bath (let to same party only).
price	£90. Singles £50.
meals	Pub/restaurant 2 miles.
closed	Christmas & New Year.
directions	From St Austell for Heligan Gardens. Follow private drive towards Heligan House. Left before white gate-posts, keep left past cottages, left after The Magnolias and follow drive.

Map 1 Entry 12

As the Wagon House lies in the centre of Heligan Gardens (just over the wall from the Sundial Garden), Charles and Mally Francis would be the first to admit that most people are here to visit their neighbour's garden rather than their own! However, their small garden will undoubtedly give encouragement to those who are just starting out with a long-neglected patch. They have eradicated the brambles and nettles, and unearthed a Mini car door from the flower bed in the process – together with some nice slate slabs. Now they are developing a garden which includes the plants that thrive in the Cornish coastal climate: hydrangeas, cordylines, griselinias and phormiums, a crinodendron and a grevillea. In spite of Heligan's popularity, the Wagon House sits in a private spot undisturbed by visitors – while a short walk (of about 400 yards) up the tree-lined drive brings you to the Gardens. Charles is a garden photographer and Mally is a botanical artist, so both are closely involved with Heligan and can provide rare insights. As they are professionally involved with the Eden Project, too, they have been part of its development from the earliest days and so are exceptional hosts.

Creed House

Lally & William Croggon
Creed House,
Creed,
Grampound,
Truro,
Cornwall TR2 4SL

tel   01872 530372

In Lally and William's lovely house and garden there's a comforting sense of all being well in England's green and pleasant land. St Crida's Church rises on tip-toes above treetops while the murmur of a lazy stream reaches your ears. Inside the 1730s house, shimmering wooden floors are covered with Persian rugs and light pours into every elegant corner. Breakfast at the mahogany table can turn into an early morning house party, such is Lally's sense of fun and spontaneity. The big guest rooms – with extra large beds – exude taste and simplicity. *Minimum stay two nights.*

rooms	3: 1 twin/double; 2 twins/doubles, each with separate bath.
price	£90. Singles by arrangement.
meals	Pub/restaurant 1 mile.
closed	Christmas & New Year.
directions	From St Austell, A390 to Grampound. Just beyond clock tower, left into Creed Lane. After 1 mile left at grass triangle opp. church. House behind 2nd white gates on left.

Map 1 Entry 13

One of Cornwall's loveliest gardens, a tribute to the enormous amount of hard work, dedication and brilliant plantsmanship devoted to these stunning seven acres. The Croggons came here in 1974 to find a Miss Havisham of a garden with a lawn like a hayfield edged in brambles, and the rest an impenetrable jungle with glimpses of 40-ft high rhododendrons, magnolia and huge stands of gunnera. Today this jungle has been transformed into a fine, gentle, old-fashioned rectory garden. Many exciting buildings have been discovered along the way, including a cobbled yard with a sunken centre and a summer house which has been restored. The mass clearance also encouraged long-dormant snowdrops and daffodils to bloom in their thousands. The tree and shrub collection is outstanding; rhododendrons, camellias, azaleas and magnolias do brilliantly and secret paths leading from the gently sloping lawns lure you deep into the woodland. So much to admire and enjoy: a circular lily pond, a swamp garden with candelabra primulas and mecanopsis, a stable yard with alpines and sun-loving plants on its raised wall beds. Lally and William are delightful, and their pleasure in their masterpiece is totally infectious. Very close to Heligan and the Eden project. *NGS County Organiser, Good Gardens Guide.*

Tregoose

Alison O'Connor
Tregoose,
Grampound,
Truro,
Cornwall TR2 4DB

tel	01726 882460
fax	01872 222427
web	www.tregoose.co.uk

At the head of the Roseland Peninsula, Tregoose is a handsome, late-Regency country house surrounded by rolling countryside. In the drawing room, where a log fire is lit on cooler evenings, a beautiful Chinese cabinet occupies one wall and in the dining room is a Malayan inscribed silk screen – a thank you present from Empire days. Upstairs the comfortable bedrooms have antique furniture, views onto the glorious garden, and pretty bathrooms with generous baths. The Eden Project and Heligan are nearby. *Children by arrangement.*

rooms	3: 1 twin, 1 four-poster; 1 double with separate bath.
price	From £86.
meals	Dinner £28. BYO. Pub/restaurant 1 mile.
closed	Christmas & Easter.
directions	A30 for Truro, at Fraddon bypass left for Grampound Rd. After 5 miles, right onto A390 for Truro; 100 yds, right where double white lines end. Between reflector posts to house, 200 yds down lane.

Map 1 Entry 14

Alison, who grew up in Cornwall, has an NDH and has created a lovely garden with a wide variety of plants, which opens under the National Gardens Scheme. Five fat Irish yews and a tumbledown wall were the starting point, but having reconstructed the walls to create a sunken garden, things started to look up. The L-shaped barn was a good backdrop for planting, so in went cotinus and yellow privet, flame-coloured alstroemerias, show-stopping *Crocosmia solfaterre* with its bronze leaves and apricot yellow flowers, and blue agapanthus for contrast. The sunken walled garden protects such tender treasures as *Aloysia citrodora*, leptospermum, and, pièce de résistance, *Acacia baileyana purpurea*. Palm-like dracaena, Monterey pines and cypresses and the Chusan palm do well, and you can't miss the spectacular magenta blooms of the 30-foot *Rhododendron arboreum* 'Cornish Red'. The woodland garden displays more muted colours, scented deciduous azaleas, and the white July-scented rhododendron 'Polar Bear'. Over 50 varieties of snowdrop flower from November to March. The potager supplies produce for dinners and flowers for the house, and Alison can supply almost any information about Cornish plants and gardens. *NGS, Cornwall Garden Society.*

Hornacott

Jos & Mary-Anne Otway-Ruthven
Hornacott,
South Petherwin,
Launceston,
Cornwall PL15 7LH

tel   01566 782461
fax   01566 782461
email   stay@hornacott.co.uk
web   www.hornacott.co.uk

The garden has seats poised to catch the evening sun: perfect after a day exploring the gardens and beaches of Cornwall. The peaceful house is named after the hill and you have a private entrance to your fresh, roomy suite: a twin-bedded room and a large, square, high sitting room with double doors, which looks onto the wooded valley. There are chocolates and magazines and a CD player, and you are utterly private; Jos, a kitchen designer, and Mary-Anne really want you to enjoy your stay. Local produce is yours for delicious breakfast and dinner.

rooms	1 suite. Child single available.
price	£76. Singles £50.
meals	Dinner £20. BYO wine. Pub/restaurant 3 miles.
closed	Christmas.
directions	B3254 Launceston-Liskeard. Through South Petherwin, down steep hill, last left before little bridge. House 1st on left.

Map 2 Entry 15

A dynamic garden where lots has been happening in recent years as Jos and Mary-Anne work their way from one area to the next. The garden is about one-and-a-half acres of sloping ground with shady spots, open sunny lawns and borders and many shrubs. A stream tumbles through the garden after heavy rain and trickles quietly by in the dryer summer months; its banks are being cleared and water-loving plants introduced. Elsewhere, clearance is underway, too, and by opening up long-hidden areas, wild flowers have been given space and light to thrive. A charming pergola with its own seat has been built at one end of the garden to add vertical interest and a touch of formality. The recent loss of some mature trees near the house has been a blessing in disguise — creating open spaces where there was once too much shade. Your hosts have been busy planting rhododendrons, azaleas, camellias and many flowering shrubs and everything is being designed to blend with the peaceful setting and the backdrop of grand old trees. A collection of David Austin roses has been introduced — his are the only ones which seem to do well here, says Mary-Anne. There's plenty of colour too, with varied colour themings from one border to the next.

Broadgate

Diana Lewthwaite
Broadgate,
Millom,
Cumbria LA18 5JY

tel   01229 716295
email   broadgatehouse@aol.com

The terrible storms two years ago felled several trees in the garden but improved the views to the woods and sea enormously; the setting is glorious. This is a classic Cumbrian country house garden, 300 years old, complete with stone balustrade and planters, box garden and fragrant roses, venerable trees and lashings of rhododendron and azalea. With the spring come wave upon wave of snowdrops (2,500 were planted last spring) and merry daffodils. A walled garden, engagingly faded in its woodland setting, tells of gardeners and summers long ago. High stone walls, covered with climbers and old roses, enclose wide herbaceous beds and an old glasshouse. At the front of the house, vivid 'Greek' blue hydrangeas make a startling contrast to the dazzling white façade and smooth green lawns, while an old palm tree adds an exotic touch. This is a garden which still needs much work to restore it but Diana has plans. Its bones are good, the position is wonderful and the potential enormous. There's masses of birdlife, too, including flycatchers and green woodpeckers. Down the lane are some interesting old buildings belonging to the estate farm, where chickens peck around under the trees and cattle graze.

rooms	4: 2 doubles sharing bath (let to same party only); 2 singles sharing shower (same party only).
price	£80. Singles £45.
meals	Supper, 3 courses, £18.50.
closed	Rarely.
directions	M6 junc. 36. After 3 miles, left slip road A590 to Barrow. After 17 miles, right A595, Workington and Millom. After 11 miles, traffic lights and bridge; 3 miles right to Broadgate.

Map 5 Entry 16

Passing white stone gate pillars, the drive sweeps up to the Georgian symmetry of a big white house – big but not intimidating. The Lewthwaites have been here for ever and the grand rooms have a lovely, lived-in feel. Guests have the whole of the third floor to themselves: gorgeous flowery bedrooms with high, comfortable beds and pretty mahogany furniture. There's a little sitting room and a breakfast room with floor-to-ceiling, china-filled cupboards. Diana, an ex-Olympic skier, is an accomplished cook. Stunning views should compensate for any traffic noise from the main road. *Children over ten welcome.*

Howe Foot

Sue & Martin Hawkard
Howe Foot,
Low Beck Bottom,
Lowick, Ulverston,
Cumbria LA12 8EA

tel	01229 885007
fax	01229 885007
email	info@howe-foot.co.uk
web	www.howe-foot.co.uk

Total independence in this thick-walled hideaway — separate from the main house and with its own secluded patio. Walk in through a dear little hall to a beamed and light sitting room with a comfy sofa, slate floor, chunky oak tables and doors, flat-screen TV and an endless supply of logs for the woodburner. The small bedroom has a firm bed, a high rounded ceiling and two windows, one overlooking the garden; the shower room is compact but perfectly formed. Nip next door for a gourmet breakfast before tackling those lakeside walks, or take in a festival at the cobbled market town of Ulveston.

rooms	Cottage with 1 double & sitting room.
price	£80–£90. Singles £50.
meals	Pubs 0.7 miles.
closed	Rarely.
directions	Through Greenodd on A5092, 2 miles to Farmer's Arms Pub. After 0.5 miles, left at crossroads up narrow fell road; 0.2 miles, 1st used track on left to house.

Map 5 Entry 17

Sue and Martin moved here four years ago to find a collapsed bridge over the beck, a lot of dead trees and some plants that were mostly unsalvageable. But what a difference they have made to this acre, with natural planting and design that slips seamlessly into native habitat and flora. A lovely paved area by the beck and the footbridge is planted with gunnera, iris, crocosmia, hostas and other damp-happy souls; this is a fine spot to dangle your toes in the cool water and admire the brown trout, or spot a freshwater salmon struggling upstream to spawn. Walk through a honeysuckle-clad pergola, wander the paths surrounded by low curved stone walls, admire the S-shaped border that brims with evergreen shrubs (providing food for a huge variety of birds), savour the scent of many roses on the evening air. Native trees include an enormous oak, a conifer which is lit up at Christmas, some acers, alder and hazel; beyond are grazing sheep. This is a true Lakeland garden, close to nature; spring brings layers of bluebells and in autumn the ferns and bracken along the lane glow a stunning dark ochre. Martin and Sue make a dream team, each adoring the tasks the other hates, and spending time reading books about gardening when they're not doing it; the result is a very young garden already with shape and structure.

Barn Close

Anne Robinson
Barn Close,
Beetham,
Cumbria LA7 7AL

tel   015395 63191 mob 07752 670658
fax   015395 63191
email   anne@nwbirds.co.uk
web   www.nwbirds.co.uk/accom.htm

A 1920s house in the village with lots of windows, high chimneys and well-proportioned rooms off long and spacious corridors. Bedrooms — one with long views over the garden — are traditional, comfortable and lack pretension; bathrooms (not huge) are spanking clean. Supper is by arrangement but will include home-grown vegetables and is taken in the dining room at a solid mahogany table. Anne is able to give her visitors lots of personal attention and this is certainly good value — perfect for bird lovers, walkers and anyone seeking a bit of peace and quiet away from the crowds. *WiFi available.*

rooms	3: 1 twin, 1 single; 1 twin with separate bath/shower.
price	£45–£60. Singles £25–£35.
meals	Supper £16. Tray snack £7–£10. Pub 300 yds.
closed	Christmas.
directions	Exit M6 junc. 35 for 4 miles. A6 north to Milnthorpe & Beetham. Left before bridge; right at Wheatsheaf pub & church. Right at end of village, over cattle grid. House at end of drive.

Map 5 Entry 18

A lovely, two-acre garden with something to interest the garden lover at any time of the year. Fantastic displays of snowdrops, aconites and bluebells in spring, a swathe of autumn colour from the surrounding mature trees, and a large herbaceous border that's stunning in June and July. Mike organises birdwatching breaks around the local area but you need not go very far: over the last ten years nearly 80 different species have been seen from or in the garden. Anne has planted teasels, acanthus, grasses and anything with seedheads to attract the birds but, needless to say, they are equally keen on her productive vegetable garden and fruit trees. The pond has been supplemented with water irises, candelabra primulas and water lilies: wildlife flourishes, particularly dragonflies, and a good number of resident butterflies. This is a beautiful unspoiled part of Cumbria (AONB), with lovely views and good walks round Morecambe Bay, famous for its huge flocks of wading birds. There are many places of interest nearby including Levens Hall, Sizergh Castle (NT) and Holker Hall, while the Lakeland Horticultural Society garden is a gem overlooking Lake Windermere. The plant centre in the village, Beetham Nurseries, won a much coveted gold medal at the Tatton RHS show 2004. *RHS, HPS, Lakeland Horticultural Society, Cumbria Gardens Trust.*

Horsleygate Hall

Robert & Margaret Ford
Horsleygate Hall,
Horsleygate Lane,
Holmesfield,
Derbyshire S18 7WD

tel   0114 289 0333
fax   0114 289 0333

Margaret and Robert are dedicated, skilful, knowledgeable gardeners and their talents are abundantly clear from the moment you arrive. Margaret is a true plantsman who knows and loves her plants; Robert is the garden architect. He has added delightful touches, including a pergola fashioned from the iron pipes of the old greenhouse heating system, a breeze house thatched in Yorkshire heather and fences made from holly poles. Exploring the garden is enormous fun – there are so many surprises. The sloping site includes a woodland garden with gazebo, hot sun terrace, rockeries, pools, a fern area, a jungle garden, mixed borders and an exquisite ornamental kitchen garden. The Fords are keen on evergreen shrubs and have an interest in euphorbias. They have a particularly unusual collection of herbaceous perennials and are always on the lookout for fresh treasures to add to their collection. Quirky statuary peeps out at you from unusual places and all around the garden are strategically placed seats where you can soak up the varied displays. The overall theme is one of informality, with walls, terraces, paths and well-planted troughs hidden from each other. Lovely in spring, gorgeous in the full flower of summer, and good for autumn colour and winter interest, too. *NGS*.

rooms	3: 1 double; 1 family room, 1 twin sharing bath.
price	£60–£70. Singles from £40.
meals	Pub/restaurant 1 mile.
closed	23 December–4 January.
directions	M1 exit 29; A617 to Chesterfield; B6051 to Millthorpe; Horsleygate Lane 1 mile on, on right.

Map 6 Entry 19

Wake up to the sounds of hens, ponies and doves as they cluck, strut and coo in a charming old stableyard outside. The house was built in 1783 as a farmhouse and substantially extended in 1856; the garden was once home to the hounds of the local hunt. The house has a warm, timeless, harmonious feel, with worn kilims on stone flags, striped and floral wallpapers, deep sofas and pools of light. Breakfast is served in the old schoolroom and is a feast of organic eggs, honey, homemade jams and fruit from Margaret's superbly maintained kitchen garden. Glorious setting... and place. *Children over five welcome.*

Cascades Gardens

Alan & Elizabeth Clements
Cascades Gardens,
Clatterway Hill,
Bonsall,
Derbyshire DE4 2EH

tel	01629 822813
fax	0115 9470014
email	enquiries@cascadesgardens.com
web	www.cascadesgardens.com

A big and successful garden, with something for everyone. Alan provides the ideas for the landscaping and the muscle to develop it, Elizabeth takes care of the planting – and does she like to plant! Over 4,000 specimens and more than 100 different perennials clamour for attention in herbaceous borders backed by large shrubs, then high banks and mature trees; copper beech, ancient yews and dozens of newcomers – planted for bark interest, blossom and autumn colour. The ruins of an old mill and a lead mine are now integral; a babbling brook, ponds and small waterfalls somersault right through the garden abundant with water plants, marginals and a host of perennials. A wild flower bank sits happily with more cultivated areas, variegated laurels and cascading plants cheer a bleak winter, hellebores and bulbs strain for spring. In summer the different parts of the garden are lush and sheltered with plenty of places to sit and admire in peace and quiet. Plants here are mostly grown from root cuttings or seed and many of them are unusual; their *Enkianthus campanulatus* was borrowed for an exhibition at the Chelsea Flower Show. In the evening, amble down to the pond and see moorhens and mallards, flitting bats and frogs galore.

rooms	2 doubles.
price	£72-£80.
meals	Pub 0.5 miles.
closed	Christmas and New Year.
directions	A6 Derby to Cromford, then Via Gellia to Bonsall. 1 mile right into village. House 800 yds on right before village green.

Map 6 Entry 20

The large and immaculate Georgian mill manager's house has a dramatic setting: a shrub-strewn cliff rising behind, lovely gardens and cascades of tumbling water down below. Alan and Elizabeth do warm, traditional B&B; breakfasts include tasty Derbyshire oat cakes, bathrooms flaunt fluffy towels. Indian and Tibetan art is a passion and each super-comfortable bedroom is filled with paintings and *objets*. No sitting room but bedrooms are well arm-chaired and the dining room is delightfully cosy, its sash bay window filled with plants. Great houses, waterways and Arkwright's Mill wait to be discovered.

Oldfield House

Edmund & Sue Jarvis
Oldfield House,
Snelston,
Ashbourne,
Derbyshire DE6 2EP

tel   01335 324510
email   s-jarvis@tiscali.co.uk

Snelston is a village of mellow, redbrick houses; Oldfield was built in the early 1700s as a small estate farm, and was later remodelled and extended. It is a handsome house with well-proportioned rooms. Two sitting rooms with log fires are filled with squashy sofas and good books, furniture gleams and there are paintings to admire. Sue and Edmund spoil you with superb breakfasts and dinners. Bedrooms have sunny views through wisteria-fringed windows, good linen, soft colours. There's walking in the Dove Valley straight from the house, fly-fishing can be arranged and the Dales are a short drive. *Ask about fishing.*

rooms	2: 1 double; 1 twin with separate bath/shower.
price	£80–£84. Singles £50–£52.
meals	Dinner £25. Pub 3 miles.
closed	Christmas & New Year.
directions	From Ashbourne, A515 for Lichfield for 3 miles, then right to Snelston for 1.25 miles to centre of village. House opp. War Memorial. Drive to rear.

Map 6 Entry 21

Both Sue and Edmund are devoted gardeners and love to share the fruits of their efforts with other garden lovers: a good one-acre plot facing south and running down to a stream, set against a landscape of estate parkland with mature trees to the horizon. A deep 'house' bed at the back is filled with climbing roses, clematis and wisteria, from which runs a huge herbaceous border of classic proportions. Facing it is a warmer west-facing shrubbery bed and a border of hot coloured perennials. Duck below a small pergola planted with early clematis and take the grassy path between stands of shrub roses onto open lawn. Here are harmoniously spaced trees, underplanted with seasonal bulbs and shade-lovers and surrounded by rare and scented roses. The visual transition from cultivated borders to parkland is seamless and leads to the stream with giant gunnera and water plants. The kitchen garden has six square beds and a cutting bed for the house. Roses are a passion: 'Fantin Latour', 'Buff Beauty', 'Ferdinand Pichard' and 'Fritz Nobis' to name but a few. This is a wonderful garden, full of charm, surprises and interest created by this hugely knowledgeable, hard working and enthusiastic couple. Garden lovers could not fail to be happy.

Tor Cottage

Maureen Rowlatt
Tor Cottage,
Chillaton,
Tavistock,
Devon PL16 0JE

tel	01822 860248
fax	01822 860126
email	info@torcottage.co.uk
web	www.torcottage.co.uk

Maureen's super-professionalism means that nothing is left to chance... bedside truffles, fresh fruit, flowers, Cava and soft robes. Each bedroom has an open fireplace, a private terrace or conservatory, a bathroom with all you need, while the woodland cabin rests in its own valley with a hammock in the trees, a covered barbecue area, a gypsy caravan to play in and steps to the stream. And the garden is full of secret corners, with a swimming pool colourfully lit at night and paths and steps to guide you through the beauty. Maureen serves delicious breakfasts in the (fountained) sunroom. *Minimum stay two nights.*

rooms	5: 2 doubles, 1 twin/double, 1 suite; 1 woodland cabin for 2 (B&B or self-catering).
price	£140. Singles £94. Suite & cabin £150.
meals	3 miles to pubs/restaurants. Tray supper by arrangement.
closed	B&B: Christmas & New Year. Self-catering: Never.
directions	In Chillaton keep pub & PO on left, up hill towards Tavistock. After 300 yds, right down bridleway.

Map 2 Entry 22

Your final approach to the house is along a half-mile, tree-lined track that's so long you'll wonder if you've taken the wrong turning. Your persistence is rewarded with a sudden burst of light and colour as you arrive at this lovely hideaway home. Birds sing, dragonflies hover over ponds and buzzards patrol the skies in that lazy way of theirs. Maureen has created this idyllic corner from what was no more than a field with a stream running through it. She has managed to make use of leylandii in such a way that even its staunchest opponent would approve, and shaped it into a perfectly manicured 20-foot-high L-shaped hedge which effectively shields the heated swimming pool and adds welcome privacy. A series of paths and steps lead you to new delights – flowers, shrubs and plants chosen for leaf texture and colour and all beautifully maintained. There are secret corners, too, particularly by the stream and in a dappled wood with its very own, wonderfully slug-free hosta garden. Two of the cleverly converted outbuildings used for bed and breakfast have their own little gardens. Natural woodland and a recently made path up the wooded hillside are bonuses. A year-round fairytale garden – from the first wild flowers of spring to the icy white of winter frosts.

Corndonford Farm

Ann & Will Williams
Corndonford Farm,
Poundsgate,
Newton Abbot,
Devon TQ13 7PP

tel   01364 631595
email   corndonford@btinternet.com

Come to be engrossed in the routines of a wild, engagingly chaotic haven. Ann and Will are friendly, kind and extrovert; guests adore them and keep coming back. There is comfort, too: warm curtains, a four-poster with lacy drapes, early morning tea. Gentle giant shire horses live at the shippon end where the cows once stood, and there's medieval magic with Bronze Age foundations. A wonderful place for those who love the rhythm and hubbub of real country life — and the Two Moors Way footpath is on the doorstep. *Children over ten by arrangement.*

rooms	2: 1 twin, 1 four-poster sharing bath.
price	£50-£60. Singles £25-£30.
meals	Pub/restaurant 2 miles.
closed	Christmas.
directions	From A38 2nd Ashburton turn for Dartmeet & Princetown. In Poundsgate pass pub on left; 3rd right on bad bend signed Corndon. Straight over x-roads, 0.5 miles, farm on left.

Map 2 Entry 23

Climb and climb the Dartmoor edge with views growing wider and wilder all the time until you reach the stone-walled lane and the sturdy granite buildings of Corndonford Farm. Roses and wisteria clamber up the rugged façade, softening the ancient strength of the house. At jam-making time the air is filled with the sweetness of an enormous pan of bubbling strawberries. Ann's jewel-like little farm garden has an arched walk of richly scented honeysuckle, roses and other climbers which leads to her very productive vegetable and soft fruit garden – the source of the berries. She knows her plants and has created a small, cottagey garden in complete harmony with its surroundings. There's a rockery and a little gravelled patio just outside the house which has been planted with charming cottage flowers. Above is a lawn edged by deep borders absolutely packed with colour and traditional cottage garden plants, including salmon-pink rhododendron, cranesbill and lupins. Do take the short walk along the lane to Ann's second garden, known locally as the "traffic calmer". Here, by the roadside, she has planted loads of rhododendrons and shrubs in a delightful display – and it really does encourage even the most hurried motorists to slow down. The views are breathtaking, the setting wonderfully peaceful, the garden as informal and welcoming as Ann and Will themselves.

Kingston House

Michael & Elizabeth Corfield
Kingston House,
Staverton,
Totnes,
Devon TQ9 6AR

tel   01803 762235
fax   01803 762444
email   info@kingston-estate.co.uk
web   www.kingston-estate.co.uk

The whole place is an absolute gem for purists and nature-lovers alike. Elizabeth's love of wildlife has made restoring the garden no easy task — she is adamant that no pesticides be used — but most of the estate was in need of a complete overhaul when she arrived. Now it is perfectly renovated and opens for the National Gardens Scheme three times a year: a rosy walled garden with peaches, pears, greengages and nectarines intertwined with roses and jasmine, beech hedging with yew arches, a formal rose garden, box topiary, a dear little summer house edged with lavender, an orchard with rare apples, and, in the South Garden, an avenue of pleached limes leading to a wild woodland. Elizabeth is also a stickler for historical accuracy. New projects include a fountain and mulberry garden and a huge patterned box parterre for either side of the front drive (4,000 plants were propagated on site) interplanted with conical yews and parrot tulips for the spring — the height of fashion when the house was built! The vegetable garden is productive and neat with a nod to the contemporary — unusually shaped twigs and branches are used as natural sculptures for supporting beans and sweet peas. *NGS*.

rooms	3: 2 doubles;
	1 double with separate bath.
price	From £150. Singles from £95.
meals	Dinner £34.50.
closed	Christmas & New Year.
directions	From A38, A384 to Staverton. At Sea Trout Inn, left fork for Kingston; halfway up hill right fork; at top, ahead at x-roads. Road goes up, then down to house; right to front of house.

Map 2 Entry 24

Gracious and grand is this impeccably-restored former home of a wealthy wool merchant with all its trappings intact. A rare marquetry staircase, an 18th-century painted china closet, marble works, original baths, galleried landings and oak panelling to gasp at. But it's not austere – the bedrooms are steeped in comfort and cushions, a fire roars in the guest sitting room (formerly the chapel), food is fresh, delicious and home-grown, and breakfasts outstanding. Rugged Dartmoor is to the north, Totnes minutes away and walks from the house through the gentle South Hams are spectacular.

Lower Norton Farmhouse

Peter & Glynis Bidwell
Lower Norton Farmhouse,
Coles Cross,
East Allington,
Totnes, Devon TQ9 7RL

tel   01548 521246
mobile   07790 288772
email   peter@lowernortonfarmhouse.co.uk
web   lowernortonfarmhouse.co.uk

Hard to believe the downstairs bedroom was a calving pen once and its smart bathroom, the dairy. Now it has a seagrass floor and a French walnut bed. All Glynis's rooms are freshly decorated and good value, and she and Peter are the most amenable hosts, genuinely happy for you to potter around all day should you wish to do so. For the more active, a yacht on the Dart and a cream Bentley are to hand, with Peter as navigator and chauffeur – rare treats. Return to gardens, paddocks, peaceful views, super dinners and a big log fire. Well off the beaten track, a tremendous find. *Children over nine welcome.*

rooms	3: 2 doubles, 1 twin.
price	From £65. Singles £55.
meals	Dinner £21. Lunch £7.50. Packed lunches £6.
closed	Rarely.
directions	From A381 at Halwell, 3rd left signed Slapton; 4th right after 2.3 miles signed Valley Springs Fishery at Wallaton Cross. House down 3rd drive on left.

Map 2 Entry 25

It's tricky to create a new garden and aim for that natural look, but Glynis and Peter have cleverly worked outwards from the house and drawn inspiration from the folds of this gentle valley. The terrace garden has a glass covered west facing seating area and an L-shaped pond brimming with marsh marigolds and lilies, with pillars supporting a campsis, the climbing rose 'Alchemist' and fragrant *Holboelia latifolia*. A shady path leads to the upper garden and its mixed borders of shrubs, wild flowers and annuals backed by mature native trees – at the top relax in the honeysuckle-smothered pergola and admire the view over the glorious South Hams. A cottage garden with penstemons and hollyhocks is developing just below the house and a peaceful sunken garden with huge ferns and a lovely laburnum; then a profusion of soft fruits and vegetables for the table. The orchard bursts with fruit trees and rhubarb and wildlife abounds – you may even meet Clarence the pheasant who takes his meals here. Like all gardeners, Glynis and Peter say there is much still to be done; thanks to their hard work and talent they do have a little slice of Eden already.

The Old Rectory

Jill Hitchins
The Old Rectory,
Diptford,
Totnes,
Devon TQ9 7NY

tel   01548 821575
email   hitchins@oldrectorydiptford.co.uk
web   www.oldrectorydiptford.co.uk

There's a tremendous feeling of space in the three-acre garden which was, Jill says, "pretty haphazard" when they took it over. Planting for structure and scent, she and John have added trees, shrubs, lawns, new flowerbeds and a romantic, back-to-nature garden. Deeply massed shrubs of varying shape, size and colour define the boundary with gently rounded fields and the green sweep of Dartmoor beyond. Amongst the trees – magnolias, oaks and a fine handkerchief tree – is a rediscovered ginkgo. There are tree ferns, too, camellias, acers and rare hellebores. An attractive pond, much visited by frogs and newts, is given extra interest by wire sculptures of chickens and cormorants. Very much alive is the family's cocker spaniel, cheerfully padding through his territory. Woodpeckers, nuthatches, owls, thrushes and bats also frequent the garden, while buzzards soar overhead. Behind the house stands Diptford church, keeping protective watch. Appropriately enough, Jill does wedding receptions here. She used to work for a television company specialising in garden films and is hugely knowledgeable and enthusiastic.

rooms	4: 2 doubles, 1 twin, 1 family suite for 4.
price	£85–£120. Singles £55–£60.
meals	Dinner, 3 courses, £25.
closed	Rarely.
directions	Avonwick to Diptford road. First house on right after village sign.

Map 2 Entry 26

Fresh flowers and 18th-century elegance… Jill and John's Regency rectory, on the edge of Diptford, was once the home of William Gregor, a vicar who discovered titanium! (There are still some titanium bowls in the large and lovely hall with its fine staircase.) You'll enjoy eating here, in the splendour of the dining room, for Jill is a superb, Leith-trained cook and a vivacious hostess. Bedrooms are all large and light; one is downstairs, another has three lovely windows with views over the garden to the moors – and a chesterfield so you can appreciate them in comfort. Pets are exceedingly welcome.

Avenue Cottage

Richard Pitts
Avenue Cottage,
Ashprington,
Totnes,
Devon TQ9 7UT

tel   01803 732769
mobile   07719 147475
email   richard.pitts@dial.pipex.com

The Turkey Oaks leading to the house were planted in 1840 by Squire Durrant; those and an enormous *Rhododendron arboreum* are all that remain of that planting. By 1987, when Richard arrived, his 11 acres were an inpenetrable forest of laurel and sycamore seedlings; learning to plant on a big scale in a big garden has been a challenge but he has no compassion for something in the wrong place. Five acres have been cleared and there are now two main paths that radiate from the house, one ending with a view of Sharpham House, the other with a view of the Dart. A spring rises and flows through two ponds; grass paths wind lazily along and there are benches and seats for the views. Richard says the most important thing has been to find plants that do well here and are happy; hydrangeas have become a great passion, *Camellia sasanqua* and scented azaleas in all their forms flourish and there is a good collection of young trees. Being a woodland garden there is plenty of wildlife; roe deer are a bit of a worry, but Richard tries to live with them all and has accepted that some plants cannot grow here. A delightful garden to visit time and time again, to be swept along by the seasons; if you ask nicely, Richard will provide secateurs and a bag for cuttings.

rooms	2: 1 twin/double; 1 double sharing shower.
price	£56–£70. Singles from £33.
meals	Pub in village.
closed	Rarely.
directions	A381 Totnes-Kingsbridge for 1 mile; left for Ashprington; into village, then left by pub ('Dead End' sign). House 0.25 miles on right.

Map 2 Entry 27

Richard came here for the garden – and so should you. The tree-lined approach is steep and spectacular; what was a thatched garden room belonging to Sharpham House is now a modern, square house surrounded by rhododendron, magnolia and wild flowers – perfect tranquillity. Do not expect state-of-the-art stylishness inside but you will find good beds and hearty breakfasts. The old-fashioned twin/double room has a huge bathroom with a faux-marble basin and a balcony with sweeping valley views; the pretty village and the pub are a short walk away.

STOP PRESS:
NO LONGER DOING B&B

This solid, early Georgian Grade II-listed country
house was originally built as a gentleman's residence
for a merchant trading in the nearby seafaring town of
Dartmouth. Everything here has an air of substance. The
bedrooms have balconies, king-sized beds or sea views.
There are open fires in the dining room and a fine library
for rainy days. There is the mood of a secret garden with
its own creeper-clad ruin... and behind it all a long valley
view bridged by a distant strip of sea.

Map 2 Entry 28

Merilyn and Philip are passionate about their eight-acre garden, always planning new features and displays to add to Wadstray's charms. When they came in the early 1990s, both house and garden needed major renovation but, on the plus side, they inherited plenty of mature planting; this was the work of Viscount Chaplin, a leading member of the Horticultural Society. He planted vigorously and well in the early 1950s, hence the profusion of good shrubs and trees including magnolia, camellias, azaleas and rhododendrons. The garden is open and sunny, with lovely valley views which they have improved by extending the lawn and moving a ha-ha fence to open up the vista even further. By the house, with its colonial veranda, Merilyn has created a gorgeous herbaceous border which blooms in profusion in summer. Spring displays get better all the time thanks to a continuing programme of bulb planting. Woodland areas have been slowly cleared to give more light, older shrubs pruned back to encourage vigorous growth. Lots of good hydrangeas — Merilyn and Philip are gradually adding to their collection because they do so well here. A new acer glade has now been established to give autumn colour. Beyond the lawn is a wildflower meadow leading to a wildlife pond and a walled garden which attracts alpinists from miles around who come to buy plants from the specialist nursery. *Devon Gardens Trust, NCCPG.*

Woodside Cottage

Tim & Sally Adams
Woodside Cottage,
Blackawton,
Dartmouth,
Devon TQ9 7BL

tel	01803 898164
mobile	07075 020769
email	stay@woodsidedartmouth.co.uk
web	www.woodsidedartmouth.co.uk

From a narrow decorative window, a charming vignette
of Devon: a winding country lane edged by fat hedgerows,
a hillside dotted with cows. The 18th-century former
gamekeeper's cottage is folded into Devon's gentle green
softness. Bedrooms are simple, fresh and charming, the
drawing and dining rooms formal and immaculate with fine
furniture, and there are gardening books galore. Tim and
Sally, both modest and beautifully mannered, may welcome
you with homemade cake, and have cuttings and jams for
sale. An excellent pub and the sea are nearby; at night see
the beam from Start Point lighthouse.

rooms	3: 2 doubles, 1 twin/double.
price	From £70. Singles by arrangement.
meals	Half-board option extra £20 p.p. for dinner with wine at village inn.
closed	Christmas.
directions	A381 from Totnes to Halwell, A3122 for Dartmouth. After Dartmouth Golf Club, right at sign to house & Blackawton; 0.3 miles before Blackawton, cottage on right.

Map 2 Entry 29

When Tim and Sally came here six years ago the garden was in a bit of a state, and difficult to manage with hardly any level ground, but conditions are favourable with a sheltered site that is almost frost free and a neutral, fertile soil. They have created three main terraces: at the top the woodland garden, designed by Sally, has curving grass paths edged with box and beds packed with shrubs, perennials and grasses. Then there is the mid terrace with a wide stone patio and plenty of seating for those long views over the valley; here a restful pond lazes with lilies and a rockery bank below is filled with bulbs and alpines. Steps down past a rhubarb bank lead to the kitchen garden terraces with greenhouse, potting shed and raised vegetable and fruit beds which provide goodies for breakfast and jams. Plenty of places to sit and quietly contemplate the beauty are dotted about and wildlife is abundant, from frogs, newts, buzzards and ducklings to white egrets, nuthatches and woodpeckers. Future plans include a water garden around the pond and perhaps a wildflower meadow, but whatever it is they will be doing it together; they are a knowledgeable couple who adore what they are doing and want to share their garden with others. Greenway, Coleton Fishacre, Overbecks and Dartington are all close.

Greenswood Farm

Mrs Helen Baron
Greenswood Farm,
Greenswood Lane,
Dartmouth,
Devon TQ6 OLY

tel	01803 712100
email	stay@greenswood.co.uk
web	www.greenswood.co.uk

A lovely, low Devon longhouse covered in wisteria, with stone flagging, deep window sills, and elegant furniture. But this is a working farm and there is no stuffiness in Helen and Roger — you will find a warm and cosy place to relax and enjoy the gorgeous valley that is now their patch. Bedrooms are feminine but not namby-pamby: huge mirrors, colourwashed walls and pretty curtains are fresh and clean, old pine chests give a solid feel and the views are special. Organic beef and lamb are reared on the farm and breakfast eggs come straight from Sally Henny Penny outside; buy some to take home — if you can drag yourself away.

rooms	3: 2 doubles, 1 twin.
price	From £75. Singles from £60. Pubs/restaurants 3 miles.
meals	Dinner (min. 4) by arrangement. Pubs/restaurants 3 miles.
closed	Rarely.
directions	A381 for Dartmouth. At Golf & Country Club right to Strete. Signpost after 1 mile.

Map 2 Entry 30

Roger has a huge interest in countryside management, having worked on The Coast Path and restoring Green Lanes in the South Hams. Helen adores growing flamboyant flowers (and arranges them skilfully in the house). When they moved here nine years ago they inherited a large garden planted on a boggy field with a stream running through and some mature shrubs and trees. South-facing and completely sheltered from any winds as it lies in a dip, the garden sweeps down from the house in a long hollow via three large ponds. Enlarged and landscaped, it has been designed to reflect the contours of its hilly, wooded outer borders. Perfect beds and borders are packed with spring bulbs, primroses, rhododendrons and azaleas, and pathways and older beds have been discovered and restored. Water lovers such as the gigantic *Gunnera manicata*, white irises, ferns and grasses hug the ponds while there are delightful secret pathways through colourful borders with large shrubs; a new path takes you across the field and through the woods. Terracing some of the steeper areas has created quiet places to sit and take in the views. The orchard is being restored, the planting around the ponds developed; the final pond is on level ground, hidden from the house with views of Greenswood Valley. Birdsong, ancient woodland, glorious peace.

Knocklayd

Susan & Jonathan Cardale
Knocklayd,
Redoubt Hill,
Kingswear,
Devon TQ6 0DA

tel   01803 752873
email   stay@knocklayd.com
web   www.knocklayd.com

When we visited, the recreation of this garden – charming in Jonathan's mother's day – was at the drawing-board stage. We include it, knowing Susan's energy will mean rapid progress, and that garden lovers will appreciate not only the destination but the journey. The starting point is an exceptional site, high above the village of Kingswear and its more bumptious neighbour Dartmouth, across the water. Gardening here must be a delight; the steep views of the town, estuary and harbour are dramatically lovely, while hoots from the steam train trundling below give a wonderfully nostalgic feel. The smallish, multi-levelled plot wraps itself comfortably around two sides of the house and the plan is to keep things simple, scented and colourful – but never brash. And also to demarcate different areas with gently shaped beds and grouped planting: spirea, agapanthus, choisya, nothing too formal or jarring on the eye. Guests will be encouraged to choose a sheltered spot – the idea is to have several – in which to sit and contemplate. This is to be a relatively low-maintenance garden with some gravel and paved areas, some gently flowing water, groundcover and shrubs (euphorbia, cistus, hebe) along with some old family favourites like cyclamen, camellia and Lady's Mantle.

rooms	3: 2 doubles, 1 twin/double.
price	£80. Singles £50.
meals	Supper & dinner from £20. Pub/restaurant 400 yds.
closed	Rarely.
directions	To Kingswear on B3205, left fork for Kingswear and Lower Ferry. Down hill, 1 mile, road climbs and becomes one way. Fork left into Higher Contour Road, half mile on left into Redoubt Hill; park by second gate; signed.

Map 2 Entry 31

Built in 1905, this family house makes the most of its extraordinary views of the estuary and harbour; the sitting rooms and pretty bedrooms each take a different angle. The dog-loving Cardales have been hard at work coordinating softly coloured fabrics, carpets and wallpapers, and arranging family furniture, prints, paintings and general 'abilia'. They've lived all over – he was a naval attaché – making this a richly comfortable place to stay. Boating can be arranged, trains met, nothing is too much trouble. And for breakfast? Locally smoked haddock, salmon and scrambled eggs, homemade jams, compotes and smoothies.

The Old Rectory

Rachel Belgrave & Heather Garner
The Old Rectory,
Widecombe in the Moor,
Devon TQ13 7TB

tel	01364 621231
fax	01364 621231
email	rachel.belgrave@care4free.net

The former home of the vicar of Widecombe with its famous fair and "Uncle Tom Cobbley and all" oozes tranquillity and calm. One of Rachel and Heather's hobbies is sculpture so although the decoration is traditional – wooden floors, pretty curtains, good furniture, family portraits – there are glimpses of well-travelled bohemianism. The dining room is iron-oxide red, there are tapestries from Ecuador and Peru, and vibrant colours glow in comfortable bedrooms. Pretty bathrooms sparkle with unusual tiles and original ceramic sinks, and there are long views from deep window seats. Charmingly relaxing and easy-going.

rooms	2: 1 double; 1 family room with separate bath & shower.
price	From £60.
meals	Pubs within 0.25 miles.
closed	November–March.
directions	From A38 Exeter to Plymouth road towards Bovey Tracey. Follow signs to Widecombe, opposite post office.

Map 2 Entry 32

Rachel has been "dotty about gardening" since she was a child and here she has used her artistic talent to create an organic cottage garden with a twist. Wanting the garden to reflect the symmetry of the house and then merge into the Dartmoor landscape, she has developed it from what was merely a field and a sloping lawn. Herbaceous borders hug the sides and are crammed with old favourites and many wild flowers. Half-way down is a sunny terrace for lounging, a border of scented roses and a heather bank reflecting the Moor. Then down through two labyrinth paths mown into the grass to a little stone circle and an open meadow that borders the woodland garden. The walled garden bursts with soft fruit and apple trees and a willow tunnel takes you to an old pond and bog garden fed by a stream and surrounded with primula, iris and other bog plants. This year has seen the new South African garden – a riot of agapanthus, crocosmia, dierama and more. Lovely arty touches everywhere – peep-holes through hedges, secret places, benches cut into the bottoms of old trees, willow structures and plenty of room for Rachel and Heather's sculptures. Rachel was told she couldn't grow roses on Dartmoor but her successes are everywhere, from the ramblers she loves to the old Georgian era varieties that go so well with the house.

Lower Hummacott

Tony & Liz Williams
Lower Hummacott,
Kings Nympton,
Umberleigh,
Devon EX37 9TU

tel   01769 581177
fax   01769 581177

The little Georgian farmhouse is as charming as its garden — and beautifully renovated by Tony and Liz. Fireplaces have been opened, shutters, panels and decorative ceilings added, new bathrooms installed, walls colourwashed. In the bedrooms are fresh fruit and flowers, antique furniture, pictures and old prints, and very comfortable beds (one king-size). The visitors' book is heaped with praise, and dinner is superb: organic and traditionally reared meats, caught-that-day fish, organic and fresh vegetables, local cheeses and free-range eggs, homemade cakes and preserves. A treat.

rooms	2 doubles.
price	£64. Singles £38.
meals	Dinner £25. Pub/restaurant 1.5 miles.
closed	Rarely.
directions	0.5 miles east of Kings Nympton village is Beara Cross; go straight over marked to Romansleigh for 0.75 miles; Hummacott is 1st entrance on left.

Map 2 Entry 33

Enthusiastic gardeners, Tony and Liz have created a fascinating garden in their seven acres on this warm, south-facing site. It's a lovely mix of the classically formal and the gently informal, a wide wildflower meadow and two acres of natural wooded parkland. They have only been here since 1999 and the work they have put into the grounds is stupendous, transforming what was until recently no more than a field. By the house is a half-acre landscaped and charmingly designed formal garden with a spring-fed pool, a lime walk, handsome borders linked with arches, a pergola of roses, wisteria, jasmine and clematis, and a new parterre garden taking shape. In direct line with the front door a bold, straight grassy avenue of chestnuts leads you down this gentle side of a little valley. Otters make their way up the brook to help themselves to the fish in the wildlife ponds fed by a new cut stream. There are ducks, dragonflies and dipping swallows. A tree-lined walk leads you to the woodland which Tony and Liz are restoring and replanting, encouraging wild spring flowers and bluebells to reappear. You may see horses or ponies in the paddock, red deer across the stream and a tawny owl who lives by the house. Wonderful.

West Bradley

Martin & Phillida Strong
West Bradley,
Templeton,
Tiverton,
Devon EX16 8BJ

tel   01884 253220
mobile   07779 241048
email   martinstrong@westbradley.eclipse.co.uk

A pretty wrought-iron gate inherited from Phillida's great grandmother tempts you into the garden, where the soft shapes and colours appear to merge into the open country beyond. Martin, who has lived here for 35 years, has created it all from scratch. The borders are full of jostling shrubs and roses, the walls are covered with climbing hydrangeas, golden hop, clematis and honeysuckle, and the curves of the lawn are dotted with the occasional statue or urn. Hedges of escallonia, beech or *Rosa rugosa* provide shelter, while a pair of wire-woven chickens make a witty addition to a corner of a flower bed. Martin loves soft fruit and grows gooseberries, raspberries, blackcurrants and blueberries in abundance (Phillida would like a proper vegetable garden but for now must make do with courgettes and tomatoes). Behind the house are trees planted when Martin first came here, recently supplemented by magnolia and arbutus; the woods are full of bluebells in the spring. There's even a sparkling stream. The rest of West Bradley's 100 acres is let to a tenant farmer; the feel is deeply, delightfully rural.

rooms	2: 1 twin/double; 1 twin with separate shower.
price	£80. Singles £45.
meals	Pubs 10-minute drive.
closed	Rarely.
directions	From Tiverton B3137 Witheridge road; on towards Rackenford & Calverleigh. After pink thatched cottage (2 miles), fork left to Templeton; West Bradley 2 miles; on left before village hall.

Map 2 Entry 34

Total immersion in beauty – doves in the farmyard, hens in the orchard, fields on either side of the long drive. Privacy, too, in your 18th-century upside-down barn on the side of the owners' Devon longhouse – and valley views; from 800 feet up, they're superb. A handmade oak staircase, oak floors, two freshly furnished bedrooms (one up, one down), a good big sitting room with a gas-fired 'woodburner' and a kitchen you are welcome to use. Phillida can bring breakfast to you here, or you can tuck into a full English in the farmhouse. There will be homemade something on arrival and a good choice of local pubs.

Regency House

Mrs Jenny Parsons
Regency House,
Hemyock,
Cullompton,
Devon EX15 3RQ

tel   01823 680238
email   jenny.parsons@btinternet.com

Rooms are beautifully proportioned in this 1855 rectory, with varnished floors and rugs downstairs. Both the music room and the drawing room have floor-to-ceiling windows overlooking the lake and the garden, and Jenny would love more visitors to play the grand piano. She adores collecting pictures and there are some interesting contemporary paintings and hunting prints around and lots of books too. The large, comfortable and light bedroom is decorated in classic pale creamy colours and still has the original shutters. You have breakfast in the dining area of the huge farmhouse kitchen warmed by the Aga.

rooms	1 double.
price	£90. Singles £45.
meals	Dinner £25. Pub 3 miles.
closed	Rarely.
directions	M5 junc. 26 for Wellington, from north. Left at roundabout; immed. right at junction, left at next junction. Right at top of hill. Left at x-roads. In Hemyock take Dunkeswell & Honiton Road. House 500 yds on right.

Map 2 Entry 35

Jenny was in the middle of her horticultural and garden design courses at Bicton when she moved here 15 years ago, so she put her increasing knowledge to immediate good use as she licked the jungle she had bought into shape. The large south-facing walled kitchen garden is old and beautiful and has been brought back into full production; nowadays Jenny rarely buys vegetables. Plum trees are fanned against the wall, and at the top a bench looks down a central espaliered apple walk. On the other side of the house an artistic son's fern sculpture attracts admiring comments, and nearby Jenny has planted a colourful bog garden around a little dew pond. However, her favourite area remains her spring garden by the drive with its *Anemone blanda* and bulbs, *Exochorda macrantha* and epimediums – an astonishing array of plants. There's restoration work going on along the fast-moving stream where a mid-19th century race and waterfall are being rebuilt. Further upstream the drive passes through a newly cobbled ford, which already looks 200 years old. It's a bit like the Good Life at Regency House: not only the garden interests her visitors but also her little Dexter cattle and Jacob sheep. *NGS.*

Applebarn Cottage

Patricia & Robert Spencer
Applebarn Cottage,
Bewley Down,
Membury, Axminster,
Devon EX13 7JX

tel	01460 220873
fax	01460 220873
email	paspenceruk@yahoo.co.uk
web	www.applebarn-cottage.co.uk

Before even setting foot in the house, the Spencers knew this was the place for them. The grounds and outlook were irresistible. Though it had become a wilderness, the garden had obviously once been well designed and stocked, and the views... on a clear day you can see Lamberts Castle and even, with binoculars, watch cricket matches on the village green. Exploring the garden is a delight, not only because of its varied nature but also because of the intoxicating scents. (Birds and butterflies seem to love it too.) In front of the house is a two-level terrace. On the upper level – a lovely place to dine on summer evenings – grow *Magnolia stellata*, Irish yew, camellias, roses and a fine show of hellebores. Lower down are more camellias, scented clarydendron and euchryphia, yucca and huge flax features. Paths and gently sloping lawns lead to a secret, paved garden, guarded by bamboos threaded through with 'Albertine' and other roses. At its heart is a two-tiered Italian fountain, surrounded by Chinese lilac and ferns; nearby stands a splendid 'wedding cake' tree. Gunnera, royal ferns and euphorbia reign supreme in the bog gardens, while the woody wild garden has magnolias, broom and monkey puzzles. And in the spring, endless drifts of primroses.

rooms	2 suites.
price	Half-board £56-£60 p.p.
meals	Dinner included. Pub/restaurant 3 miles.
closed	Last two weeks November up to 1 March.
directions	A30 from Chard, signed Honiton. Left at top of hill signed Wambrook/Stockland. After 3 miles pass Ferne Animal Sanctuary. Straight on at next x-roads (Membury); 0.75 miles, left, signed Cotley/Ridge. Past Hartshill Boarding Kennels; signed 2nd right.

Map 2 Entry 36

A tree-lined drive leads to a long white wall; a gate in the wall opens to an explosion of colour – the garden. Come for a deliciously restful place and the nicest hosts. The wisteria-covered 17th-century cottage is full of books, flowers and paintings, and bedrooms are large, traditional and wonderfully comfortable, with all-white bathrooms. One of the rooms is in an extension but blends in beautifully. Breakfast, served in a lovely slate-floored dining room, includes a neighbour's homemade honey. Eat in if you can: dinner is superb and includes vegetables and fruits from the garden.

Woodwalls House

Sally & Tony Valdes-Scott
Woodwalls House,
Corscombe,
Dorchester,
Dorset DT2 0NT

tel	01935 891477
fax	01935 891477
web	www.woodwallshouse.co.uk

Quiet seclusion among birds, badgers and wildflowers. The 1806 keeper's cottage sits in its own 12 acres of deepest Dorset where lovely walks lead in all directions. A pretty garden, a sheltered, wisteria-fringed terrace and two cosy bedrooms with lace bedspreads, garden views and a little cream sofa in the twin. It is all thoroughly comforting and welcoming, and your kind, wildlife-loving hosts rustle up fine breakfasts of Beaminster bangers and honey from their bees. Hone your skills for the vicious game that is croquet, and if you fancy tennis, the court is yours to borrow. *Minimum stay two nights.*

rooms	2: 1 double; 1 twin with separate bath/shower.
price	£80. Singles £50.
meals	Pub 5-minute walk.
closed	Christmas.
directions	Leave Yeovil on A37 to Dorchester. After 1 mile, right for Corscombe; 6 miles to Corscombe; left after village sign down Norwood Lane; 300 yds, 1st white gate on right.

Map 2 Entry 37

A pretty garden surrounds the house: mainly laid to lawn with some mature shrubs and magnificent trees, including three types of Chilean beech, and not too many flower beds make it relatively low maintenance. When Tony and Sally decided to extend their garden the fields surrounding the house had been farmed intensively for many years, ancient hedges had been removed and the wildlife that once populated them had seriously declined. They have spent the last 20 years trying hard to reverse this damage and to provide an environmentally friendly habitat for all the flora and fauna which are returning. They haven't used any commercial fertilisers and — without any seed at all — the hay meadows are once again a mass of wild flowers in May and June; several ancient species of grass have also recolonised. Jacob sheep graze the meadows and provide manure, hedges have been carefully planted and managed, and there is an active programme for encouraging birds which includes leaving the hay uncut until mid-July to allow ground-nesting species to breed safely. Successes include a mass of cowslips in one meadow and several varieties of orchids in another. And birds are back in abundance, thrushes, yellowhammers, skylarks, tits and owls among the list. Nature lovers will adore it here, especially in the spring, and there isn't much local history that Tony doesn't know about — just ask!

The Dairy House

Paul & Penny Burns
The Dairy House,
Stowell,
Sherborne,
Dorset DT9 4PD

tel   01963 370754
email   paul.burns@totalise.co.uk

The Georgian-Victorian dairy-cottage, whose additions (studios, study, art gallery) extend in several directions, is a warm and unfussy home. Come not for luxury but for a bohemian kitchen whose shelves burst with pink and white china, a cosy sitting room shared with the owners, a fun family room with space in which to romp, and a faded but friendly twin. Penny and Paul – artistic, energetic, youthful – run an easy-going household and have a stunning garden to boot. Breakfast is the full Monty, dinner is traditional and delicious, and nearby Sherborne offers the Abbey, galleries, castles, cafés and more.

rooms	3: 1 twin; 1 family room with separate shower; 1 twin sharing shower.
price	From £50. Singles £35.
meals	Dinner £18. BYO. Pubs/restaurants 2.5 miles.
closed	Occasionally.
directions	From A303, south on A357 for 3 miles; right at 2nd sign to Stowell, by lodge on left. After 1 mile pass church; after 800 yds, 1st two-storey house on left.

At the Dairy House, conservation is taken seriously in the house and garden. Water is heated by solar energy, there are six large water butts in the garden, three compost heaps and many butterfly-attracting plants. Three hundred trees have been planted, along with a 'brash'-filled hedge to encourage insects.

Map 2 Entry 38

Paul is the gardener. When he was 12 years old he helped to landscape his parents' garden and was smitten. Here he has created a number of distinctive garden rooms connected by paths and walkways through woodland and under arches. Collecting unusual things for the garden is another hobby; the potting-shed windows were the lavatory windows from the Salisbury workhouse, 50p each! The terrace just outside the house has stone flags from the kitchen leading to the first path, past an old sundial, then through a pergola tunnel smothered in white rambling roses. A lawned area is interspersed with many herbaceous borders, while beautiful wrought-iron and wooden archways lead to a woodland garden filled with 20-year-old trees. As the path continues through the woods the sunlight breaks through the tree canopy to reveal the woodland floor of periwinkle and hardy geraniums; beyond, fields stretch in every direction. A pond is guarded by yellow flag irises, and there's a 200-yard-long trellis made from pollarded branches from the wood flanked by a stream — the first tributary of the river Yeo. There are soft fruit bushes for the kitchen and many birds thrive, including greenfinches, goldfinches, wrens, two species of woodpecker and, occasionally, a little owl. A new gravel area lends a tranquil touch of zen. A fascinating and artistic place to wander and ponder. *HPS*.

Lytchett Hard

David & Elizabeth Collinson
Lytchett Hard,
Beach Road,
Upton,
Poole,
Dorset BH16 5NA

tel   01202 622297
fax   01202 632716
email   lytchetthard@ntlworld.com

One fascinating acre adjoins a reeded inlet of Poole harbour plus their own SSSI where, if you're lucky, you'll spot a Dartford Warbler among the gorse. The garden has been created from scratch over the past 30 years and carefully designed to make the most of the views over heathland — haunt of two species of lizard — and water. Liz is a trained horticulturist and she and David have capitalised on the mild weather here to grow tender plants; copious additions of compost and horse manure have improved the sandy soil. These tender treasures thrive gloriously and are unusually large — you're greeted by a huge phormium in the pretty entrance garden by the drive; the terrace is a stone and gravel Mediterranean garden. Acid-lovers are happy, so there are fine displays of camellias and rhododendrons among hosts of daffodil and tulips once the sweeps of snowdrops have finished. Three borders are colour-themed, each representing a wedding anniversary: silver, pearl and ruby. Kitchen gardeners will be interested in the productive potager. Play croquet on the large lawn, explore the private woodland where David has created winding paths, relax in the shade of the gazebo or in the warmth of the working conservatory, admire the many unusual plants, or simply sit back and enjoy that shimmering view. *RHS.*

rooms	3: 1 twin, 1 double, 1 four-poster.
price	£60-£85. Singles £40-£60.
meals	Dinner £15-£25. Pub 1 mile.
closed	Occasionally.
directions	From Upton x-roads (0.5 miles SE of A35/A350 interchange), west into Dorchester Rd; 2nd left into Seaview Rd; cross junc. over Sandy Lane into Slough Lane; immed. 1st left into Beach Rd. 150 yds on, on right.

Map 3 Entry 39

The house takes its name from the place where fishermen brought their craft ashore, in the unspoilt upper reaches of Poole harbour. The three guest bedrooms all face south and make the most of the main garden below and the views beyond. Elizabeth and David's green fingers conjure up a mass of home-grown produce as well as flowers – vegetables, jams, herbs and fruit. Guests can linger in the antique oak dining room; there are log fires and a lovely, huggable pointer called Coco.

Mount Hall

Sue & James Carbutt
Mount Hall,
Great Horkesley,
Colchester,
Essex CO6 4BZ

tel   01206 271359
email   suecarbutt@yahoo.co.uk

An immaculate Queen Anne listed house. Two upstairs rooms
are large, light, quietly elegant and deeply comfortable, with
garden views, but it is the private, ground-floor annexe that
Sue enthuses about most. She particularly enjoys welcoming
those in wheelchairs, children and dogs – there is even a
door out to a separate secure garden for visiting pooches.
You get twin zip-link beds, two futons for families, a huge
sofa, masses of lovely books to browse, spoiling touches
everywhere and homemade jams for breakfast. Set out from
this peaceful place to explore Constable country – and the
Beth Chatto Gardens.

rooms	3: 1 twin, 1 single. Annexe: 1 twin/double, 2 futons.
price	£70. Singles £35.
meals	Pub 0.5 miles.
closed	Rarely.
directions	A134 through Great Horkesley to Rose & Crown pub, left (London Rd). 1st left marked West Bergholt; 2nd drive on left.

Map 4 Entry 40

The drive sweeps you around and up to the handsome pillared and stuccoed front porch of Mount Hall, overlooking a wide lawn flanked by mature trees and shrubs. Sue has a great interest in trees and the many well-established varieties act as a dramatic backdrop to the labour-saving foliage plants which speak for themselves through their different shapes and shades of green and yellow. This is a place for retreat, very tranquil, with plenty of seats under trees, or by the pool. The walled pool garden is totally secluded and private, a haven of peace watched over by a huge eucalyptus; again, Sue prefers calm, cool and subdued colours in her planting. A beautiful evergreen tapestry border is of year-round interest in muted greens; elsewhere greys and whites, pale blues and silver predominate, most of the plants coming from the Beth Chatto Gardens eight miles away. The pool was an erstwhile swimming pool: the formal rectangular shape has been kept, but now teems with wildlife. Nicknamed her "gosh" pool after her visitors' first reactions, the fish and frogs have bred and multiplied well since its conversion. So peaceful, four miles from the edge of the Dedham Vale, and close to the oldest recorded town of Colchester. *HPS.*

Drakestone House

Hugh & Crystal Mildmay
Drakestone House,
Stinchcombe,
Dursley,
Gloucestershire GL11 6AS

tel   01453 542140
fax   01453 542140

The hauntingly atmospheric Edwardian landscaped grounds would make a perfect setting for open-air Shakespeare – rather apposite since it's said that young Shakespeare roamed the hills around Stinchcombe. Hugh's grandparents laid out the grounds, influenced by a love of Italian gardens and admiration for Gertrude Jekyll. When Hugh and Crystal moved here, the garden was distressed and needed attention, particularly the magnificent topiary. The beautifully varied, lofty, sculptural yew and box hedges, domes and busbies dominating the view from the house are restored to perfection, creating a series of garden rooms with a backdrop of woodland. Paths and a romantic Irish yew walk invite you to wander as you move from one compartment to the next. By the house, a pergola is covered with wisteria in spring and rambling roses in summer, near displays of lovely old roses underplanted with lavender. Crystal describes these two acres as informally formal or formally informal – she can't quite decide which. But it's that elegant Edwardian design with its Mediterranean mood that makes Drakestone House so special. The best moments to enjoy the grounds are on sunny days when the shadows play strange tricks with the sculptured hedges and trees… expect Puck or Arial to make a dramatic entrance at any moment!

rooms	3: 1 twin/double with separate shower; 1 double, 1 twin, sharing bath.
price	£76. Singles £48.
meals	Dinner £25. BYO wine.
closed	December-January.
directions	B4060 from Stinchcombe to Wotton-under-Edge. 0.25 miles out of Stinchcombe village. Driveway on left marked, before long bend.

Map 2 Entry 41

Utterly delightful people with wide-ranging interests (ex-British Council and college lecturing; arts, travel, gardening...) in a manor-type house full of beautiful furniture. A treat. The house was born of the Arts and Crafts movement and remains fascinating: wood panels painted green, a log-fired drawing-room for guests, quarry tiles on window sills, handsome old furniture, comfortable proportions... elegant but human, refined but easy. And the garden's massive clipped hedges are superb.

Pauntley Court

Mrs Christine Skelding
Pauntley Court,
Pauntley,
Redmarley d'Abitot,
Gloucestershire GL19 3JA

tel   01531 820344

Reputedly the house where Dick Whittington was born; certainly his family lived here for 300 years and there is still a wise-looking cat! Christine, a cello player, is elegant and kind: sharing her home with guests comes naturally, and the huge old quarry tiled kitchen and dining room are perfect for large gatherings. Everything is in character: wooden floors, plastered walls between ancient beams, roaring log fires, a gorgeous hand-painted ceiling and wall paintings that are expanding along a corridor. Bedrooms are large and filled with bowls of flowers, linen is crisp and the views from all windows are stunning.

rooms	2: 1 double, 1 twin/double.
price	£80.
meals	Pub 5 miles.
closed	October-February.
directions	M50 junc. 2 for Gloucester; through Redmarley d'Abitot, for Newent; 3 miles to Pauntley; past church, down 'no through road' and over cattle grid to house.

Map 2 Entry 42

Christine has been here since 1990 and has meticulously restored the garden with an Elizabethan feel to reflect the history. A young orchard lines the left hand side of the drive and, as you approach through the iron gates, an intimate courtyard has pretty lawns outlined in box. A secret and sheltered herb garden sits outside the kitchen door, and four standard figs stand proudly in terracotta pots. To the south east of the house is a cloister garden planted with pleached hornbeams and two deep herbaceous beds backed by very old brick walls. The sunken garden has beds planted with tulips, alliums and roses, and lovely oak balustrading. From here is a marvellous view down to the lake (fed by a natural spring) and new woodland right down to the boundary, formed by the river Leadon. The Ruin Garden is planted around what historians believe was a great stone building started by the Marquis of Somerset but never completed; specialist plans have been drawn up and the foundations are represented in yew. A delighted memorial garden, planted in honour of Mr Thornton, who lived here and devoted himself to the house and garden restoration, has a sculpted bowl at its centre with a natural water feature. From here, more fabulous views. This is a special garden with plenty of interest and a serene atmosphere.

Ivydene House

Rosemary Gallagher
Ivydene House,
Uckinghall,
Tewkesbury,
Gloucestershire GL20 6ES

tel	01684 592453
email	rosemaryg@fsmail.net
web	www.ivydenehouse.net

An attractive red-brick 1790 house on the border of
Gloucestershire and Worcestershire; close to the motorway
but with a rural feel. Rosemary greets guests with tea and
homemade cake, to enjoy in the garden or by the sitting
room fire. Downstairs is traditional and comfortable with
pictures, fresh flowers and books to read. Bedrooms have a
more contemporary feel – are swish even – with plain grey
bedspreads spruced up with silky cushions. Sparkling
bathrooms, crisp white linen and smashing squidgy pillows
on good beds mean you will rest well. Good walking
straight from the house or a game of tennis in the garden.

rooms	2: 1 twin/double, 1 double.
price	From £60. Singles from £40.
meals	Pub within walking distance.
closed	Christmas.
directions	M5 junc. 8 onto M50. Exit junc. 1 onto A38 north, then 1st left to Ripple.

Map 3 Entry 43

When Rosemary and Pete arrived eight years ago the 'garden' was an expanse of mud, weeds, stones and rubble – with a few asbestos sheds and bonfire remnants thrown in for good measure. So, apart from a sprinkling of old apple trees, everything in this gorgeous, informal, country garden has been planned and planted by the Gallaghers. Rectangular, flanked on two sides by farmland and divided by a shrub-filled island bed so large it has gravel paths through it, the garden is something special. The formal part is to one side: huge bed, pristine lavender walk and smooth lawn – broken up by a yew-hedge archway leading to a pond, with plenty of seating areas, a water feature and a pergola. The pond is surrounded by water lovers and is left alone to encourage wildlife, there are some good trees like robinia, elder and eucalyptus dotted about, and a pretty row of hydrangea 'Annabel'. The other side of the garden is wilder: mown paths swoop through a wood of about 300 English trees, all surrounded by a hawthorn hedge and with a trampoline in the middle. A south-facing terrace cluttered with happy pots has more seating areas; a sunny conservatory hugs the house. Rosemary doesn't like gardens filled with colourful annuals and prefers something more subtle; this she has achieved. Future plans include building a small jetty to hang over the pond. This is a young garden worth watching.

Clapton Manor

Karin & James Bolton
Clapton Manor,
Clapton-on-the-Hill,
Bourton on the Water,
Gloucestershire GL54 2LG

tel	01451 810202
mobile	07967 144416
email	bandb@claptonmanor.co.uk
web	www.claptonmanor.co.uk

Like Wilde's reformed Selfish Giant, the house chuckles 'under the influence' of children. Relaxed and inviting, the 16th-century manor is as all homes should be: loved and lived-in. Yet, with three-foot-thick walls, a flagstoned hall, sit-in fireplaces and stone-mullioned windows, it's an impressive pile. One bedroom has a secret door that leads to an unexpected fuchsia-pink bathroom; the other, smaller, has wonderful garden views. Gaze over the garden wall as you breakfast on home-laid eggs and homemade jams. A lovely, easy-going house with a family, and dogs, to match.

rooms	2: 1 double, 1 twin/double.
price	From £90. Singles £80.
meals	Dinner by arrangement. Pub/restaurants within 15-minute drive.
closed	Christmas & New Year.
directions	A429 Cirencester-Stow. Right signed Sherborne & Clapton. In village, pass grassy area to left, postbox in one corner; house straight ahead on left on corner.

Map 3 Entry 44

James abandoned his life in the City in order to garden. Now he runs his own garden tours business and lectures extensively for NADFAS and the NACF, as well as designing gardens with his wife Karin. They have created a delightfully informal garden here, with a formal touch or two: a perspective path between the double borders; a pyramid of Portuguese laurel with pruned Moorish 'doors'. The gently sloping garden wraps itself around the lovely old manor house and is divided into compartments defined by ancient Cotswold stone walls and hedges of yew, hornbeam, box and cotoneaster. And there's a wildflower meadow with its own mound from which you can survey the surrounding hills. The garden is planned for year-round interest, with sparkling displays of rare snowdrops, narcissi and hellebores in winter and spring. Summer sees masses of old roses climbing through trees, over arches and in the tiny orchard surrounding the children's Wendy house, smothered in 'Mrs Honey Dyson'. Later in the year, the double borders with their perennials come into their own. It is a lovingly designed garden where the four Bolton children and their three dogs play rugby and cricket in among the flowers and hens… in spite of which B&B guests still manage to relax and enjoy this fine collection of plants in a beautiful setting.

Lower Farm House

Nicholas & Zelie Mason
Lower Farm House,
Adlestrop,
Moreton-in-Marsh,
Gloucestershire GL56 0YR

tel	01608 658756
fax	01608 659458
email	zelie.mason@talk21.com

Jane Austen used to stay in Adlestrop and Fanny would surely have found it 'most agreeable' and chosen kedgeree for breakfast. Once the Home Farm of the Leigh estate, Lower Farm House has a perfect Georgian feel – high ceilings, sash windows, and well-proportioned rooms graciously furnished yet not dauntingly formal. Nicholas and Zelie are both charming and articulate and love entertaining. Their pale-carpeted guest bedrooms are softly serene with fine garden views. Meals – everything as organic and locally sourced as possible – sound superb; cooking and gardening are Zelie's passions.

rooms	2: 1 double, 1 twin.
price	£90-£96. Singles £55.
meals	Dinner, 3 courses, £30. Pubs/restaurants 1-5 miles.
closed	Rarely.
directions	A436 from Stow; after 3 miles, left to Adlestrop; right at T-junc; after double bend, drive 50 yds on right; sign at end of drive.

Map 3 Entry 45

Borders here are seasonal and colour themed: white and blue in early spring, red and yellow going into summer when things get hot and frothy with penstemons, delphiniums, roses and lavender. There's a huge terrace where you can sit and admire the setting sun, or wander past the pond and into woodland to watch the evening flight of birds over the spring-fed lake. Although these two acres of garden have evolved gradually since Zelie and Nicholas started from scratch, when they moved here in 1991, they are maturing fast. The result is an open and flowing country garden to complement the long and lovely views and the soft stone of well-maintained walls that provide a wonderful backdrop to the many climbers, including clematis and honeysuckle. Other good structure comes from fine pleached hornbeam and yew hedges. Mown paths lead to Zelie's flourishing vegetable garden; if you choose to eat in, you'll reap the rewards of her labours at dinner. The next project is underway and the picture is continually evolving. A gently restful, and supremely comfortable place to round off the day after taking in other Cotswold charmers; Hidcote, Kiftsgate and Bourton are close by and on the urban front Cheltenham, Stratford, and Oxford.

Mizzards Farm

Harriet & Julian Francis
Mizzards Farm,
Rogate,
Petersfield,
Hampshire GU31 5HS

tel   01730 821656
fax   01730 821655
email   francis@mizzards.co.uk

Wow! The central hall is three storeys high, its vaulted roof open to the rafters – a splendid spot for bacon and eggs. This is the oldest (and medieval) part of this lovely, rambling, mostly 16th-century farmhouse, with its huge fireplace and stone-flagged floor, covered by a large Persian rug. A four-poster on a raised dias in the main bedroom has switches in the bedhead to operate curtains and bathroom light... the sumptuousness continues with a multi-mirrored, marble bathroom, an upstairs conservatory for tea, a drawing room for concerts, croquet in the grounds and a covered, heated pool.

rooms	3: 1 double, 1 twin, 1 four-poster.
price	£75-£80. Singles £50-£55.
meals	Pub 0.5 miles.
closed	Christmas & New Year.
directions	From A272 at Rogate, turn for Harting & Nyewood. Cross humpback bridge; drive signed to right after 300 yds.

Map 3 Entry 46

The Francis family have derived huge pleasure from this garden – set in a deeply rural part of Hampshire – for more than a quarter century. A series of sweeping terraced lawns flow down to a peaceful lake and woodland stream. Not only is there a heated and covered swimming pool (that you, too, may use) but there's a chess set beside it, its squares painted on a concrete base, its wooden pieces two feet high. Stroll across the terrace on the other side of the house, peer round the box parterre, and you find a croquet lawn. And if you'd like a quiet spot from which to watch others play – or you wish to read – just make for the gazebo at the end of the lawn. When deciding to create a garden from a field, Harriet deliberately chose not to divide the area into rooms, but, to keep the natural vista to lake and stream. Over the years she has developed a series of colour coordinated borders, terraces and island beds. Today the garden plays host to a series of charity concerts; members of the audience bring their own picnics and everyone is served with strawberries and cream. A mini-Glyndebourne in a fine garden in Hampshire.

Bollingham House

Stephanie & John Grant
Bollingham House,
Eardisley,
Herefordshire HR5 3LE

tel   01544 327326
email   grant@bollinghamhouse.com
web   www.bollinghamhouse.com

A Georgian jewel in a delightful, lofty – 600 feet above sea level – setting.
When they arrived, John and Stephanie carefully studied the garden around
the house and set to work with huge gusto. The result is a well-considered,
four-acre garden. The master plan was to create gardens within a garden,
always with labour-saving ideas in mind. The gardens at the front of the house
are a formal introduction to the stunning views, and terraced front lawns
sweep down to meet the sight of the Wye Valley and the Black Mountains.
Beyond is a wildflower meadow divided into two terraces, one of which is
guarded by a magnificent sweet-chestnut tree. The old walled garden is
approached through a Millennium iron gate and leads to a perfumed avenue of
old roses and a sequence of formal parterres. There's a Moghul-influenced area
edged by a rectangular rill that contrasts with the silent pool; water features use
modern pump technology to create yesterday's classic effects. A well-stocked
fish pond leads to a bog garden planted with willow and water-loving plants
including a gigantic gunnera, and to the shady shrubbery. The final flourish
behind the house and its 14th-century barn – decorated as a splendid party hall
– is a motte-and-bailey topped with an ancient water tower and dovecote.

rooms	2: 1 twin; 1 double with separate bath.
price	From £70. Singles from £35.
meals	Dinner £22. Packed lunch £5.
closed	Occasionally.
directions	A438 Hereford to Brecon road, towards Kington on A4111; through Eardisley; house 2 miles up hill on left, behind long line of conifers.

Map 2 Entry 47

From the sofa in your comfortable bedroom you can gaze out on the Malvern Hills and the Black Mountains. In spite of the grandeur of this Georgian house it feels like a lived-in home with large rooms graciously furnished, and some contemporary touches. Fascinating features and furniture everywhere: a timbered frame wall from the original 14th-century house, wide elm floorboards upstairs and a dining room table reputed to be an Irish 'coffin table' which John found in Dublin. Your hosts are delightful and Stephanie's Aga cooking excellent.

Winforton Court

Jackie Kingdon
Winforton Court,
Winforton,
Herefordshire HR3 6EA

tel   01544 328498
fax   01544 328498
web   www.winfortoncourt.co.uk

A delightful little walled garden greets you, its path edged with profuse purple and green sage studded with perennial geraniums. When Jackie arrived, all the grounds were down to grass with some mature trees and with fine views across the Wye Valley to the Black Mountains – there's a lovely walk to the river. She took heaps of cuttings from her previous home, created borders, planted vigorously and transformed her big new garden. The sunny courtyard behind the house has a fruit-covered fig tree and mature magnolia, flowering shrubs in containers, cherubs on walls and a fountain brought from Portugal. Beyond lies her open, terraced garden dominated by a weeping willow, with an ancient standing stone on a ley line shaded by a tall horse chestnut, emerald lawns, flower-packed beds and, below, a stream and small water garden. She has even planted the edge of the parking area with colourful sun-lovers thrusting through the gravel. Jackie aimed to make a garden to complement Winforton Court's dreamy architecture, and that's what she has achieved. Guests love it here – regulars come bearing gifts to add to her collection, and are sometimes generously given cuttings so a little bit of Winforton Court will grow in their garden and give them pleasure for years to come.

rooms	3: 1 double, 1 four-poster, 1 four-poster suite.
price	£75-£90. Singles £60.
meals	Pub 2-minute walk.
closed	Christmas.
directions	From Hereford, A438 into village. House on left with a green sign & iron gates.

Map 2 Entry 48

The staircase, mentioned in Pevsner's, is 17th century. Most of this half-timbered house was built in 1500 and is breathtaking in its ancient dignity, its undulating floors, its wonderful thick walls and its great oak beams. Take a book from the small library and settle into a window seat overlooking the gardens. There is a guest sitting room too, festooned with works of art by local artists. The two four-postered bedrooms verge on the luxurious; so does the double, and all have fruit juice and sherry. Gorgeous.

Brobury House

Pru Cartwright
Brobury House,
Brobury,
By Bredwardine,
Herefordshire HR3 6BS

tel	01981 500229
email	enquiries@broburyhouse.co.uk
web	www.broburyhouse.co.uk

Here are emerald-green riverbanks, and a huge handsome house dominated by a wisteria-cloaked folly. The ancient mulberry tree on the lawn was planted by Victorian diarist Francis Kilvert, who lived across the river. Super big bedrooms with traditional wallpapers, polished furniture and carpeted floors have country or garden views — and it's a short dash to the twins' smart shower rooms. After a perfect night's sleep, tuck into locally sourced organic breakfasts on the terrace or in the conservatory — light and lovely, with comfortable seating. Conveniently close to bookish, eccentric Hay-on-Wye, and the Tudor village of Weobley.

rooms	3: 1 double; 1 twin, 1 twin/double each with separate shower.
price	From £60. Singles from £45.
meals	Pub 2.5 miles.
closed	Occasionally including Christmas & New Year.
directions	Turn south off A438, 10 miles west of Hereford, signed 'Bredwardine & Brobury'. Continue 1 mile. House on left before bridge. Large car park for visitors.

Map 2 Entry 49

Enthusiastic, energetic Pru and Keith are passionate about these gardens that sweep down to the Wye, and have won Green Tourism and Wildlife Action awards for their work. Together with designer Peter Antonius, they are continuing to expand and develop the graceful tree-filled terraces, laid out in the 1880s to make the most of the views. Open to the public (hence the car park at the front and the green signs), this spectacular, waterside setting has plenty to explore and places in which to sit and muse. Close to the house the grounds are formal: a south-facing lawn, an acacia-shaded lily pond and a Lutyens-inspired pool with parterre, all overlooking more lawns, and copper beeches, lavender, climbing roses and clipped hornbeam hedges. Rose beds, magnolias, asters and dahlias zing with colour around a pretty pergola and a dramatic Bodmin standing stone. The grounds were once part of a large kitchen garden and vegetables flourish in the original Victorian greenhouses. At the outer reaches, formal gardens give way to the wild, with a natural pond, a mature orchard and a fern garden. The river views take in the church, the ice house and the rectory on the opposite bank where Kilvert lived and is buried. Wildlife thrives on the riverbank: kingfishers are common and you may even spot an otter.

The Old Rectory

Jenny Juckes
The Old Rectory,
Ewyas Harold,
Herefordshire HR2 0TX

tel   01981 240498
fax   01981 240498
email   jenny.juckes@btopenworld.com
web   www.theoldrectory.org.uk

Wonderful for walkers and garden lovers, a Georgian rectory at the foot of the Black Mountains, in the 'golden valley' where Wales and England converge. Inside, stags' heads, family portraits, stuffed birds and a wagging spaniel give a traditional, homely feel. Bedrooms are large, airy and filled with good furniture, lots of books and big windows with garden views. The feel is not plush or luxurious but relaxed, and there is an elegant sitting room with a grand piano which guests are welcome to play. The dining room has a roaring fire in winter and French windows that open onto the bucolic garden in warmer weather.

rooms	3 doubles.
price	From £52. Singles from £32.
meals	Pub in village 4-minute walk.
closed	Rarely.
directions	A465 to Abergavenny. 12 miles from Hereford, right on B4347. After 1.5 miles, left into village, then right by Temple Bar Pub. Left at top of road (School Road). House 1st on right.

The aim is to save energy, use less water, recycle waste and encourage wildlife in the garden. Environmental policies include the use of light bulbs, buying in bulk and saving packaging, supporting a towel and linen agreement, and informing guests of their active participation in the green tourism scheme.

Map 2 Entry 50

A secluded three-acre garden which Jenny got her hands on 12 years ago. Then it was just a sloping wilderness of long grass and brambles which had to be hacked back and cleared. Once that was done she started planning: good mature trees like conifers, oak, ash and acacias provide the basic backdrop, and now there are well tended lawns, large beds near the house filled to bursting with a huge variety of plants of many colours, a pond which is home to newts and frogs where irises and king cups flourish, and a lovingly tended croquet lawn. The house has some well-pruned roses scrambling up it, and great views of the surrounding countryside from the terrace which give a wonderful feeling of space – in spite of those huge trees. Plenty of evergreens give joy in winter and they have 'Kiftsgate' roses and others clambering up them to show off in spring and summer; huge swathes of lawn are left unmown to protect spring bulbs like daffodils, jonquils and fritillaries. Intentionally leaving some areas untouched has earned the Juckes a wildlife award from the Herefordshire Nature Trust. This garden reflects the character of its owners: relaxed, informal and deeply comfortable.

Dippersmoor Manor

Hexie and Amanda Millais
Dippersmoor Manor,
Kilpeck,
Herefordshire HR2 9DW

tel   01981 570209
email   hmm@dippersmoor.eclipse.co.uk
web   www.dippersmoor.com

Dating in parts back to the 15th century, the red sandstone house is flanked by a magnificent brick and timber long barn. The bedrooms are traditional, airy and spacious with crisp white linen and views to woodland and pasture towards the south, and mountains to the west. Breakfast is in the dining room, where the fireplace was once used for curing bacon, or out under the pergola; on warm evenings, dinners of local produce and homegrown vegetables can be taken outside under the vine in candlelit privacy, or with the charming Hexie and Amanda.

rooms	2: 1 double; 1 twin, sharing bath (let to same party only).
price	From £70. Singles from £36.
meals	Dinner £25 by arrangement. Pub 3 miles.
closed	Rarely.
directions	Turn left 7 miles south of Hereford on A465 to Kilpeck. Through village past Red Lion. Fork left on sharp bend signed village hall. Turn right over cattle grid 100 yds past village hall up a poplar lined drive.

Map 2 Entry 51

Robinia, catalpa, rowan and tulip trees dot the main lawn, buzzards float overhead and owls and bats roost in the barn. This big, secluded, hillside garden, with wonderful views to the Black Mountains, was virtually a field when Amanda and Hexie arrived 25 years ago. It was they who planted the avenue of poplars curving up to the house. A flagstone path leads you through a knot garden to the door, overhung by a vine which has been there since the 1920s. Roses, wisteria, quince and hydrangea scramble haphazardly up the walls and everywhere there are things to engage the eye. At the centre of a terraced lawn stands a stone cider press brimming with plants; next door is a box-hedged rose garden. More roses, lavender and sweet peas scent a square, pretty garden in front of the stone summer house, where swallows nest. (You can play table tennis here too.) The old stables provide a good backdrop to a bright border and pleached limes screen off an area destined to be a vegetable garden. Old cider orchards and a bluebell wood are fine places to explore, a pergola festooned with vines and clematis provides dappled shade – just the place to sit with a drink.

Hall End House

Angela & Hugh Jefferson
Hall End House,
Kynaston,
Ledbury,
Herefordshire HR8 2PD

tel	01531 670225
fax	01531 670747
email	khjefferson@hallend91.freeserve.co.uk
web	www.hallendhouse.com

All the grandeur you could ask for from the moment you enter. The airy hall has a handsome staircase leading to wide landings and the bedrooms upstairs. They are large and elegant, with rich curtains, comfortable beds and immaculate new bath/shower rooms. The dining and drawing rooms echo the mood of classic English elegance. A friendly welcome from a couple who have devoted an enormous amount of care and energy to the restoration of both house and garden. Lamb and other produce from this extremely well-managed farm is used when in season. *Children over 12 welcome.*

rooms	2: 1 twin, 1 four-poster.
price	£85–£99. Singles £60.
meals	Dinner, 3 courses, £22.50. BYO wine. Pub/restaurant 2.5 miles.
closed	Christmas & New Year.
directions	From Ledbury, A449 west, towards Ross-on-Wye. In Much Marcle, right between garage and stores. Right after 300 yds, follow lane for 2.5 miles, drive is on left.

Map 2 Entry 52

It is an especial treat for garden lovers to visit a garden in the making –
particularly one with plans as ambitious as those that Angela is developing with
the help of a talented young designer (Josie Anderson from Cheltenham). What
was once a run-down farmyard is being transformed into a large, open, elegant,
feature-packed garden, that perfectly complements the grand listed Georgian
farmhouse that Angela and Hugh have restored so brilliantly. A neglected pond at
the front has been cleared and planted with water-loving beauties; a second has
been created nearby so that as you approach up the drive you see the house in
reflection. And so much to enjoy once you arrive: a designer kitchen garden, a
herb garden, a formal rose garden with the finest roses, a croquet lawn to add
greenness and space. Angela loves flowers and her beds and borders are brimming
with the loveliest plants. There's a tennis court for the energetic, a summer house
in which to unwind and a large conservatory – relax and gaze at the splendours
outside. On a sunny day, take a dip in the striking, L-shaped (heated) pool lined in
deepest blue. The setting, in 500 acres of farmland, is a delight: views everywhere
– of woodland, open countryside and parkland – and one of the loveliest corners
of Herefordshire.

Homestead Farm

Joanna & Iain MacLeod
Homestead Farm,
Canon Frome,
Ledbury,
Herefordshire HR8 2TG

tel   01531 670268
fax   01531 670210

Gorgeous. A Roderick James oak-framed barn joined to a 16th-century keeper's cottage: light, airy and with soft views over cider orchards and hop fields. Lulu the Tibetan spaniel will give you an exuberant welcome while you admire the creative use of colour, attractive pictures and books, open fireplace and a gorgeous drawing room. Bedrooms are unfussy: pale green carpet, crisp white linen, aqua-blue tongue and groove panelling round the baths, vertical beams, dazzling light and a designer feel. An attractive veranda outside and balcony above cunningly melt a 500-year age difference into nothing at all.

rooms	2: 1 double, 1 twin.
price	£80. Singles £45.
meals	Pub/restaurant 3 miles.
closed	Christmas, New Year & occasionally.
directions	A438 west from Ledbury, north on A417 for 2 miles. At UK garage right to Canon Frome. After 0.75 miles, right in front of red brick gates of Rochester House; house 0.5 miles at end of track.

Map 2 Entry 53

An enchanting mix of terrace, sunken garden, vegetable garden, a field with a folly, a lake, mown paths, matrix-planted trees as windbreaks and the fabulous long distance views. All totally created by Iain and Joanna, who arrived clutching some pots from their old home and began with the terrace, flagstoned with a rectangular pond and a bubbly fountain. Along paths and across the garden are mounded metal arches planted with roses and clematis, a rope swag (once the Mallaig ferry's rope) is blue-smothered in 'Prince Charles' clematis and bushes of white *spinosissima* roses. A honeysuckle hedge, a greenhouse with a fanned nectarine and an abundant vine, a fruit cage with 'Autumn Bliss' raspberries and wild strawberries grown from seed. The field is mown with paths, cut for hay in the autumn, and contains a thousand trees planted for the millennium. Some trees are planted as a shelter belt, some in avenues and Iain's "folly" is a circle of pleached rowans with a stockade of 20 young oaks — donated by the architect to replace those cut down for the house. Views are created everywhere; across the length of the field towards the lake there's another avenue of *Malus coronaria* 'Charlottae' alternating with bird cherries. Two thousand snowdrops have been planted with wild daffodils and a carpet of bluebells — never mind June, spring will be busting out all over. *RHS.*

North Court

John & Christine Harrison
North Court,
Shorwell,
Isle of Wight PO30 3JG

tel   01983 740415
mobile   07955 174699
email   christine@northcourt.info
web   www.northcourt.info

North Court's astonishing 15 acres have developed over the last four centuries into a garden of historical interest and a paradise for plantsmen. The Isle of Wight remains warm well into the autumn, and in its downland-sheltered position the garden exploits its micro-climate to the full. Able to specialise in such exotics as bananas and echiums, the Harrisons have developed a sub-tropical garden; higher up the slope behind are Mediterranean terraces. There's extensive variety: the chalk stream surrounded with bog plants, the knot garden planted with herbs, the walled rose garden, the sunken garden, the one-acre kitchen garden, a Himalayan glade and a maritime area. All this represents a collection of 10,000 plants, some occasionally for sale – how do they do it? Modest John, the plantsman, says it is the good soil and atmosphere that allows everything to grow naturally and in profusion. But that is only half the story – he has left out the back-breakingly hard work and committment that have gone into it. They are knowledgeable too – he a leading light in the Isle of Wight Gardens Trust, she once the NGS county organiser for the island. Between them they have done a huge amount to encourage horticultural excellence in the area. *NGS, Good Gardens Guide, RHS, Isle of Wight Gardens Trust.*

rooms	6 twins/doubles.
price	£64–£80. Singles from £40.
meals	Light meals available. Pub 3-minute walk through garden.
closed	Christmas.
directions	From Newport, drive into Shorwell; down a steep hill, under a rustic bridge & right opp. thatched cottage. Signed.

Map 3 Entry 54

Think big and think Jacobean – built in 1615 by the then deputy governor of the Isle of Wight, North Court was once the manor house of a 2,000-acre estate. Extensively modified in the 18th century, the house has 80 rooms including a library housing a full-sized snooker table (yes, you may use it), and a 32-foot music room (you may play the piano, too). Bedrooms are large, in two separate wings, but although it all sounds terribly grand, this is a warm and informal family home – and your hosts more than likely to be found in gardening clothes. Autumn is an excellent and less busy time to visit.

Worples Field

Sue & Alastair Marr
Worples Field,
Farley Common,
Westerham,
Kent TN16 1UB

tel   01959 562869
email   marr@worplesfield.com
web   www.worplesfield.com

Sue is likely to greet guests in her wellies and gardening clothes at her home above a steep valley. Black rams with curving horns graze the paddock, and, unlikely as it seems, you are only 22 miles from central London, immersed in much of historical, geological and architectural interest. All the rooms in this wonderful, traditional 1920s house are light, airy and comfortable, towels are soft, colours restful and the rooms that share the bathroom have bucolic views. Play tennis or croquet, stroll into Westerham, or just relax in the garden room full of scented plants. Sue, full of fun and sparkle, will spoil you with homemade treats.
Minimum stay two nights at weekends.

rooms	3: 1 double, 1 twin, sharing bath; 1 double with separate bath.
price	£60-£65. Singles £55-£60.
meals	Pub/restaurant 0.5 miles.
closed	Rarely.
directions	From M25 junc. 6 to Westerham (A25). After town sign & 30mph sign, 1st left into Farley Lane. After 200 yds, left at top, then left again.

Map 4 Entry 55

Is the sensually undulating lawn just an example of modernistic landscaping? Not a bit of it. Worples is a corruption of 'wurples', Kentish for ridge-and-furrow; the wave-like lawn patterns around which Sue has built her garden are far from modern, and hugely intriguing. Sue is a garden designer and makes interesting use of large garden 'furniture' – a traditional Shepherd's hut here, a little 100-year-old summer house from Alastair's grandmother's garden there. And that's just the start. In 1997 she began a serious re-design of these three-acres with their beautiful views across the valley; no corner is untouched by her flair and her plans are bearing fruit. The new orchard is underplanted with bulbs, the trees and fine shrubs she has introduced are fleshing out beds and borders. There's a lily-pad shaped pond for frogs, newts and damselflies and a mixed, colourful avenue planted with Himalayan birch and azaleas. The original sunken garden just below the house is being lovingly re-designed into a 'planet' garden with sparkling surprises. The vegetable garden has been transformed into an ornamental potager. Every feature enhances the view and entrances, and each season is a delight in this young garden. *RHS, Westerham Horticultural Society.*

Hoath House

Mr & Mrs Mervyn Streatfeild
Hoath House,
Chiddingstone Hoath,
Edenbridge,
Kent TN8 7DB

tel   01342 850362
email   jstreatfeild@hoath-house.freeserve.co.uk

Mervyn and Jane live in a fascinating house which creaks under its own history, twisting, turning, rising and falling, and takes you on a journey through medieval, Tudor and Edwardian times. Breakfast in what was a medieval hall, all heavy panelling, low ceilings and small, leaded windows, entertained by your local historian and film extra host. Ancestors gaze down from the walls; dark staircases wind up to big bedrooms with views to Ashdown Forest. There are few modern embellishments – other than an unexpected Art Deco bathroom suite. For the curious and the robust. *Minimum stay two nights at weekends.*

rooms	2 twins sharing bath.
price	£65. Singles £35-£37.50.
meals	Supper from £9. Dinner from £16. Pub/restaurant 2 miles.
closed	Christmas & New Year.
directions	From A21, Hildenborough exit. Signs to Penshurst Place; pass vineyard; right at T-junc. for Edenbridge; through village, bear left, for Edenbridge. House 0.5 miles on left.

Map 4 Entry 56

The garden was designed in the 1930s – so vast, it was maintained by seven gardeners! No more. Mervyn and Jane today devote their energies to what they call "gardening on a shoestring". Their 20 rolling acres of fields, 'pleasure gardens', kitchen garden, wild garden and a secret garden over the road will be admired by every garden lover. The grounds reflect the house – rambling, time-worn, romantic. Avenues are cut through deep grasses to emphasise glorious views, and deep borders are piled high with witch hazel, evening primrose, lavender and shocking-pink peonies. Jane's greatest love is the steep wildlife garden where she is cutting her way through a jungle of rhododendrons and azaleas. Herringbone-brick paths are being rediscovered after years of neglect, water features cleared and restored. This wild area was – and still is – a place where children are at their happiest and which is shared with wildlife. Acid lovers thrive; magnolias and camellias do especially well. Now Jane is devoting more and more of her time to the challenge, and her enthusiasm shows in every distant corner. Nothing fussy, everything informal, a laid-back approach to developing the grounds with limited manpower. Don't expect showiness, do enjoy the atmosphere of a garden that has been blessed with a new lease of life.

Sunninglye Farmhouse

John & Susie Petrie
Sunninglye Farmhouse,
Bells Yew Green,
Tunbridge Wells,
Kent TN3 9AG

tel   01892 542894
email   jrwpetrie@aol.com

More a retreat than a B&B. The house, dating from
the 15th century, is in the countryside yet a few miles
from Tunbridge Wells. Higgledy-piggledy floors and walls,
ancient beams, wide fireplaces and lots of rugs make the
downstairs cosy and welcoming, and bedrooms are plain
and simple: iron bedsteads, an 18th-century lattice window,
a complete absence of frilly bits, perhaps a heated brick
floor. John and Susie already look after 42 Shetland sheep,
two horses, two dogs, two cats and a flurry of chickens,
but they are eager to share all this with their guests, and
nurture you with organic and home-grown food.

rooms	2: 1 double, 1 twin.
price	From £70. Singles from £45.
meals	Supper from £15.
closed	October-March.
directions	M25. junc. 5 south on A21 for 16 miles. At roundabout right to Frant Station. After 2.3 miles left on farm track. Take right fork in track.

Map 4 Entry 57

When John and Susie arrived – 27 years ago – the garden was in a state.
And those who prefer clipped edges, pristine gaps, well-behaved plants and
everything tickety-boo may still think it's in one! Let us call it 'laissez-faire'
instead: if a stray twirl of clematis decides to make a dash up a bush, then the
Petries will let it, if a self-seeded something pops up in a bed then they will
encourage it. Everlasting sweet peas peep in the front kitchen window, an
arch of tumbling banksia roses marks the entrance into the garden, daisies
and foxgloves flourish where an old oil tank used to stand, a smooth lawn sits in
the middle. The kitchen garden is the main focus. John is a member of HDRA
and they have always followed organic principles, growing masses of fruit and
vegetables for the table and for preserves. This year's crop includes golden
beetroot, celeriac, artichokes, squashes and every kind of green bean you can
imagine, all from the three kitchen gardens – one of which is neatly surrounded
by a clipped holly hedge. One of the outlying fields is registered with the Weald
Meadow Initiative and has been certified as ancient pasture; wild flowers burst
through in spring and summer. Plenty of good public gardens to visit nearby;
this one is open regularly under HDRA's Organic Gardens Open Weekends.

Wickham Lodge

Richard & Cherith Bourne
Wickham Lodge,
The Quay,
73 High Street,
Aylesford, Kent ME20 7AY

tel   01622 717267
fax   01622 792855
email   wickhamlodge@aol.com
web   www.wickhamlodge.co.uk

The onetime gatehouse to the big house on the hill looks Georgian, but started life Tudor: two lodges woven into one. It's a super house with a special garden that Cherith has loved since she was a young woman. Be spoiled by traditional comforts, a riverside setting and greenery from every window. The room overlooking the river is fresh and airy with linen quilts on white metal beds; the Tudor Room is low-ceilinged with pretty pine and Victorian-style 'rain bath' (amazing). Have breakfast in the garden, lunch in Canterbury and supper in the village; its two old pubs and 14th-century bridge ooze history and charm.

rooms	3: 1 double, 1 twin/double, 1 single.
price	£70-£80. Singles £40-£50.
meals	Pubs/restaurants within easy walking distance.
closed	Rarely.
directions	From M20 junc. 5. Follow signs for Aylesford. Over crossing and bridge. At T- junc. left into village. Left 100 yds after traffic lights, directly after the Chequers Pub.

Map 4 Entry 58

Who would believe so much fecundity could be squeezed into one half acre? Cherith has known and loved this walled garden – 14 small gardens that flow into one – for 40 years. Many plants were used in Tudor times (the business of identification is unfaltering), with Victorian cottage-garden plants being popped in over the years. Starting at the top end is the kitchen garden, a horn of plenty sprinkled with spring bulbs and cultivated wisely, 'companion planting' controlling pests and diseases. Then a fruit grove, a secret garden, a Cornish haven, a rose walk fragrant with Tudor and French shrub roses. In the Japanese garden, a stairway of railway sleepers topped with pebbles winds serenely up to a circular terrace enfolded by winter flowering shrubs. Later this transforms into a cool green oasis, while the most central section of the garden opens up to its summery palette of purples, pinks, whites and blues. Wander further… to the gravelled hop garden, where a rustic pergola supports hops from the river bank, and a topiary terrace (with goldfish pond) nudges the Tudor back of the house. To the front, a boatyard garden by the river – boats bob by at high tide, birds at low. The drive is edged with lavender and you park among vines.

Rock Farm House

Mrs Sue Corfe
Rock Farm House,
Gibbs Hill,
Nettlestead,
Maidstone,
Kent ME18 5HT

tel   01622 812244
fax   01622 812244
web   www.rockfarmhousebandb.co.uk

Plantsmen will be happy here. In the Seventies, when her children were young, Sue ran a nursery at Rock Farm that built up a considerable reputation. It closed in 2000, but her collection of interesting plants continues to be celebrated in her own garden. She knows from experience what plants grow best in these alkaline conditions, and they perform for her. The evergreen *Berberis stenophylla* provides a striking backdrop to the large herbaceous border – 90-foot long and, in places, 35-foot wide. Bulbs grown along the hedge are superceded by herbaceous plants; as these grow, the dying bulb foliage behind is neatly hidden from view. The oriental poppies in May herald the outburst of colour that lasts from June to September, and, to encourage wildlife, cutting down is delayed until January. The bog garden that lies below the house is filled with candelabra primulas, trollius, astilbes, day lilies, gunnera, lythrum, filipendulas and arum lilies: a continuous flowering from April to July. In a further area – around two natural ponds – contrasting conifer foliage interplanted with herbaceous perennials is set against a backdrop of Kentish woodland; superb groupings of hostas and ferns grow in shady areas. A delightful spot. *NGS, Good Gardens Guide, RHS Garden Finder.*

rooms	3: 1 double, 1 twin; 1 twin with separate bath/shower.
price	£60. Singles £35.
meals	Restaurant within 1 mile.
closed	Christmas Day.
directions	From Maidstone A26 to Tonbridge. At Wateringbury lights, left B2015. Right up Gibbs Hill; 1st right down drive, past converted oast house on right. Farm next.

Map 4 Entry 59

A charming Kentish farmhouse, with beams fashioned from recycled ships' timbers from Chatham dockyard. Bedrooms are simple, traditional, exquisite, one with a four-poster bed. Walls are pale or pure white, bedheads floral, furniture antique; the bedroom in the Victorian extension has a barrel ceiling and two big windows that look eastwards over the bog garden to the glorious Kentish Weald. Stairs lead down into the dining room with its lovely old log fire. Free-range eggs from the farm, homemade jams and local honey for breakfast.

Boyton Court

Richard & Patricia Stileman
Boyton Court,
Sutton Valence,
Kent ME17 3BY

tel   01622 844065
fax   01622 843913
email   richstileman@aol.com

Higgledy-piggledy but immaculate. A truly handsome Grade II-listed house – 16th century brick-and-tile-hung, with Victorian additions. Richard and Patricia are helpful and friendly and have created a comfortable, elegant and relaxing home. There's a dining room with a fabulous, original black and terracotta tiled floor, a soft-blue drawing room with views over the garden and stacks of books. Breakfast is cooked on the Aga – sausages with hops and other local produce. Soft colours in the bedrooms too – terracotta or cool lavender – with pretty tiles in the sparkling bathrooms. Super views from both. *Minimum stay two nights at weekends.*

rooms	2: 1 double, 1 twin.
price	£90. Singles £55.
meals	Pubs 1 mile.
closed	Christmas & New Year.
directions	From M20, junc. 8, A20. Right at r'bout onto B2163, left onto A274. In S. Valence left at King's Head. Through village with chapel on right. After 0.5 miles right at 1st x-roads; house on left past barn.

Map 4 Entry 60

A stunning series of slopes and terraces that swoop southwards with breathtaking views over the Weald to Tenterden and Sissinghurst. A natural spring feeds a series of four ponds packed around with primulas and other damp-loving plants; the top pond takes the Alhambra in Granada as a source, giving a Moorish feel. An octagonal pool with a fountain forms a striking centre piece surrounded by a very pretty parterre garden – designed on a paper tablecloth in New York when Richard was briefly stranded there after 9/11. Water flows down a stepped rill to the lower level: a rectangular pond full of fish and water lilies, an iris bed with *Verbena bonariensis* for late summer interest. The bottom, separate pond is wilder with a rowing boat, willows and *Betula jacquemontii*. Below the house is a bog garden with a mass of arum lilies, filipendula, eupatorium and other damp-loving varieties. Gaze over the blue and purple striped lavender bank from the terrace, enjoy a new border with drifts of grasses – especially interesting in late summer – and an exquisite rose garden with a selection of David Austin repeat-flowering roses underplanted with hardy geraniums. Perfection in two-and-a-half acres. *NGS.*

Cloth Hall Oast

Mrs Katherine Morgan
Cloth Hall Oast,
Cranbrook,
Kent TN17 3NR

tel   01580 712220
fax   01580 712220
email   clothhalloast@aol.com

Light shimmers through swathes of glass in the dining room of this immaculate Kentish oast house and barn; there are off-white walls and pale beams that soar from floor to rafter. Discuss in the morning what you'd like for dinner – duck with cherries, sole Véronique; later you dine at an antique table gleaming with crystal and candelabra. Choose from a huge four-poster on the ground floor, a triple or large double on the first; all have soft colours, laundered linen on fine mattresses, flowered chintz and good bathrooms. And there's a sitting room for guests, made snug by a log fire on winter nights.

rooms	3: 1 four-poster, 1 triple, 1 double.
price	£90–£130.
meals	Dinner £22–£25. Pub 1 mile.
closed	Christmas.
directions	Leave village with windmill on left, taking Golford Road east for Tenterden. After a mile, right, before cemetery. Signed right.

Map 4 Entry 61

For 40 years Mrs Morgan lived in the 15th-century manor next door where she tended the garden which was open for charity; now she has turned her perfectionist's eye upon these five acres. Out of a hard tennis court and wild surroundings she has created well-groomed lawns, a carp-filled pond, pergola, summer house, heated pool and flower beds — two of orange and yellow, four all-white. Packed planting from the rhododendrons sweeping along the drive to the colour-themed beds of lilies, delphiniums, tulips, agapanthus and roses ensures masses of interest at every time of year — and there are structural delights too. A ha-ha has been dug to separate the garden from the field, the swimming pool is sheltered on two sides by a neat yew hedge, the original beech hedge from the tennis court is well-established and there are fruit trees leading to the wild garden. The pond is brimming with fish and has an island in the middle with a willow; the curved decking edge is surrounded by gunnera and grasses with spots of colour from crocosmia. A line of boxed beds with a weeping pear in the middle gives a nod to formality and the smart terraces are perfectly placed for sitting with an evening drink and keeping an eye on the pond — look out for the heron.

Pope's Hall

William Wakeley
Pope's Hall,
The Street,
Hartlip,
Sittingbourne,
Kent ME9 7TL

| tel | 01795 842315 |
| email | william.wakeley@btinternet.com |

Wind through the charming village to this listed house that
dates from 1212, with a madly sloping roof, uneven floors
and a riot of beams and timber inside. Step down into the
salmon-pink dining room for a breakfast of local produce
served at a solid oak table; William and Veronica are cheerful
and welcoming. Old-fashioned bedrooms are a good size and
deeply comfortable; bathrooms are spanking clean and sport
thick towels, lovely soaps. This is a pleasant antidote to bling
culture, so come to unwind — and it's only 40 minutes from
the Channel tunnel.

rooms	3: 1 twin; 1 double, 1 twin sharing bath.
price	£55–£75.
meals	Pubs/restaurants in village.
closed	Rarely.
directions	From M2, A249 towards Sittingbourne. 1st left at roundabout on A2 through Newington, then 1st left to Hartlip.

Map 4 Entry 62

Veronica and William came here in 1961 when the house and garden were almost derelict. Now these beautiful two-and-a half acres are separated into three areas and, apart from a large oak and two yews, Veronica has planted everything herself, from seeds and cuttings grown in the greenhouse. The pond garden has a top pond with a small waterfall; a sturdy cherub clutches a goose from whose mouth water cascades. Amble round the lower pond to admire the ornamental planting and fat water lilies while listening to the call ducks. Other touches of formality include the terracotta pot-lined drive, bursting with agapanthus in summer, a courtyard with stone troughs and a variegated maple; from there, an archway of roses and honeysuckle leads to the main garden. Relax among smooth lawns, shrub areas, roses and trees, which in turn lead down to an elegant display of birch trees, underplanted with snowdrops and dogwood. Hydrangeas do well, growing along the old wall that hides the swimming pool, and beside a very large old Kentish barn. Rhododendrons and azaleas thrive, wildlife twitters and swoops, and two friendly terriers laze beneath the spreading horse chestnut tree next to a circle of box hedging. Come for more than one night and you can stay all day – bliss.

Bunkers Hill

Nicola Harris
Bunkers Hill,
Lenham,
Kent ME17 2EE

tel   01622 858259

The garden room is an inspiration: not technically a conservatory, but a room extended into the garden, with windows all round, and doors onto the terrace. Breakfast (with eggs from the chickens) and dinner are served in here among the pots of jasmine and mimosa. Leading off it, the sitting room is low-beamed, and the oak panelling has decorative Tudor-style friezes: very cosy with a woodburning stove. A little sofa by the upstairs landing window is a sunny place for morning letter-writing, and the classic pale colours of the pretty bedroom give a bright welcome in the afternoons – along with good books to read.

rooms	1 twin, with separate bath & shower.
price	£75. Singles £50.
meals	Dinner £20. Pub/restaurant 0.25 miles.
closed	Christmas & New Year.
directions	From M20 junc. 8, A20 east for Ashford. At Lenham, left to Warren St. On for 1 mile. Harrow pub on right. Bear left. After 300 yds, 3-way junc, sharp left. House 4th on left.

Map 4 Entry 63

From seats in different rooms in this treeful garden, you particularly notice the birdlife. The golden robinia framed against dark, spreading yew attracts many species to its bird feeder, and there are busy flutterings in and out of mature trees and shrubs all over the garden. The terrace is planted with pots of lilies, roses and fuchsia, and from here the eye is drawn down between yew hedges and two pairs of swelling conifers to the little white dovecote at the end. Behind it, the layers of white blooms on the massive *Viburnum plicatum* 'Mariesii' are the spring focal point. Down between mixed borders and a tapestry beech hedge dividing the garden into two halves, round a mound of wisteria, or behind a thicket of hydrangeas, rhododendrons and hollies, sits another bench in a sunny clearing. Scent rises from the border of shrub roses in this little secret garden: a 'Paul's Himalayan Musk' has dived up a silver birch, and 'Wedding Day' has taken over an old prunus. Nicola took over her mother-in-law's garden when she moved here: rather than make drastic changes she has gently nurtured and gradually developed her inheritance, and the garden reflects her quiet affection for it.

Woodmans

Sarah Rainbird
Woodmans,
Hassell Street,
Hastingleigh,
Ashford,
Kent TN25 5JE

tel   01233 750250
mobile   07836 505575

Not only are you in the depths of the countryside but you feel very private: your ground-floor bedroom is reached via a corner of the delightful garden with a seating area all your own. Step past greenery to the breakfast room, cosy with old pine table, dresser and flowers, for your bacon and eggs; if you don't feel like emerging, you may have breakfast brought to your room. This is a good stopover point for trips across the Channel – and you're a 15-minute drive from Canterbury and its glorious cathedral. *Babies welcome.*

rooms	1 double.
price	£60.
meals	Dinner, 3 courses, £22.50. Packed lunch £6.50. Pub/restaurant 1 mile.
closed	Rarely.
directions	From A2, 2nd exit to Canterbury. Follow ring road & B2068 for Hythe. Over A2, through Lower Hardres, past Granville pub. Right to Waltham; 1.5 miles after Waltham, right into Hassell St; 4th on left.

Map 4 Entry 64

A leafy, colourful garden of about three quarters of an acre surrounded by paddocks. Sarah got the gardening bug from her parents, so when she found a garden that was already designed she felt confident about making a few changes. It feels rather Edwardian and old-fashioned, with long stretches of well-maintained lawn and a series of 'rooms' with large round shrub-filled beds – some winter-flowering and heavily scented. The whole garden is contained by mature trees and some pretty cross-hatch fencing forms a boundary between the garden and the fields beyond that open onto farmland. Colour is gentle: soft pink and cream tiles on the patio, faded wooden seats and tables, ancient lilac trees and the subtle blending of all that green. A stone bird bath sits on the lawn, there are some interesting stone statues, a raised pond with a small fountain tinkles away and there's a pretty rockery with wooden edges. The front garden faces north and is filled with things that thrive there, including hydrangeas. Roses and clematis tumble from many of the trees wafting their delicious scent in early summer, pots and hanging baskets are filled with flowers. Traditionalists will be happy here; it is amazingly peaceful.

Little Mystole

Hugh & Patricia Tennent
Little Mystole,
Mystole Park,
Canterbury, Kent CT4 7DB

tel   01227 738210
fax   01227 738210
email   little_mystole@yahoo.co.uk
web   www.littlemystole.co.uk

A graceful Georgian house and much loved family home; the Tennents, your retired army hosts, have lived here for years. A charming drawing room for guests is full of family photographs and looks onto the garden. Cosy, comfortable bedrooms with touches of chintz and frill have views of fields and woods; the double has an extra single bed in its dressing room, the twin, an alcove with a sofa by the window. A handsome dining room, plump sofas, gilt-framed portraits and pretty flower arrangements set the scene, you are ten minutes from Canterbury, 30 from ferries and tunnel. The dog Pippin will greet you with as much pleasure as your hosts. *Children over eight welcome.*

rooms	2: 1 double with extra single bed, 1 twin.
price	£80. Singles £15-£46.
meals	Occasionally. Pub/restaurant 1.5 miles.
closed	Christmas & Easter.
directions	A28 Canterbury-Ashford. Left to Shalmsford Street; right immed. after post office at Bobbin Lodge Hill. Road bends left, then right at T-junc.; 2nd drive on left at junc. with Pickelden Lane.

Map 4 Entry 65

A garden with which owners of smaller gardens can identify. Hugh and Patricia call their half-acre-plus a cottage garden, but they wear their experience and achievements lightly. It's actually more of a small country-house garden, in two parts. As you approach, a path passes between a mature herbaceous border and a curving rockery, then follows a long wall up to an old mulberry tree. This stands opposite the entrance to the walled garden, right by the house. White, scented 'Rambling Rector' frames the summer house in the corner, and 'Galway Bay' and clematis 'Perle d'Azur' romp up a wall. There's a cottagey and relaxed feel to this delightful planting and people are more than happy to enjoy it from the comfy garden chairs. Hugh and Patricia love plants in pots, and their groupings by the house include white lacecap hydrangeas, fuchsias, an all-white display of pelargoniums, lobelia and impatiens and the softly pink 'Queen Mother' rose flanking the front door. They like groupings of the same colours: a pretty pink bed of hydrangeas and hardy geraniums lies under the dining room window. A secluded haven in an Area of Outstanding Natural Beauty, among the parkland, orchards and hop gardens of Kent.

Hornbeams

Alison Crawley
Hornbeams,
Jesses Hill, Kingston,
Canterbury,
Kent CT4 6JD

tel	01227 830119
mobile	07798 601016
email	alison@hornbeams.co.uk
web	www.hornbeams.co.uk

Rolling hills and woodland, long views over luscious Kent, and a lovely garden that Alison has created entirely herself. This is a modern bungalow, a rare phenomenon in this book, a Scandia house brick-built from a Swedish kit. It is brilliant for wheelchair users and altogether easy and comfortable to be in, with floral-covered sofas and chairs and plain reproduction furniture. Alison, a beauty therapist and massuese, is friendly and gracious. The house is so close to Dover that it is worth staying here for the night before embarking on the ferry fray.

rooms	3: 1 double; 1 twin with separate bath/shower; 1 single (let to same party only).
price	£70. Singles £40.
meals	Occasional dinner. Pubs 1 mile.
closed	Christmas.
directions	From A2 Canterbury-Dover, towards Barham & Kingston. Right at bottom of hill by shelter, into The Street, Kingston to top of hill & right fork. 1st left on sharp right bend. Left into farm, keep right of barn.

Map 4 Entry 66

Perfectly designed, brilliantly executed – Alison has come a long way since this garden was a field. She used to picnic here as a child, admire the view and dream about living here... The garden now surrounds the house and is bursting with plants. At the front are roses, camellias, lavender and acers in pots; a blackthorn and hawthorn hedge is grown through with golden hop, vines and more roses. By the front gate is a spring bed, then a purple bed leading to a white-scented border of winter flowering clematis and magnolias. An immaculate herb garden is spiked with tall fennel, the vegetable garden has raised beds and a morello cherry tree, and the orchard hums with fecundity. Winter and autumn beds are filled with interest and colour: snake-bark maple, dusky pink chrysanthemums, witch hazel and red-stemmed cornus. The herbaceous border is a triumph – colours move from pinks, purples and blues through apricots, creams and whites to the 'hot' end, and self-seeded intruders are swiftly dealt with. A little waterfall surrounded by lilies sits in the pond garden and rockery where hostas, ferns, astilbes, gunnera, bamboo and lilac compete for space. Rejoice in the knowledge that someone who has achieved their dream is so happy to share it with others. *RHS, Barham Horticultural Society.*

The Ridges

John & Barbara Barlow
The Ridges ,
Weavers Brow,
Limbrick,
Chorley,
Lancashire PR6 9EB

tel   01257 279981
email   barbara@barlowridges.co.uk
web   www.bedbreakfast-gardenvisits.com

The story of Barbara's garden starts in the 1970s when she used to help her mother with their garden centre in the back garden. The more she learned, the more her interest grew: by the time her children had grown and flown she was hooked. Realising the potential of the garden, she began restoring and developing. Original apple trees lining the path were pruned, but otherwise you wouldn't recognise the back garden now: dense cottage garden planting demonstrates Barbara's eye for combinations of colour, form, and foliage. Through a laburnum arch, a lawned area is fringed with bright foliaged specimen trees cleverly positioned to shine against dark copper beech, holly and rhododendron. This shelter protects such tender plants as windmill palm and *Magnolia grandiflora*, and provides a lovely setting for a Victorian-style glass house used for entertaining. In a natural stream garden damp-loving plants such as rodgersia and gunnera grow down towards a pool, and a 'Paul's Himalayan Musk' runs rampant over trellis and trees. An old buttressed wall has been uncovered to create a new, naturally planted quiet area, with scented plants and herbs to attract butterflies and bees. Barbara's horticultural achievement is to be admired and enjoyed. *NGS, Good Gardens Guide.*

rooms	3: 1 double; 1 twin/double, 1 single with separate shared bath.
price	From £70. Singles from £40.
meals	Pub within walking distance.
closed	Rarely.
directions	M6 junc. 27 or M61 junc. 8 for Chorley. Follow A6 ring road, taking mini r'bout for Cowling & Rivington. On down Cowling Brow, past Spinners Arms pub. House a few hundred yds further, on right.

Map 6 Entry 67

John and Barbara used to do B&B in the separate Coach House but now you are looked after in the lovely old mill-owner's house, built in 1880 and bought by Barbara's family in 1951. Bedrooms are upstairs and cottagey with pale colours, flowery curtains and covers, traditional furniture; breakfast is downstairs in a beamed room with a log burner for chilly mornings. The magnificent West Pennine Moors are great for walkers and cyclists – either hardy ones who want to try the Commonwealth Games Course or pootlers who can amble along the woods and reservoirs below the Pike.

Baumber Park

Clare Harrison
Baumber Park,
Baumber,
Horncastle,
Lincolnshire LN9 5NE

tel	01507 578235
mobile	07977 722776
email	baumberpark@amserve.com
web	www.baumberpark.com

If I were a bird I would go and live in this garden. Just over an acre of delicious smelling flowers, shrubs and hedges (sea buckthorn because the thrushes like the berries). "Scent is the thing," says Clare and even her favourite daffodil, 'Pheasants Eye', smells lovely. Follow a formal gravel front bordered by lonicera hedges, under a solid pergola over which golden hop and honeysuckle battle for the sky, to lawn and large borders full of sweet-smelling roses, eleagnus, buddleia, sedum and a maturing pocket handkerchief tree – planted to commemorate an anniversary! A box parterre is being created in the vegetable garden and beds are full, colourful and scented – thousands of bulbs pop up in the spring. There's a vast cherry tree underplanted with more bulbs, periwinkles and holly, a peony bed interplanted with sweet-smelling viburnum, and then a lovely whitebeam arch through which peeps a wildflower meadow. Few large trees have been planted so views are un-hindered and an old pond is planted around with native species only – for the wildlife, lucky things. A small quantity of interesting plants are for sale – propagated by Clare. *Trustee of Lincolnshire Wildlife Trust and manager of one of their nature reserves locally.*

rooms	3: 2 doubles, 1 twin.
price	£58–£62. Singles £30–£40.
meals	Pub/restaurants 3.5 miles.
closed	Christmas & New Year.
directions	From A158 in Baumber take road towards Wispington & Bardney. House 300 yds down on right.

Map 7 Entry 68

Lincoln red cows and Longwool sheep ruminate in the fields around this rosy-brick farmhouse – once a stud that bred a Derby winner. The old watering pond is now a haven for frogs, newts and toads; birds sing lustily. Maran hens conjure delicious eggs and Clare – a botanist – is hugely knowledgeable about the area. Bedrooms are light and traditional with mahogany furniture, and there is a heart-stopping view through an arched landing window. And a grass tennis court, a guest sitting room with log fire, and a dining room with local books. This is good walking, riding and cycling country, with quiet lanes. *Minimum stay two nights weekends in high season.*

Kelling House

Ms Sue Evans
Kelling House,
17 West Street,
Barkston, Grantham,
Lincolnshire NG32 2NL

tel	01400 251440
fax	01400 251440
email	sue.evans7@btopenworld.com
web	www.kellinghouse.co.uk

Once three cottages dating from 1785, it is now a long, low house of gentle rubble stone with a pantile roof. Its gable end faces up the street and it has a pretty painted gate with lolling hollyhocks. Well-proportioned rooms have good English furniture, well-made heavy curtains and interesting paintings. The creamy sitting room overlooks the quiet street on one side and the garden on the other. Bedrooms are freshly traditional with a pretty mix of checks, stripes and plain white cotton. Sue is delightful and looks after you without fuss.

rooms	3: 1 double; 1 double with separate bath; 1 single sharing bath (let to same party only).
price	From £75. Singles from £45.
meals	Dinner £20, by arrangement. Packed lunch £7.50. Pub/restaurant 3-minute walk.
closed	Rarely.
directions	From A1, B1174 for Grantham; then A607 for Belton & Barkston. In Barkston, 2nd left on to West Street opp. village green and Stag pub. House on left opp. green cottage.

Map 6 Entry 69

When Sue arrived in 1999 she kept only a few good shrubs and mature trees; the rest she bulldozed. Now French windows and doors lead directly onto the generous flagged terrace with its young box-edged parterre filled with herbs. Clumps of lavender, rosemary and sage give a mediterranean feel and scent the house but it is also a lovely place to sit and admire the rest – in particular, the wide bed of summer-flowering perennials: sweet-scented white phlox, elegant perovskia with its lavender blue spikes and grey foliage, and dramatic acanthus. From here the lawn runs to the southern boundary, while a curving herbaceous border softens the eastern boundary and leads to a small area of young ornamental trees. The western beds reveal tulip and walnut trees interspersed with shrubs and grasses. This is a young garden but it's charming and well planted with good lawns and unexpected surprises that invite inspection… there are interesting small trees and flowering shrubs that include grey-leafed cistus, santolina and rue. In summer, colours are pink, white and blue. Belvoir Castle is worth visiting – as are the magnificent cathedrals of Lincoln and Peterborough.

The Old Vicarage

Mrs Liz Dixon-Spain
The Old Vicarage,
Low Road,
Holbeach Hurn,
Spalding,
Lincolnshire PE12 8JN

tel	01406 424148
fax	01406 426676
email	lizds@ukonline.co.uk

One of Liz's sons is an artist and his work appears all over her lovely, relaxed home. Although her children are now grown up, a family atmosphere prevails and all is practical rather than frilly: a combination of antique and modern furniture, ethnic rugs, spider plants and bamboo, and squashy sofas in the drawing room. Bedrooms are sunny, covered in an eclectic mix of artwork and the twin has floral quilts with matching curtains and cushions. Liz is friendly and will spoil you with a good breakfast including homemade jam and marmalade.

rooms	2: 1 twin; 1 double with separate shower.
price	£60. Singles £35.
meals	Pub 2 miles.
closed	Mid-December–mid-March.
directions	Off A17 north to Holbeach Hurn, past post box in middle of village, 1st right into Low Road. Old Vicarage 400 yds on right.

Map 7 Entry 70

Trained as a dress designer, Liz swapped her needle for a spade and created this two-acre garden around her old family home from scratch. A large job to tackle but Liz is a natural; not only does she look after her own garden but she works her magic for other people, including winning a Bronze medal at Hampton Court for 'Paddington's Marmalade Garden'. In her own, she has concentrated on a not-too-formal look that requires the minimum of maintenance. Some older trees were cleared – some stumps cleverly carved into rustic seats – but plenty of mature trees and shrubs form the backdrop including a 50-ft tulip tree. Ideas have also grown by themselves, like the wisteria which covered its arch and then shot up a nearby holly – a stunning display in late spring. Liz is always on the look-out for new plants but gives them a gentle start by re-potting them first in a mix of her homemade compost and soil and planting them out the following year; she rarely loses anything. Grasses are a favourite, mixed with colourful shrubs, roses, perennials and bulbs. There's a surprise around every corner: a croquet lawn, a pond and bog garden, a wild and wooded area, a south-facing terrace and plenty of vegetables and fruit trees. Birds love it here and no chemicals are used. Special. *NGS, Lincolnshire Gardens Trust.*

Winkle Haworth
38 Killieser Avenue,
Streatham,
London SW2 4NT

tel   020 8671 4196
fax   020 8761 4196
email   winklehaworth@hotmail.com

Winkle is a gardener to the last tip of her green fingers. She is devoted to gardening, garden details, design, collecting unusual plants and the pleasure of creating ever more displays. Hence this ravishing garden in Streatham's delightful conservation area. There are myriad lessons to be learned for town gardeners the moment you step into this south-facing plot. The simple, long rectangle of the garden's space has been magicked into three compartments, each with a character of its own, each decorated with the finest plants. Certain items stand out: a lofty rose arch, water features, a carefully worked parterre and a new dry gravel garden with drought tolerant plants. Deep, deep borders, a sequence of intimate areas, topiary to give form, sweet peas rising up rockets, wonderful old roses, mostly courtesy of Peter Beales, fine shrubs. A blacksmith forged the gothic garden seat where you sit surrounded by colour and scent. A pink wisteria adorns the back of the pretty Victorian house; old London bricks form patterns on the final terrace. Containers are stuffed with agapanthus and other beauties around the patio, a perfect place to relax. Winkle has won first prize in the English Garden best town garden award. *NGS, Good Gardens Guide.*

rooms	2: 1 twin; 1 single with separate bath.
price	£90-£95. Singles from £50.
meals	Dinner £25.
closed	Occasionally.
directions	3-minute walk from Streatham station (15 minutes to Victoria); 15-minute walk from Balham tube.

Map 3 Entry 71

The Haworths – early Streatham pioneers – have brought country-house chic to South London. Few people do things with as much natural good humour and style as Winkle. The house glows yellow, and you breakfast in the rug-strewn, wooden-floored, farmhouse kitchen. Bedrooms are big, grand and homely: more rugs, comfy beds, lamb's wool blankets, loads of books, waffle bathrobes, beautiful linen. Even the single is generous. All on a quiet residential street, and Streatham Hill station a three-minute walk; you can be in Victoria in 15 minutes. Brilliant. *Children over 12 welcome.*

24 Fox Hill

Sue & Tim Haigh
24 Fox Hill,
Crystal Palace,
London SE19 2XE

tel   020 8768 0059
email   suehaigh@hotmail.co.uk
web   www.foxhill-bandb.co.uk

This part of London is full of sky, trees and wildlife; Pissarro captured on canvas the view up the hill in 1870 and the original painting can be seen in the National Gallery. There's good stuff everywhere – things hang off walls and peep over the tops of dressers; bedrooms are stunning, with antiques, textiles, paintings and big, firm beds. Sue, a graduate of Chelsea College of Art, puts guests at ease with intelligence and good humour and has created a very special garden, too. She will cook supper (sea bass, maybe, stuffed with herbs); Tim often helps with breakfasts.

rooms	3: 1 twin/double; 1 double, 1 twin sharing shower.
price	From £80. Singles £50.
meals	Dinner, 2-3 courses, £25-£30.
closed	Rarely.
directions	Train: Crystal Palace (7-min. walk). Collection possible. Good buses to West End & Westminster.

Map 3 Entry 72

The Haighs home in the sweet seclusion of Fox Hill has a small gravelled front garden with bobbles of box and a standard holly – an eye-catching frontage for the pretty Victorian house – but there's much, much more to come. The long rectangular back garden has been completely re-designed and now bursts with colour and interest in every direction. Sue, who once worked at the Chelsea Physic Garden and is a true plant-lover, has cleared and re-planted paved areas by the house and built a raised pond for her beloved fish. The delicate water plants are guarded by tall, spiky agaves that thrust skywards from their containers. Climbers snake up walls, trellises and an arch, while water cascades soothingly from a waterfall into the pond. She has nurtured a few of the plants that were there when she arrived, a thriving ceanothus and a weeping pear tree among them, but otherwise started with a clean slate. To add a final flourish and to mark her pleasure at having her first-ever garden shed to play with, she has planted a 'Liquid Amber' sweet gum outside its door. This is a relatively young garden packed with promise.

Mill Common House

Mrs Wendy Pugh
Mill Common House,
Ridlington,
North Walsham,
Norfolk NR28 9TY

tel	01692 650792
fax	01692 651480
email	johnpugh@millcommon.freeserve.co.uk
web	www.millcommonhouse.co.uk

The house is an elegant Georgian conversion and expansion
of an older cottage. There are gorgeous chintzes throughout,
and the bedrooms have a luxurious feel with toile de Jouy
patchwork bedspreads and masses of cushions. Bathrooms
have easy chairs, and the one overlooking the walled garden,
a sumptuous freestanding bath. Aga-cooked breakfasts taken
in the pretty conservatory are a treat – Wendy is a Cordon
Bleu cook. Flowers everywhere, log fires, French windows
that lead onto the terrace: this is a cossetting place to stay in
undiscovered Norfolk. There are plenty of inspirational
gardens and historic houses and churches nearby.

rooms	2: 1 twin; 1 double with separate bath.
price	From £70. Singles £45.
meals	Dinner from £25. Pub/restaurant 5 miles.
closed	Christmas.
directions	A1151 from Norwich through Wroxham. Left to Walcott. At T-junc. left for Walcott. After 3.5 miles, pass Lighthouse Inn on right. Left, 1 mile to the Y-junc.; house on left at next Y-junc.

Inside the house the Pughs use low-
energy light bulbs throughout, all is
recycled including old soap and other used
beauty products, the roof is massively
insulated to help with energy conservation
and food miles are calculated and kept
as low as possible. Outside there are
conservation paddock areas and a whole
lot of composting going on.

Map 7 Entry 73

John and Wendy have always treated their guests like friends; not surprisingly, their walled garden receives a similar level of tender loving care. The garden is protected from the salty north-east wind by a thick 30-foot-high conifer hedge; this allows a wide variety of flowering shrubs to flourish – hydrangeas do particularly well here – interspersed with Wendy's favourite annuals such as *Nicotiana silvestris* and *Verbena bonariensis*. Roses scramble through trees, over walls, and up the extensive 200-year-old brick and flint barns. 'New Dawn' frames the front door. To the front of the house the old farm pond is surrounded by grasses, camassias, phormiums and valerian; to the rear, a new *Viburnum tinus* hedge has been planted for the planned extension to the garden. In the large Victorian-style conservatory, plumbago and passion flowers weave their way through the wall trellis, and the many geraniums and orchids add colour to the sills. Wendy is a talented flower arranger and loves to grow herbs, lavender, agapanthus and lilies in artistically arranged pots around the terrace. *RHS, The Royal National Rose Society, NT, The Norwich Cathedral Flower Guild, Norfolk Gardens Trust.*

Litcham Hall

John & Hermione Birkbeck
Litcham Hall,
Litcham,
Swaffham,
Norfolk PE32 2QQ

tel   01328 701389
fax   01328 701164
email   h.birkbeck67@amserve.com

For the whole of the 19th century this was Litcham's doctor's house and today, over 200 years after it was built, the red-brick Hall remains at the centre of the community. This is a thoroughly English home with elegant proportions; the hall, drawing room and dining room are gracious and beautifully furnished. The big-windowed guest rooms look onto the stunning garden where church fêtes are held in summer. Household hens lay the breakfast eggs, and the garden provides soft fruit for the table in season. John and Hermione are friendly and charming. *Children, dogs & use of pool, by arrangement.*

rooms	3: 1 double, 1 twin; 1 twin with separate bath.
price	£60-£80.
meals	Dinner occasionally, by arrangement. Pub/restaurant 3 miles.
closed	Christmas.
directions	From Swaffham, A1065 north for 5 miles, then right to Litcham on B1145. House on left on entering village. Georgian red-brick with stone balls on gatepost.

Map 7 Entry 74

This superb garden has given the family a lot of pleasure over the 37 years since they came to Litcham Hall. The swimming pool has provided fun for children and visitors, but John and Hermione have found the design and planting of their garden from scratch the most satisfying project. Yew hedges make a dramatic backdrop for herbaceous borders and the framework for a sunken area with a little lily pond and fountain. Strolling along mown paths through their wild garden is a delight in spring when the snowdrops, azaleas and bluebells are out: in summer you emerge from this spinney through a pergola covered in climbing roses. Behind the house the swimming pool is sheltered in part of a double-walled garden, with a brick-arched veranda loggia down one side — a wonderful spot for relaxing in mediterranean weather. The walled Italian garden was inspired by the desire to put to best use some beautiful inherited stone urns. Now artfully positioned in a parterre of lavender-filled, box-edged beds, the urns make an elegant finishing touch to a formal composition entirely suited to the period of the house. *Open occasionally for the Red Cross and NGS.*

The Old Rectory

Mrs Caroline Brennan
The Old Rectory,
Caston,
Attleborough,
Norfolk NR17 1DL

tel   01953 488084
email   caroline@stayincaston.co.uk

A very English, wisteria-clad Queen Anne rectory with a
Georgian stable block and an attractive French lump clay
barn. Inside: stone flagging, Japanese wallpaper, huge views
through long windows, a library with oodles of books,
a dining room big enough to cope with an Adam Calkin
trompe d'oeil on all its walls and deep, deep sofas by
roaring fires. Upstairs is sumptuous too with fine linen,
a blue roll top bath, thick velvet curtains and fluffy towels.
A serious, locally-sourced breakfast can be taken in that
beautiful dining room, and Caroline, charming and kind,
absolutely loves her garden.

rooms	2: 1 double, 1 twin sharing bath.
price	£100–£120. Singles £75.
meals	Supper occasionally by invitation, £20. Pub within walking distance.
closed	Christmas & Easter.
directions	A11, after Thetford A1075 10 miles. After Breckles, 3rd small lane on right to Stow Bedon. Caston about 1 mile. Church on right, The Old Rectory opposite Red Lion.

Map 7 Entry 75

When Caroline isn't busy looking after you in the house, you will find her somewhere in this five-acre Georgian flower and vegetable garden. Explore sweeping lawns, take afternoon tea on the large west-facing terrace, stroll through the secret garden at twilight to hear the shriek of a barn owl or spot a great crested newt in the pond; there's a lot to admire here so do take the time. The front and two sides of the house are surrounded by old yews, box trees and hedges of holly, chestnut, beech and ash; a large black walnut and an old English mulberry are well established. The thriving vegetable garden also produces soft fruit for jams and compotes and is separated from the flower garden by an ancient wall. Most flowers are grown from cuttings and all else from seeds (including melons!); unusual plants include four shades of hibiscus, a white weeping mulberry, a *Cardiocrinum giganteum* and a collection of 200 old shrub roses in pretty pinks. Caroline never thinks of her creation as finished, she's always seeking to improve on what is there, but she admits that her favourite task is sitting down at the end of the day and admiring all her hard work.

Sallowfield Cottage

Caroline Musker
Sallowfield Cottage,
Wattlefield,
Wymondham,
Norfolk NR18 9PA

tel	01953 605086
mobile	07778 316616
email	caroline.musker@tesco.net
web	www.sallowfieldcottage.co.uk

So many interesting objects it takes time to absorb the splendour; in the drawing room, gorgeous prints and paintings, unusual furniture, decorative lamps… Caroline has a fine eye for detail. The guest room has a Regency-style canopied king-size bed and decoration to suit the era of the house (1850). The large garden is just as fascinating, with rooms and a very large, jungly pond that slinks between the trees. You can eat in the courtyard or the conservatory; Caroline prepares lovely dinners using much local produce. *Children over nine welcome.*

rooms	2: 1 double, 1 double with separate bath.
price	£50. Singles £25-£35.
meals	Lunch £10. Dinner £15.
closed	Christmas & New Year.
directions	A11 Attleborough to Wymondham road. Take Spooner Row sign. Over x-roads by Three Boars pub. 1 mile on, left at T-junc. to Wymondham for 1 mile. Look for rusty barrel on left. Turn into farm track.

Map 7 Entry 76

A deceptive one acre, but the beautiful large pond in front of the house acts as a huge mirror and reflects tall trees, island beds and the building itself, giving a Norwegian 'lake impression' of space and green. When Caroline arrived it was swamped and overgrown; hacking her way through, she only left what she decided was interesting. This included an impressive swamp cypress, a weeping ash, lots of viburnums, magnolias, a chimonanthus and an as yet unidentified acer she calls the "firework tree" because of its fiery autumn colour. There are also some very old trees: an enormous willow and a vast ash. Caroline adores plants and has a real knack for positioning – they all thrive where they're placed and look good together; lilacs and pinks, shades of green from shrubs and the odd splash of dark red or yellow against the perfect backdrop. An old ditch has been turned into a sunken path with a trimmed hedge on one side and a herbaceous bank on the other. Clematis and honeysuckle wind through trees and shrubs, shade and water-loving plants are deeply content, and all the shapes and colours are soft – there's no ugly rigidity. A tiny, enclosed courtyard has been constructed against one wall of the house and a very pretty pink *Clematis texensis* shoots up it; another wall is capped by curly tiles and there are pots filled with hostas. The pale terracotta-floored conservatory is prettily canopied with vine leaves.

Conifer Hill

Mrs Patricia Lombe Taylor
Conifer Hill,
Low Road,
Starston,
Harleston,
Norfolk IP20 9NT

tel	01379 852393
fax	01379 852393
email	richard.taylor55@virgin.net

A house on a hill – unusual for East Anglia; the lawns fall away and views stretch out over farmland. Richard and Patricia are utterly charming and so easy to talk to; their respective passions are fishing and gardening and the garden is superb. In the house: fresh flowers, family photographs, agricultural prints, a feeling of light and space. The guest sitting room is generously furnished and Patricia will light a fire for you if its chilly. The double, predominantly green bedroom is the biggest; all have thick carpets and a quiet Victorian elegance.

rooms	2: 1 twin/double with separate bath; 1 double let to same party only.
price	£70. Singles £35.
meals	Pub/restaurant 1 mile.
closed	Rarely.
directions	A143 Diss/Yarmouth for 9 miles. At r'bout left for Harleston; immed. left to Starston. Over x-roads, into village, over bridge, immed. right. After 0.5 miles, drive on left with white railings.

Map 4 Entry 77

Built by Richard's grandfather in 1880, Conifer Hill's garden was laid out at the same time. When the 1987 hurricane destroyed 40 mature trees, the Lombe Taylors decided to give the three acres a complete overhaul, and in the process discovered the original layout of beds and shrub borders. Horticultural taste has changed since Victorian times, so you won't find the mass of bedding plants you'd have seen here a century ago; and being practical, Patricia says she is in any case less interested in labour-intensive plants these days. This is nevertheless a much loved garden and it celebrates family rites-of-passage as well. It wasn't only the Queen who celebrated her Golden Jubilee in 2002: the golden wedding anniversary at Conifer Hill was marked by a new border of golden shrubs underplanted with grey. The Lombe Taylors' silver wedding anniversary bed of roses is flourishing too. A recent project brings the garden right up to date: a modern sculpture created by a local craftsman displayed in a roundel of yew hedge; children find the five-foot-tall copper resin sculpture with its abstract verdigris curves irresistible to touch. This is a family garden with much to interest the plantsman. *RHS, The Norfolk & Norwich Horticultural Society.*

Westfield

Dr & Mrs C B Mynott
Westfield,
36 Main Road,
Crick,
Northampton,
Northamptonshire NN6 7TX

tel   01788 822313
email   cbm@mynott.com

The surprises come thick and fast. First, after a rather
unexceptional approach, the charm of the village. Then,
behind a modern entrance, a rambling period house which
was once two cottages. One, 18th-century and stone, has
flagstone floors and its original pump; the other, Victorian
and brick, has been joined to an outbuilding by an atrium-
style extension so that its kitchen and living area seem
almost part of the garden. Bedrooms are traditional,
comfortable and have tea trays with bone china. You are
welcomed by wonderful, down-to-earth people – this is a
delightful place to stay.

rooms	2 twins/doubles sharing bath.
price	£60. Singles £35.
meals	Pubs/restaurants within walking distance.
closed	Christmas & Boxing Day.
directions	Proceed East from M1, junc. 18. In village of Crick, park near church (spire visible); walk 100 yds to house.

Map 3 Entry 78

When Colin and Vicky arrived here 35 years ago, the half-acre garden was a random forest of native trees. Drastic culling helped to give much-needed structure: they left a few indigenous trees and planted ornamental species (Indian bean tree, liquidamber, Ponderosa pine, black walnut). Then they set about creating three separate areas. The result is a meandering, engaging garden, completely surrounded by high walls or impenetrable hedge, which is stunning in spring, summer and autumn. Shrubs – philadelphus, weigelia, deutzia – mass together and deep borders glow with rare French irises, day lilies, penstemon or superb hellebores. The collection of unusual plants is growing all the time. Beside the new extension is a terrace which drops away to three walled areas with more beds and a weeping pear tree. Emma, Vicky's mother, came to live with them a couple of years ago and is obviously a presiding genius. Her pride and joy is the Victorian greenhouse, where she cherishes rare scented geraniums, jasmines and orchids. She is quite capable of putting in six hours gardening during the day before retiring to write her book on Chaucer. Two dogs and two cats keep a proprietorial eye and the birds are truly prolific.

Guilsborough Lodge

Mrs Tricia Hastings
Guilsborough Lodge,
Guilsborough,
Northamptonshire NN6 8RB

tel   01604 740450

There are always fresh flowers in Tricia's house: her style is a blend of the fresh and chintzy as well as the horsey, with an eclectic mix of sporting prints on the walls. Stripped pine windows, and both sitting and drawing rooms opening onto the terrace. A roaring log fire in the dining room in winter, and you'll notice the unusual kilim or Chinese tapestry covered fireside stools that Tricia and a friend trade in. The bedrooms still have their original little Victorian fireplaces, and both rooms have lovely views towards the church.

rooms	2: 1 twin with separate shower; 1 twin with separate bath & wc.
price	£80. Singles £45.
meals	Pub/restaurant 1.5 miles.
closed	Christmas & Easter.
directions	A14 junc. 1 (A5199); 2.5 miles to Northampton; right to Guilsborough.

Map 3 Entry 79

Built in the 1890s as a hunting box for the Pytchley Hunt, Guilsborough Lodge makes a handsome focal point for the garden with its mellow brick and tall chimneys. In a commanding position 600 feet up, these south-facing two acres have lovely views to the church and over a reservoir that attracts masses of wildlife. Tricia was for many years a professional flower arranger, so the gentle palette of blooms in her herbaceous border, dotted with the occasional bright splash, are selected for cutting: she loves phlox, stocks and pinks, and anything that has good structure or a wonderful scent. The border leads down to a hidden sunken garden by the tennis court, planted with more soft pastel colours. When the weather's lovely, breakfast can be served on the terrace, with perhaps fresh garden fruits in season; you can even have a game of croquet on the lawn at the front, where there's a growing collection of old-fashioned roses. To the side of the house is a beautiful billowing cloud of 'Wedding Day' — and a small paddock housing hens and four horses; lovely to lean against the fence and dream.
A peaceful spot to stay in an area rich in well-known gardens to visit: Coton Manor Gardens and Cottesbrooke Hall to mention but two.

Coton Lodge

Joanne de Nobriga
Coton Lodge,
West Haddon Road,
Guilsborough,
Northamptonshire NN6 8QE

tel   01604 740215
fax   01604 743515
email   jo@cotonlodge.co.uk
web   www.cotonlodge.co.uk

Hidden at the end of a mile-long drive, a handsome, wisteria-clad farmhouse surrounded by enchanting gardens, ancient sycamores, horse chestnuts and limes. The elegant, early 19th-century rooms have space, light, archways, sash windows and bags of character, and look out across the beautiful valley beyond. Bedrooms are softly decorated, utterly comfortable and spotless; one bathroom has a washbasin with a marvellous view. Sleep in deep rural peace, then wake to birdsong and a delicious breakfast of muffins, smoothies, fresh eggs from the farm and homemade jams. *Children over 12 welcome.*

rooms	2: 1 double, 1 twin.
price	From £70. Singles £50.
meals	Pub 3 miles.
closed	Rarely.
directions	From M1 junc. 18 follow signs for Crick & W. Haddon. Bypass W. Haddon following signs to Guilsborough. After fork right to Guilsborough, Coton Lodge 0.75 miles on right.

Map 3 Entry 80

A fabulous garden that was created over a period of 30 years by Jo's mother, Ann; now Peter and Jo dedicate themselves to continuing the good work. To the front of the house is a formal semi-circular parterre bordered with box hedging, which leads down to a lower terrace edged with alpine phlox and aubretia. Views from here are over old iron park railings to mature trees and open fields. To the side of the house, a series of rooms are entered through trellising which spills over with cream, yellow and white roses: a silver garden, a cutting garden packed with annuals and an area of shade with hostas and ferns. Here a little brook wanders along towards the hellibore-fringed pond. These small, intimate spaces give way to huge sweeps of lawn; the sunken garden has a small raised pond with a fountain and a sculpture of two seated figures on a bench by Jonathan Nelson admire it all. Planting is carefully organised to make each season a treat, starting with mass tulips for bold spring colour and moving on to hardy and half-hardy annuals for cutting. The woodland, planted by Jo's mother, is now fully mature and provides shelter from the wind; unusual trees include *Taxodium distichum* and early flowering *Prunus mume* 'Beni-chidori'. *NGS.*

Ashdene

David Herbert
Ashdene,
Halam,
Southwell,
Nottinghamshire NG22 8AH

tel   01636 812335
email   david@herbert.newsurf.net

A mile west of bustling Southwell and its lovely Minster, this stunning rosy-bricked house was once the old manor house of Halam and dates from 1520. Much travelled, David and Glenys have packed their big, friendly, family house with wonderful paintings, samplers, embroidery, books on history and travel, lovely old rugs and comfortable furniture. Guests have their own drawing room with open fire and the bedrooms are gorgeous: pretty white bed linen, spotless bathrooms with fluffy towels and relaxing, neutral colours. Don't creep around on egg shells, come and go as you like – but do ask about the area, they know it well.

rooms	4: 2 doubles, 1 twin, 1 single.
price	£60. Single £40.
meals	Pub 4-minute walk.
closed	Occasionally.
directions	A1, then A617/A612 to Southwell. Take sign to Farnsfield. In Halam left at crossroads, past church, house 200 yds on left.

Map 6 Entry 81

An imaginative, really special garden – with a huge 60-year-old paulownia which – excitingly – flowered recently. Both David and Glenys have done the hard work: gravel and boulder garden tucked around the front of the house has scented plants for spring and autumn, two huge yews have been cut to tall stumps, then their later sproutings coaxed and designed by David, one into a spiral, the other into a witty Rastafarian topknot. There's a white spring garden and a woodland walk along serpentine brick paths with precisely coppiced hazels. A long grass walk up a slope takes you away from the house and is edged with hornbeam – rest at the top, a favourite quiet spot. There are over 50 species of damask roses, paths through brick-raised beds of mixed planting and a central circle of five pillars around an Ali Baba urn. Trellises, covered in scented roses, create hidden corners and add height. The vegetable garden is fecund but neat, the sunken garden and the terrace by the house have good seating areas. David's topiary is artistic and striking, including using an unusual muehlenbeckia; he's nicked a juniper into a table (his Chinese libation cup) and is training ivy along a tunnel of wire like a long roll of carpet – so this is what retired surgeons do! Their use of chemical help with all this? None. An organic garden which attracts many birds (38 nests at the last count) and a centuries-old colony of bees. *NGS, RHS. Open for garden clubs & charities.*

South Newington House

Roberta & John Ainley
South Newington House,
South Newington,
Banbury,
Oxfordshire OX15 4JW

tel   01295 721207
email   rojoainley@btinternet.com
web   www.southnewingtonhouse.co.uk

Roberta and John are generous hosts and great fun. Their charming, listed, 17th-century hall house has a ground-floor cottage annexe, prettily furnished with its own little sitting room looking out over the walled garden; a private haven for two. Bedrooms are immaculate with crisp linen on good beds and views to the garden and fields beyond. Enjoy breakfast in the fragrant conservatory or on the terrace in summer – all will be delicious; eggs from the hens, honey from the bees, local Gloucester Old Spot sausages and bacon, homemade bread and preserves. *Discounts for two or more nights.*

rooms	4: 2 doubles, 1 twin, each with separate bath. Cottage: 1 double.
price	From £80. Singles from £50.
meals	Pub/restaurant 1.5 miles.
closed	Rarely.
directions	A361 Banbury to Chipping Norton. In South Newington 3rd left signed 'The Barfords'. 1st left down tree-lined drive.

Map 3 Entry 82

Arrive down the drive in June and you are engulfed by colour and scent — and roses wafting in that gentle, English-garden way. The Ainleys are a great team, work well together as organisers for the National Gardens Scheme, and have created two very special acres of garden in five acres of paddocks and grounds. A walled garden (its gate leading to a field of sheep) is surrounded by honeyed Hornton stone — an idyllic backdrop for roses and wisteria. Here a parterre has been created with Box topiary. The themed borders on the other side of the house are profusely and subtly planted, making this a garden for all seasons. Hellebores, winter-flowering honeysuckle and cornus stems brighten winter days and the orchard is carpeted with snowdrops; daffodils and primroses welcome the spring. By summer the pond is a riot of water lilies and brightly-coloured damselflies; misty autumn mornings shimmer with colour. The conservatory is filled with fragrant hoya, plumbago, stephanotis and jasmine: it's the perfect place to sit and view the garden. The huge kitchen garden provides a range of organic vegetables and soft fruit — asparagus and artichokes among other delights. Roberta's "gardeners" are her bantams: eggs don't come fresher or more free-range. *NGS, RHS.*

Manor Farmhouse

Helen Stevenson
Manor Farmhouse,
Manor Road,
Bladon, Woodstock,
Oxfordshire OX20 1RU

tel	01993 812168
fax	01993 812168
email	helstevenson@hotmail.com
web	www.oxlink.co.uk/woodstock/manor-farmhouse/

Many are the plants in this garden which encourage and feed birds and other wildlife – including the deer which regularly chew the 'Kiftsgate' rose climbing the old apple tree. This charmingly informal garden was created from scratch after the Stevensons arrived in the mid-70s. Helen planted interesting shrubs and trees right at the start but further plans had to be shelved for years as children romped in their garden playground. Now Helen has found more time to focus on gardening and developing this third of an acre surrounded by fields. In spring, the grounds sparkle with snowdrops, crocus, pulmonaria, sweeps of aconite and drifts of daffodils. Her beloved bluebells are allowed to do their own thing. Those first plantings of trees and shrubs – presided over by an eye-catching golden *Acer platanoides drummondii* – have now come into their own and create areas of dappled light and a fresh, natural feel. Her chemical-free, curved borders and raised beds behind low stone walls are packed with colour – she's a great bargain hunter and eagerly swoops on the plant stalls at her local gardening club. When we visited she was gleefully ripping out a leylandii hedge to replace it with a handsome stone wall – another pleasing touch for her colourful, informal English country garden.

rooms	2: 1 double, 1 twin, sharing shower.
price	£62–£75.
meals	Pub 5-minute walk.
closed	Christmas.
directions	A44 north from Oxford's ring road. At r'bout, 1 mile before Woodstock, left onto A4095 into Bladon. Last left in village; house on 2nd bend in road, with iron railings.

Map 3 Entry 83

Hand-painted Portuguese pottery sits on the dresser in the bright dining room and over breakfast you'll be watched by a collection of wooden birds including an inquisitive lapwing and avocet. The main double room has had a makeover courtesy of a Laura Ashley catalogue and is as pretty as you'd expect. Guests share a large shower room, so Manor Farmhouse is ideal for families or friends travelling together; the spiral staircase to the small twin is steep, but the room feels nicely private. The restaurants and inns of lovely old Woodstock are a mile off and Blenheim Castle is close by.

Lakeside Town Farm

Theresa & Jim Clark
Lakeside Town Farm,
Brook Street,
Kingston Blount,
Oxfordshire OX39 4RZ

tel	01844 352152
fax	01844 352152
email	townfarmcottage@oxfree.com
web	www.townfarmcottage.co.uk

A dream setting – and a picture-perfect farmhouse, built along traditional lines, hidden at the bottom of a quiet lane beside the lakes. The guest drawing room is large and light with sofas and chairs for lounging and a door to the garden for sunny evenings. Bedrooms have garden views, Victorian brass beds, pretty cushions and fresh flowers; there's even a little decanter of sherry and a fridge outside for your own bottles of wine. Wake up to the smell of freshly baked bread, and fill up on Jim's hearty farmhouse breakfast served on blue Spode china. *Minimum stay two nights.*

rooms	2: 1 double, 1 twin.
price	From £75. Singles from £50.
meals	Pubs/restaurants 600 yds.
closed	Rarely.
directions	M40 junc. 6, B4009 for Princes Risborough; 2 miles, then 1st left in Kingston Blount for 300 yds, right into Brook Street, then immediately left down drive to last house, through automatic-opening wooden gates.

Map 3 Entry 84

Theresa started taking gardening seriously years ago, when she and Jim moved into their home on their Oxfordshire farm. It all began with a rockery and is now a maturing multi-dimensional plant paradise. What was once sheep pasture is now one and a half acres of superbly planted, well-designed areas that range from the formal to the wonderfully wild. Theresa has created rockeries, scree beds and dramatic borders as well as a restful waterfall and two lakes. The garden, featured in *Ideal Home* last year, is divided into a series of well-defined areas, each with a mood of its own and with witty decorations including an old telephone kiosk and street lamp. You'll find a rose-smothered pergola, an ornamental grass border, specimen trees, manicured lawns and a glorious vegetable garden. Theresa is a self-confessed plantaholic and avidly collects new treasures – no wonder the garden has also been featured in the *Sunday Telegraph* and on *Gardener's World*! 'Albertine' roses wind through apple trees, a vigorous 'American Pillar' decorates an arch. Best of all is Theresa's supreme wildflower garden surrounding one of the ponds: a snowy mass of ox-eye daisies studded with corn cockle, corn marigolds and other wild beauties. A gem. *RHS*.

Larchdown Farm

David & Cally Horton
Larchdown Farm,
Whitehall Lane,
Checkendon, Reading,
Oxfordshire RG8 0TT

tel	01491 682282
fax	01491 682282
email	larchdown@onetel.com
web	www.larchdown.com

There's a huge wow factor here, and indeed the sight of honey-coloured rafters to the ceiling and the polished ash floor and balusters along the gallery in the entrance hall is breathtaking. This open space connects the two ends of the house: visitors have the right-hand end to themselves, with their own drawing room where breakfast is also served. An extremely comfortable family home with lovely pictures and books: the dining table is beautifully laid in preparation for the Horton mega-breakfast. The large ground floor bedroom leads out to a wild area of the garden that attracts many birds.

rooms	4: 2 doubles; 2 singles sharing bath.
price	From £80. Singles £35-£65.
meals	Pub/restaurant 1 mile.
closed	Christmas & New Year.
directions	A4074 to Oxford; right to Checkendon. In village pass pub, church & cricket pitch; right after red phone box. Whitehall Lane out of Checkendon, Larchdown 400 yards on right.

Map 3 Entry 85

'Capability' Brown is alive and well and living in Oxfordshire! When the Hortons
had finished extending and remodelling the house they bought 12 years ago,
David's attention turned to the surrounding three acres. JCBs were brought in to
dig ponds and landscape the levels, and with the help of copious amounts of
manure, the different areas responded quickly with profuse colour. Cally
produces the plants in large quantities, David builds and also looks after the
enormous kitchen garden and polytunnel which extends the produce season;
jointly they maintain the borders. The Hortons' energy and imagination seems
boundless and they cater for all gardening tastes. You can now choose to linger in
the formal sunken garden with pergola on two sides and formal boxed hedge and
lavender parterre in the centre, or stroll along the newly planted terrace garden,
which has access from the car park for wheelchair users. You might cross the
bridge over the man-made stream to the ponds, enjoy the wild life garden,
yellow with daffodils in spring, or you could saunter up the pleached lime walk
to the octagonal trellised area where climbers such as vine, golden hop and roses
are planted. You are now near the large open lawned area where marquees for
weddings and parties are erected. It has been planted with many new specimen
English trees, fruit trees and there's a walk where juniperus, thuja [Western Red
Cedar], and a catalpa [Indian Bean Tree] grow.

Hernes

Richard & Gillian Ovey
Hernes,
Henley-on-Thames,
Oxfordshire RG9 4NT

tel   01491 573245
fax   01491 574645
email   oveyhernes@aol.com
web   www.herneshenley.com

Ramble through the ages in Hernes, home to five generations of the family. A stately but comfortable place to stay: a panelled hall with open fire and grand piano, a drawing room with original inglenook fireplace, a billiard room with easy chairs by a log stove. Large bedrooms overlook the garden; one has a fine four-poster, another a large sleigh bed. Long soaks in the Victorian blue claw-foot bath are a treat. On Sundays tuck into the traditional Ovey breakfast of porridge (in winter), kedgeree and boiled eggs – served in the dining room hung with family portraits.

rooms	3: 1 twin/double, 1 four-poster; 1 double with separate bath.
price	From £85. Singles from £60.
meals	Pub & restaurants within 1 mile.
closed	December-mid-January & occasionally.
directions	Straight over lights in centre of Henley as far as Town Hall. Right into carpark, drive through then right into Greys Rd for 2 miles. 300 yds after 30mph zone, 2nd drive on right signed Herne estate, private drive to main house.

Map 3 Entry 86

In 1968 Gillian and Richard took over the family estate with two full-time gardeners to look after the huge Victorian garden. When one of them died unexpectedly the then somewhat unhorticultural Gillian, with three children under four, knew something had to change. More than 30 years on the garden is mercifully a little smaller but it is in extremely capable hands. Some elements of the original Victorian layout remain: the wisteria arbour, the nut walk, the croquet lawn and the wild garden – Gillian's favourite spot. The garden has many family associations and memories: majestic Wellingtonias that mark the 21st birthdays of elder sons, the holly 'house' and the giant toadstool on which children love to perch like pixies, the ha-ha looking out to the old cricket meadow, the carpets of bulbs under the trees. New since the 1960s are the pool garden, the rose arbour (planted to celebrate Gillian's retirement as a school governor) and the hornbeam walk. The vegetable garden continues to supply delicious produce, and while Gillian plans new projects for the future (ask her about her philosophical "labyrinth of life"), she remains realistic about all that maintenance. This garden is essentially a gentle place for peaceful contemplation.

The Wilderness

Peter & Tarn Dearden
The Wilderness,
Empingham,
Oakham,
Rutland LE15 8PS

tel   01780 460180
fax   01780 460121
email   dearden@empingham.fsnet.co.uk
web   www.rutnet.co.uk/wilderness

Peter's grandfather was a great collector of seeds and cuttings from all over the world which encouraged his enthusiasm for growing things. Six years ago the garden was re-designed by Peter and Tarn; they have added walkways and pergolas to link the different rooms, then planted new beds and – Tarn's great love – old-fashioned roses. They have achieved what they wanted, a garden that looks both natural and stylish. A huge bouncy lawn leads to long pergola walkways with borders in front and behind, all smothered in roses, and a shrubbery with mounds of hebe, mahonia and climbing hydrangea. The croquet lawn looks out to an SSSI (with some rare wild orchids) and is bounded by a mixed beech and copper beech hedge, walnut and horse chestnut trees, a colourful shrub bed and a woodland bed with roses under a line of sycamores. An old espaliered pear climbs up the side of the house and there is a peaceful orchard, guarded by larger trees and an ancient folly. Bounded on one whole side by an ancient yew hedge the garden is protected and a haven for birds: pheasant, partridge and woodpeckers which potter and swoop alongside the smaller species. Geoff Hamilton's amazing Barnsdale garden is close by: a 'theme park' for gardeners.

rooms	2: 1 twin/double with separate bath, 1 twin/double with separate shower.
price	£95.
meals	Pub in village or within 5 miles.
closed	Christmas & New Year.
directions	From A1 to Empingham, into village, 250 yds past 30mph sign, house on right behind stone wall with yew hedge – 50 Main Street – opposite School Lane.

Map 6 Entry 87

Lawley House

Jackie & Jim Scarratt
Lawley House,
Smethcott,
Church Stretton,
Shropshire SY6 6NX

tel   01694 751236
mobile   07980 331792
email   jscarratt@onetel.com
web   www.lawleyhouse.co.uk

More than 50 types of rose bloom in wild profusion – including a 'Paul's Himalayan Musk' that vigorously scrambles through an acacia. Deep herbaceous borders glow with colour and the secret pond garden sparkles with water lilies. This was a weed-choked three acres of sloping ground when Jim and Jackie came 30 years ago. Since then they have gardened devotedly and imaginatively, creating a richly planted design of lawns, beds, trees and shrubs to draw the eye across the valley to the hill scenery beyond. They began with a massive clearance programme which unearthed stone steps and the now restored pond. Today the mood is sunny, delightfully informal and traditional – they love scent and have carefully planted for year round interest among different sections divided by immaculately tended lawns. Acid-lovers, including rhododendrons and camellias, thrive and so do the traditional garden flowers: lupins, sweet peas and delphiniums. A lovely country-house garden with long views – the Wrekin, Lawley and Caradoc hills are all in view and you can even spot distant Clee Hill on a clear day.

rooms	3: 1 twin/double, 1 twin; 1 double with separate bath/shower.
price	£50–£70. Singles £35–£50.
meals	Pub/restaurant 1.5 miles.
closed	Christmas & New Year.
directions	From Shrewsbury, south on A49. Ignore turn in Dorrington, keep on for 3 miles. 0.5 miles before Leebotwood, right to Smethcott. Follow signs uphill for 2 miles; drive on left just before Smethcott.

Map 5 Entry 88

The Wilderness awaits you in a quietly elegant way. The pretty, secluded stone house dates from 1690 (although with some Georgian tampering) and is in a quiet village close to Rutland Water. The entrance hall is stone-flagged, the pale blue drawing room (with roaring fire for chilly days) is large and inviting with books and games, and the dining room is grand with high ceiling and huge windows. You're spoiled in the bedrooms – one pink and flouncy with Colefax & Fowler fabrics, the other bright lemon – and the bathrooms, with their power showers and fluffy robes. Tarn is glamorous and fun, and Peter is charming.

Built on the lower slopes of north Long Mynd to take in the view, this imposing Victorian house is large and comfortable. You can lie in bed in the morning with the sunlight streaming in and gaze over beautiful countryside – or enjoy it all from the proper timber conservatory downstairs. William Morris fabrics and big furniture give a traditional feel. There's a sense of privacy too – you have your own staircase – while bedrooms welcome you with flowers, bathrobes, books, duckdown pillows... Jackie and Jim are delightful hosts and great fun. *Helicopter landing available.*

Acton Pigot

John & Hildegard Owen
Acton Pigot,
Acton Burnell,
Shrewsbury,
Shropshire SY5 7PH

tel	01694 731209
mobile	07850 124000
email	acton@farmline.com
web	www.actonpigot.co.uk

Ferocious fecundity – as if the entire two-acre garden had been magically manured and then left to marinade. John's mother is a great gardener (if you want another treat ask to see her next-door paradise) and she laid out the structure. John and Hildegard have worked hard to bring it into line and the results are magnificent. Dividing the garden into sections the drive up to the house is heaving with huge euphorbias in raised aubretia-clad stone beds, there are thousands of bulbs, an iris bed, large shrubs planted through with ramblers and lovely giant yew balls for structure. The front garden is enclosed with a lawn (croquet in summer) and a huge late-flowering magnolia leans against the almost green house; the back section is all mixed borders with a walled garden by an old swimming pool where sun-lovers are planted. A vegetable, fruit and herb garden provides goodies for the kitchen. There are many rare shrubs and trees, and a wood for each of their three children. Scent is important, especially near the terrace – a wonderful spot for alfresco meals or simply sitting. The garden gently peters out with no boundary to open fields and a lake where ducks, geese, curlews and other water birds flap happily – go quietly and you will hear that lark rising. Hildegard says "you can't force nature" but she has done a jolly good persuading job.

rooms	3: 1 double, 1 twin/double, 1 family room.
price	£70. Singles £45.
meals	Supper or dinner from £15. Pub/restaurant 3 miles.
closed	Christmas.
directions	From A5 & Shrewsbury, onto A458 for Bridgnorth; 200 yds on, right to Acton Burnell. Entering Acton Burnell, left to Kenley; 0.5 miles, left to Acton Pigot; house 1st on left.

Map 6 Entry 89

From the double room, with hand-printed wallpaper and oak chests, you look to Acton Burnell hill — England's first parliament was held here. The yellow room has lovely views of a lake, the garden and the Welsh hills; sunsets can be spectacular. Wooden doors, floors, carved settle and chests sit well with elegant furniture, fine prints and photographs. Happy in their role of hosts, the Owens spoil you with afternoon tea before a log fire, and their suppers are delicious. Parts of the house were built in 1660; the site is mentioned in the Domesday book. A restorative place run by lovely people.

Coston Manor

James and Alex Beazley
Coston Manor,
Aston on Clun,
Craven Arms,
Shropshire SY7 8EJ

tel   01588 660697
email   james.coston@btinternet.com

Bowl along a narrow lane through the verdant Clun valley
then through the iron gates and a gravelled sweep to the
front of the house, the core of which dates back to the 15th
century. Alex and James are gradually bringing the inside
up to date but retaining the family pictures and furniture
which give it such character. It's comfortable too, with
squashy sofas, good beds, gleaming bathrooms and fine
views through long windows. This is such a peaceful part of
England and the house is so quiet you can forget about any
urban worries; the perfect spot for recuperation, and walks
long or short.

rooms	3: 1 double, 1 family suite (1 double, 1 twin).
price	£85.
meals	Dinner by arrangement. Pub 1.5 miles. Restaurants in Ludlow, 8 miles.
closed	Rarely.
directions	From Craven Arms, take B4368 for Clun. In Aston on Clun turn left immediately (before Kangaroo pub). After 250 yds, turn right up inconspicuous tarmac road, 1 mile.

Map 2 Entry 90

The house looks out over the valley and down to the river Clun. At the front of the house is a smooth lawn leading down to a ha-ha, then bucolic views across fields with grazing cattle; to the side is another lawn and a pool which is fed by a spring and drains out through an old bog garden. Rose-coloured old brick walls enclose the lawn to the north guarding a long herbaceous border which is being brought back to former splendour; the large, lazy pond is planted round with hostas and is home to a family of ducks. More lawn runs up the side of the house to the productive flower, fruit and vegetable beds. Beyond the pond is the wood, which has a stream running through it and huge gunnera growing in the dappled light; sit in the shade and read a book in the quiet or peek at the pond from here. Mature shrubs and trees rub shoulders with statues and stonework and there are lovely walks along paths. January heralds a triumphant display of snowdrops and aconites, hundreds of daffodils are followed by bluebells and aubretia-clad walls; lilacs and rhododendrons come later. Alex and James have only been back here for eight months but plan to give the garden year-round interest.

The Croft Cottage

Elizabeth and David Hatchell
The Croft Cottage,
Cumberley Lane,
Knowbury,
Ludlow,
Shropshire SY8 3LJ

tel	01584 890664
email	garden@croftcottagebedandbreakfast.co.uk
web	www.croftcottagebedandbreakfast.co.uk

The Colly Brook bisects the property, tumbling some 350 yards through the south-facing garden created over ten years by Elizabeth and David; a real joint effort. Five bridges now connect the parts of the garden to one another; to the west is a vegetable patch, some herbaceous borders, a willow tunnel and a hazel coppice; to the east are the cottage, more borders, the orchard, the reflective garden and a duck house for the Indian runner ducks who keep the slugs at bay. Further upstream is the goose field with bee hives, geese, chickens and a wildflower meadow which bursts with orchids in June. Beyond this is the wood where there is an observation hide for watching the badgers. A wetland meadow has a pond which is home to moorhens, minnows and dragonflies; hundreds of hedging trees have been planted to create a perfect windbreak. Because Elizabeth keeps bees, most of the plants are old cottage-type nectar or pollen producers; colour-themed beds include one devoted to hot yellows, reds and purples, another mainly to blues, pinks and whites. You are welcome to stay all day in this paradise if you like – have a picnic just outside your room and then badger-watch in the evening. It is a gorgeous, peaceful spot.

rooms	2: 1 double, 1 twin/double sharing bath (let to same party only).
price	£60.
meals	Pub 5-minute walk across fields.
closed	Christmas.
directions	From Clee Hill, south for Knowbury. One mile, left Hope Bagot Lane, second right Cumberley Lane. Under bridge, past Cumberley, 100 yds to The Croft Cottage.

Map 2 Entry 91

Drop from the heights of Clee Hill down narrowing lanes and a secluded valley to find this old estate worker's cottage beside a stream; its new extension is where you will stay with complete independence. Breakfast is locally sourced with eggs from the Hatchell's own hens and ducks and honey from their bees; enjoy it while watching the ducks through the full-length glass in the dining room. Bedrooms are clean, pine-bedded and old-fashioned – not for style fanatics – with comfortable chairs; one has doors to the glorious garden. The quiet is palpable.

The Old Priory

Jane Forshaw
The Old Priory,
Dunster,
Somerset TA24 6RY

tel   01643 821540
web   www.theoldpriory-dunster.co.uk

Ancient, rambling, beamed and flagstoned, Jane's 12th-century home is as much a haven for reflection and good company today as it was to the monastic community who once lived here. Both house and hostess are dignified, unpretentious and friendly; Jane adds her own special flair with artistic touches here and there, and books and dogs for company. There are funky Venetian-red walls in the low-ceilinged, time-worn living room with its magnificent stone 14th-century fireplace and, in one bedroom, decoratively painted wardrobe doors. The big bedroom — undulating oaken floor and four-poster — is deeply authentic.

rooms	3: 1 twin, 1 four-poster; 1 double with separate shower.
price	£70–£75. Singles by arrangement.
meals	Pub 0.25 miles.
closed	Christmas.
directions	From A39 into Dunster, right at blue sign 'unsuitable for goods vehicles'. Follow until church; house adjoined.

Jane tries very hard to keep nature's balance. All produce is either home-grown and reared or bought locally (organic preferably). Environmentally-friendly cleaning products are used , low-energy bulbs installed and there is springwater. Composting is taken seriously and the garden is completely organic.

Map 2 Entry 92

Jane Forshaw's bewitching walled garden in the beautiful Somerset town of Dunster is a wonderfully personal creation. You'll discover a bounteous blend of formal touches with shrubs, small trees and climbers which are allowed to express themselves freely. The garden perfectly complements her ancient priory home… a place of reflection, seclusion and peace. A tall mimosa greets you at the little gate on a lane overlooked by the Castle, mature espaliered fruit trees line the garden path and then comes Jane's most formal touch, the square, knee-high hedged box garden. The shrubs for this were rescued from the Castle's 'Dream Garden' when the National Trust abandoned it because they thought it would be too labour-consuming to maintain. Jane piled as many of the uprooted shrubs as she could into the back of a van, heeled them into some empty land and later arranged them into their present design. Informally planted herbaceous borders and a small lawn in front of the house complete the picture. Through an archway you wander into the church grounds with stunning long beds which Jane helps maintain. When the writer Simon Jenkins drew up his list of the best churches in England, Dunster received star billing and the grounds did even better. He described it as the most delightful church garden in England… see if you agree.

Hartwood House

David & Rosemary Freemantle
Hartwood House,
Crowcombe Heathfield,
Taunton,
Somerset TA4 4BS

tel   01984 667202
fax   01984 667508
email   hartwoodhouse@hotmail.com

Having run 'Gardens of Somerset' tours, David and
Rosemary are experts at both looking after their guests (tea
and homemade cakes on arrival, delicious breakfasts) and
showing them West Somerset's loveliest corners. The house
exudes warmth and comfort, and guests have a large sitting
room, a cosy woodburner, a sprawl of easy chairs, and stacks
of books and jigsaw puzzles. Bedrooms are comfortable,
traditional and spacious with good mattresses, fresh flowers
and garden views. Nights are exceptionally quiet: you may
hear owls and the occasional vixen. Immaculately kept and
everything works properly – a joy in itself.

rooms	4: 3 twins/doubles; 1 single with separate bath.
price	£70. Singles from £35.
meals	Occasional dinner £25. Pub 1 mile.
closed	Occasionally.
directions	From Taunton, A358, for 9 miles, then left signed Crowcombe Station. Over railway bridge; right at T-junction. Last house on left after about 400 yds.

Map 2 Entry 93

This peaceful garden is set within a sheltered glade of beech trees – a glorious setting. It is a garden of many parts. From the house you gaze over the croquet lawn down past an unusual selection of young flourishing shrubs and trees to a magnificent 300-year-old oak. Wander back up the woodland path, edged with primulas and lilies of the valley, through camellias, rhododendrons and azaleas (and hydrangeas in summer) to the formal garden of circles. Here is lush planting within a planned colour scheme. In the centre, an armillary within a stone circle surrounded by pillars up which grow 'Dublin Bay' roses. Duck under a rose and clematis arch to find yourself in David's vegetable garden: a joy to look at and a joy to work in. Here, narrow brick-edged borders guard vegetables of every description, a circular greenhouse nurtures tomatoes, melons, peppers and aubergines, there are beds for asparagus and raspberries, and a fine runner-bean arch – Rosemary's favourite. And there's a large and splendid davidia, whose seeds are now growing to provide a half avenue up the drive. In spring, an old and prolific mulberry tree protects a carpet of fritillaries, while the bank beside the yew is drenched with snowdrops and the field is bright with daffodils.

Montys Court

Major & Mrs A C W Mitford-Slade
Montys Court,
Norton Fitzwarren,
Taunton,
Somerset TA4 1BT

tel   01823 432255
fax   01823 433623
email   mitfordslade@montyscourt.freeserve.co.uk

A mansion in the grand manner, the Union Jack flying for your arrival. The dining room's great windows look out over the rose garden and ancestral portraits gaze down from the walls. The big, light, double drawing room has tall windows, family photographs and a baby grand piano. There are always lovely flowers in the large entrance hall; here the main feature is the magnificent staircase. Bedrooms are fairly plain and old-fashioned but beds are comfortable and bathrooms charmingly 50s. Dawn cooks a splendid breakfast with eggs from their own hens, and there are bridge suppers in the winter evenings. *Pets by arrangement.*

rooms	3: 2 double, 1 twin with separate bath & shower.
price	£75. Singles £40.
meals	Dinner £15, October-March. Pub 2 miles.
closed	Christmas.
directions	M5 exit 25, A358 towards Minehead. B3227 at Cross Keys Roundabout through Norton Fitzwarran. House 1 mile further on left opposite Wick Lane.

Map 2 Entry 94

Dawn manages the flowers and beds while the Major mows, copiously. The stately mature trees give an indication of the atmosphere and origins of Montys Court (the name derived from the Saxon word 'muntior', meaning a house in a glade). The lovely house was built by one of Tony's forebears in 1838 after a successful military campaign, and the collection of specimen trees was planted at the same time to create a park-like environment. The garden looks its best in spring and summer with standard roses to welcome you up the drive – but Montys Court's main glory is its elaborate formal rose garden, consisting of 16 beds laid out in the Victorian era in the shape of a Maltese cross around a sundial. It's a splendid sight in spring when the 1,600 underplanted tulips give a massed display. Two tennis courts and a heated swimming pool are tucked in a secluded area sheltered by shrubs and roses, and a patio under a magnificent oak tree provides a pleasant sitting area with views over the garden and park. This is also an ideal stage for open-air performances: plays are performed here in aid of charity, the ample lawns accommodating audiences of over 200 quite comfortably. Views to the Blackdown and Quantock hills call to the walker from every corner of this lovely garden. *NGS.*

King Ina's Palace

Mrs Shirley Brown
King Ina's Palace,
Silver Street,
South Petherton,
Somerset TA13 5BY

tel   01460 240603
email   trevor.brown2@tinyworld.co.uk

Shirley and Trevor have done an amazing restoration job on their garden. When they first arrived 17 years ago there was much out-of-control yew; now clipped hedges and topiary shapes give a superb framework for Shirley's talented and artistic plantsmanship. Her passion for plants, originally inspired by her father, is evident, and she loves colour coordinating borders; blue flowers are her favourite. Hence the gold/yellow/blue bed of corydalis, iris, aconite and tradescantia mixed with golden elder, cotinus and the unusual yellow magnolia 'Butterflies'. A blue and white garden features a magnificent wedding cake tree (*Cornus controversa variegata*), and, from an old sundial, a yew arch frames the entire length of the garden. A 30-foot rose arbour smothered in 'Crimson Shower' leads to a sunken garden with hostas, ferns and rodgersia. In September, come for the massed display of cyclamen. This immaculate garden has been featured in Amateur Gardening, 'gorgeous gardens'. And when you have explored the garden here, you are within striking distance of Tintinhull, Forde Abbey with its arboretum and nut walk, and of course the delightful East Lambrook Manor; this is the perfect base for visiting Somerset gardens. *NGS*.

rooms	1 twin.
price	£68. Singles £50.
meals	Pubs/restaurants 5-minute drive.
closed	Christmas.
directions	A303 roundabout at eastern end of Illminster bypass, follow signs to South Petherton village. Through village; right to 'East Lambrook'. House down hill on left.

Map 2 Entry 95

In case you're wondering, Ina was a Saxon king of Wessex, but this heavenly house, Grade II*-listed, didn't get going until the late 14th century. It was given its romantic name in the 16th century, and was majorly renovated in Victorian times. The medieval banqueting hall, with Victorian carved fireplace, is now the sitting room. There are tall windows and a medieval fireplace in the dining room, and a half-panelled oak staircase that leads to the bedrooms, fittingly furnished with Victorian-style pieces. Shirley and Trevor are warm hosts, and justifiably proud of their loving restoration.

Carpenters

Mike & Christabel Cumberlege
Carpenters,
Norton-sub-Hamdon,
Somerset TA14 6SN

tel   01935 881255
fax   01935 881255
email   mikecumbo@hotmail.com
web   www.carpentersbb.co.uk

Down a sleepy lane in a hamstone village lies a house heavy
with history. A purple wisteria embraces the front door of
Carpenters which dates from the 1700s and, until the
1930s, was a carpenter's home; the sunny sitting room
where guests are welcomed was the workshop. Christabel
places posies from the garden in every room and, on the day
we visited, deliciously scented daphne cuttings in the hall.
The house is immaculately cared for with soft-coloured
carpets and pretty wallpapers hung in bright bedrooms.
Traditional breakfasts with local produce are served in the
large kitchen, once used by the village baker. *Children by
arrangement.*

rooms	3: 1 twin, 1 single, 1 child's room, all sharing bath.
price	£70. Singles £45.
meals	Pub/restaurant 5-minute walk.
closed	24 December-2 January.
directions	From A303, A356 for Crewkerne. Ignore turn to Stoke-sub-Hamdon; on for 1 mile to x-roads. Left into Norton-sub-Hamdon, 1st right into Higher St. Up to bend, straight through gate by small greenhouse.

Map 2 Entry 96

Christabel once worked at the plant centre at nearby Montacute House; she and lawnsman/pruner Mike are an excellent team. When they came to Carpenters 18 years ago they inherited a highly-managed, sloping garden enclosed by local hamstone walls with views to Ham and the Chiselborough hills. Over the years they have added unusual trees and shrubs to create height and structure; the catalpa they planted at the start is now large enough to sit under on a summer's evening – and enjoy a glass of Mike's delicious home-made wine. (His half-acre vineyard lies just beyond the garden.) Formally shaped borders have been informally planted with hardy geraniums, shrub roses and as many violas and other favourites as Christabel can pack in, while striking architectural plants, like acanthus and phormiums, tower above. A climbing frame is festooned with 'Sander's White Rambler', clematis and honeysuckle. Mike keeps the lawns in pristine condition, prunes trees and shrubs and has carved a straggling yew hedge into dramatic, sentinel-like shapes beyond the double borders. From the first spring flowers to the late autumn blaze of acer, this garden holds your interest. The sole exception to Mike and Christabel's organic rule is the occasional anti-slug offensive in their vegetable garden. *RHS, HPS.*

The Firs

Dr & Mrs R B O Sutton
The Firs,
Lower Odcombe,
Yeovil,
Somerset BA22 8TY

tel   01935 862189

Deep in gorgeous south Somerset, this 16th-century listed
building has 'new' additions that are 200 years old,
flagstoned floors and lovely leaded windows with stone
mullions and pale beams. Your intelligent, interesting hosts,
who have both retired early, have stamped their personality
and exquisite taste all over the house with fine furniture,
good pictures and comfortable, mellow colours. You will
be spoiled with local produce for breakfast, and bedrooms
are large and bright: excellent beds and linen, tapestry
cushions, plain warm colours, sparkling bath and shower
rooms. Relax and enjoy the experience.

rooms	3: 1 double, 1 twin; 1 family room with separate shower downstairs.
price	From £65. Singles from £40.
meals	Pub/restaurant 300 yds.
closed	6 December–6 January.
directions	From A303, take A3088 for Montacute. 1st right, drive through Montacute, continue to roundabout. Right to Odcombe, 1st right Lower Odcombe. 1st house on left.

Map 2 Entry 97

Impossible to picture this lovely garden as being the derelict jungle it once was. When the Suttons arrived here ten years ago all the dry stone walls had fallen down and sheep and horses were happily grazing. They spent a lot of time devising a garden plan, then promptly lost it! But they have managed beautifully without, creating a large, wide swathe of well-cut lawns and beds surrounded by old brick outbuildings, perfectly re-constructed walls and some thick hedges with wild plums growing in them. The area just beside the house is a sheltered, south-facing sun trap with masses of pots filled with annuals for colour. Heather doesn't like vibrant colours and opts instead for softest blues, whites, creams and mauves which go well with the bluey-green of the house paintwork – very rustic French. Scent is important: lavender, rosemary, lilies and honeysuckle; in summer roses clamber everywhere. Steps (built by Heather) lead up to a wider area and some good mature trees: a huge copper beech, silver birch, magnolia and mimosa. A thriving vegetable patch and good fruit trees rescued from the orchard keeps them, and probably half the village, away from the greengrocers for much of the year. As well as being an excellent brickie, Heather makes sculptures (she modestly calls them structures) out of chicken wire; she is also a dab hand at topiary and her fan-tailed rabbit is magnificent. A delightful garden.

Higher Hurcott House

Julia Apps
Higher Hurcott House,
Hurcott,
Somerset TA11 6AA

tel   01458 274541
email   julia.apps@btinternet.com
web   www.sensuousgardens.co.uk

In 1993, the Apps took on two acres of south-facing, gently sloping, jungle and clay. The first thing they did was to curve the drive and 'lose' it down the slope. Gravel paths, pond and lawns followed and a braided hornbeam hedge, with porthole, was planted to enclose the nucleus of the garden. Now cowslips and orchids bloom under a spreading cotoneaster in spring. There are spaces to sit and contemplate: a guilded cage 'sitooterie' beside the bog garden; a gazebo by the pond; a deck shaded by laurel for breakfast out. The area below the driveway is field-grass, mown creatively, studded with native trees and shrubs, with a wildflower meadow as you come in, a small orchard and, tucked away, a tiny wildlife pond, created after a fish in the top pond ate everything in sight. Julia's garden look is loose and informal – don't expect weed-free and manicured but a vibrant space designed to attract wildlife and keep the eco-system in balance. She grows labiates for nectar, salvias for the humming-bird hawk moth and lavender. A self-confessed 'hortibore', Julia has a passion for growing from seed – and for close-up photography – and is delighted to help plan garden days out. She runs a garden consultancy, belongs to the Private Nature Reserve network and is a volunteer Garden Steward at East Lambrook.

rooms	1 twin.
price	£70–£80. Singles £40–50.
meals	Pub/restaurant 6 miles.
closed	Christmas & New Year.
directions	From A3151, A3153 signed Lytes Cary for 0.6m. 2nd turning to Hurcott on left. House after embankment bridge on left.

Map 2 Entry 98

Minutes from mellow Somerton is a peaceful old farmhouse with views onto wooded hills. A twin room with a sitting area in tranquil blues and whites has plump duvets, gardening books and treats — an aromatherapy pillow to scent your sleep if you wish and a fresh single bloom in the spotless shower room. Breakfast when you like it in front of the cosy Rayburn: feasts of compotes from Julia's orchard, homemade muffins, fresh farm eggs and bacon, kidneys and sausages from the nearby farm shop. Julia, a well-travelled Garden Doctor and a Cordon Bleu chef, takes beautiful care of guests and plants alike. *Minimum stay two nights.*

Starsky's Hutch

Joseph Mallard William Starsky
Starsky's Hutch,
Quack Quay,
Billfeather,
Somerset QU4 4CK

tel   0 – # please hold, caller...
email   allquackedup@webfooted.org.anism
web   www.withawaddleandaquack...

The tiniest timber-framed structure ever inspected, built with machine-like precision to a traditional formula that dates back decades or less. Time and energy have been poured into the hutch itself, an almost literal interpretation of 'living in a box', with clever post-industrial inclusion of some fine mesh window features that make mullion look mundane. A few feathers were ruffled when this radical departure from the norm was unveiled to a gob-smacked public, but we like it for its simple, unpretentious in-one's-faceness. Don't forget when you arrive at its lowly, humble entrance – duck.

rooms	1 room with lush, grassy, open front.
price	Many types of grain and small insects accepted.
meals	Dabble for your dinner - you'll be surprised...
closed	Only in summer.
directions	Follow river up to bend, emerge onto bank and shake dry. Hutch can be found a short waddle away.

Map 0.5 Entry 99

Almost lost in a willow-draped scene that could be – from any section – the English bucolic repertoire, the grounds of Starsky's just make you want to waddle into the water and splash it all over your back. Take in the scent of the bull-rushed banks and enjoy squelching your feet into the soft mud. Who needs to go messing about in a boat when you can delight in your own buoyancy on this peaceful stretch of river? And once the pleasures of bobbing about and dabbling for aquatic life have expended your interest, shuffle up onto the grassy bank and fold yourself up for a quiet kip. You'll not be disturbed by other guests – as likely as not they will all be doing the same. You might want to watch out for unwelcome predatory visitors, but they have a hard time beating the hutch's security features, so once you've wallowed by the willows long enough, toddle on over and you'll be able to snuggle into a bed of organic material, lined with the downy contributions of previous visitors, since departed to colder climes. On waking, you'll have a view of the river almost from river-level. The hutch is designed, controversially, to "bring the inside out", which can cause trouble if you have to share. But this place is so perfectly suited to its clientele that they return year after year after year. *Minimum stay one winter.*

Rectory Farm House

Michael & Lavinia Dewar
Rectory Farm House,
Charlton Musgrove,
Wincanton,
Somerset BA9 8ET

tel   01963 34599
email   mike@oneismore.com
web   www.rectoryfarmhouse.com

The Dewars started from scratch – this was just a series of fields around the house. Now it is a beautiful, formal-looking garden and the house is wisteria-clad. Lavinia calls it a low-maintenance garden: she has created a series of 'rooms' by planting yew hedges; they are maturing nicely and act as good windbreaks, too. The house is surrounded by some mature trees and flowering shrubs for every month of the year, mostly highly scented: choisya, *Viburnum tinus*, old English lavender and *Philadelphus coronarius*. A huge swathe of lawn at the back of the house is divided by more yew hedges and there are two weathered stone urns guarding white flowers – lovely in the evening light. An avenue of two conical hornbeams and lime trees is stunning; spring heralds an explosion of colour from bulbs, including wild daffodils; further hedging is in the traditional Georgian style of five trees: nut, beech, blackthorn, maple and whitethorn. Roses are a particular love of Lavinia's: a 'Rambling Rector' (of course) for the east-facing side of the house, and, in other beds, 'Fragrant Memory', 'Mary Rose' and 'Queen of Denmark'. Sheep in the fields, a copse at the far boundary and long views to the hills of Stourhead and King Alfred's Tower make this a magical garden.

rooms	3: 1 double; 1 twin/double, 1 double sharing bath (let to members of same party only).
price	From £84. Singles from £50.
meals	Pub 0.5 miles.
closed	Rarely.
directions	From the east, exit A303 on to B3081 for Bruton. After 1 mile left into Rectory Lane. House 0.25 miles on right.

Map 2 Entry 100

A mile off a fairly main road but as peaceful as can be. Lavinia has showered love and attention on her early Georgian house and garden in a landscape that has changed little since the 18th century. Beams, sash windows, wood fires and high ceilings are the backdrop for gleaming family furniture, paintings and delightfully arranged flowers. Good-sized bedrooms in restful colours have starched linen, fluffy bathrobes and binoculars for watching wildlife from wide windows; spot deer, badgers, foxes, hares, buzzards. Breakfast is so local it could walk to the table on its own, and includes homemade marmalade and jams.

Pennard House

Martin & Susie Dearden
Pennard House,
East Pennard,
Shepton Mallet,
Somerset BA4 6TP

tel   01749 860266
fax   01749 860700
email   susie.d@ukonline.co.uk

One of the grandest houses in this book, Pennard has been in Susie's family since the 17th century — the cellars date from then. The superstructure is stately, lofty Georgian, but the Deardens are delightfully unstuffy. Guests have the run of the library, formal drawing room, billiard room and garden with a freshwater Victorian swimming pool. Or walk in 300 acres of cider orchards, meadows and woods. Martin runs his antique business from the house; Susie was born and brought up here and knows the area well. All is warm and civilised, and the mahogany beds are made up to perfection. *Tennis court available.*

rooms	3: 1 double, 1 twin; 1 twin/double with separate bath/shower.
price	From £80. Singles £40.
meals	Pub/restaurant 1 mile.
closed	Rarely.
directions	From Shepton Mallet south on A37, through Pylle, over hill & next right to East Pennard. After 500 yds, right & follow lane past church to T-junc. at very top. House on left.

Map 2 Entry 101

Sweeping lawns, mature trees, a 14th-century church below, a south-facing suntrap terrace, a formal rose garden, pools and curious topiary... Pennard House is one of those dreamy landscape gardens straight from the pages of P G Wodehouse. All seems serene, graceful, easy – and on a grand scale – yet a huge amount of time and hard work has gone into developing and restoring the grounds of Susie's family home. Shady laurels and yews were the dominant feature until the couple launched a clearance and restoration campaign after taking advice from expert friends. Pennard House has, in fact, two gardens within a garden, divided by a little lane. There are the open, sunny lawns of the house garden and, across the road, a second garden with clipped hedges, a formal rose garden and that inviting spring-fed pool which in turn feeds a series of ponds below. Don't miss the witty topiary cottage, rabbit and other creatures which the gardener has created over the years. Susie always has some new project afoot – a recent success was ripping out cotoneaster below the terrace and replacing it with a formally-planted combination of rosemary, roses and lavender. Knock a few balls around on the grass court, swim in the crystal clear water of the pool, or simply stroll among the colour, the scents and the blooms.

Beryl

Holly Nowell
Beryl,
Wells,
Somerset BA5 3JP

tel	01749 678738
fax	01749 670508
email	stay@beryl-wells.co.uk
web	www.beryl-wells.co.uk

A lofty, mullioned, low-windowed home – light, bright, and devoid of Victorian gloom. Holly and her daughter Mary Ellen have filled it with a fine collection of antiques and every bedroom has a talking point… a four-poster here, a time-worn baby's cot there. The flowery top-floor rooms in the attic have a 'Gothic revival' feel with arched doorways; one first-floor room has a stunning old bath, sumptuously clad in mahogany and with its very own tiny staircase. Delicious breakfasts in the sunny dining room, a drink in the richly elegant drawing room. All this and the wonders of Wells just below.

rooms	8: 3 doubles, 3 twins, 2 four-posters.
price	£75–£110. Singles £55–£75.
meals	Pubs/restaurants in Wells within a mile.
closed	Christmas.
directions	From Wells, B3139 for Radstock. Follow sign 'H' for hospital & The Horringtons. Left into Hawkers Lane. Follow lane to top & signposted.

Map 2 Entry 102

Holly says 'Beryl' means a meeting of hills; it is also a precious gem in a perfect setting. Beryl is a small, early-Victorian mansion with south-facing grounds gazing down to dreamy Wells Cathedral. Holly and her late husband Eddie have devoted countless hours to the restoration of the grounds from an overgrown shambles to their original Victorian splendour. A broad terrace leads to open lawns, a formal staircase and a wildlife pool, while avenues draw the eye towards the views. Beyond lies well-tended woodland planted with more than 4,000 trees with wild daffodils strewn among them – and Beryl's most ravishing feature, the very large walled garden. There are garden rooms and deep, generously planted borders intersected by paths edged by catmint and low box hedges. A cutting bed provides a rich supply of flowers for the house. Fifty white hydrangeas were planted to celebrate Holly's 50th birthday and, of course, there is a large collection of hollies. Victorian garden elegance, flowers in profusion, magical woodland walks... no wonder Beryl's charity open days are such a celebration.

Brambles

Genny Jakobson
Brambles,
Worlington,
Bury St Edmunds,
Suffolk IP28 8RY

tel   01638 713121
fax   01638 713121
email   genny@trjakobson.freenetname.co.uk

Genny's love for her timber-clad home surrounded by
flat-racing country is as evident as her enthusiasm for her
garden. She has decorated the big, sunny rooms with thought
and care, supplying every treat a guest could want, as well as
books and magazines. In the hall a large mirror reflects the
light, and the house is filled with flowers. Tony is a racing
journalist and can take you to the Newmarket gallops if you're
up for an early start. As you relax in the drawing room by the
log fire you may ask, "Why haven't we organised things like
this at home?" *Children over eight welcome.*

rooms	3: 2 doubles; 1 twin with separate bath.
price	£75. Singles £50.
meals	Pub in village within walking distance.
closed	Christmas & New Year.
directions	From A11 (for Thetford & Norwich) B1085 to Red Lodge & Worlington. Right at T-junc. through village; house 200 yds on right.

Map 4 Entry 103

Some gardeners design gardens in rooms, and some prefer to remain unrestrained. Genny falls into the latter category – she loves space. And space she has: the lawn sweeps down to a stream, framed by copses of trees to right and left. The garden at Brambles had already been landscaped when the Jakobsons moved in 14 years ago, and Genny has worked along similar lines since, adding her own touches gradually. To give height to the rose garden she and Tony introduced a four-pillared gazebo, clothed it in summer jasmine and clematis, and underplanted it with delphiniums to add depth of colour. The dark hedge of yew round the rose garden makes the perfect backdrop to three colourful herbaceous beds. In the sunken garden, with its lily pond, Genny allows verbena, evening primroses and pale Californian poppies to self-seed in the gravel. Her relaxed touch has also allowed the drive to reinvent itself as a gravel garden: pretty cross-bred poppies, campanulas and sisyrinchium seed themselves here and there from surrounding borders. Snowdrops, aconites and hellebores carpet the one-acre dell garden, so even early in the season you can expect a floral welcome.

May Cottage

Judy & John James
May Cottage,
Hall Road,
Bedingfield,
Eye,
Suffolk IP23 7QE

tel   01728 628705

Judy vividly remembers their first glimpse of the garden: silver birches glowing
on the lawn against a dark backdrop of woodland, shrubs clustering sociably
around the house, and a stout native hedgerow encircling it all. Despite two-
metre high nettles in some areas and a general air of neglect, she and John fell
instantly in love with it. That was in 2001. Since then, determined to restore and
develop the garden along natural lines, they've created swathes of wildflower
meadow, full of meadowsweet, campion and ox-eye daisies. Woodpeckers,
songbirds and a pair of spotted flycatchers visit regularly. Nearer the house,
where some older shrubs have had to be replaced, Judy has used bamboo,
grasses, *Rhubus thibetanus* and dogwood to great effect; where nettles once
were, hostas and ligularia now flourish. Sit beneath the blackthorn canopy or on
a Lutyens bench under the bay tree and enjoy it all. Although there are plenty of
mature trees (including a Bramley of unbelievable antiquity) the garden still has
a young, hopeful feel. There's nothing grandiose or startling: it's tranquil and
full of wildlife. The area has an abundance of excellent nurseries and gardens:
Judy knows most of them and will be delighted to help you plan your visit.

rooms	1 double.
price	£50. Singles £30.
meals	Packed lunch £5. Pub/restaurant 2 miles.
closed	Rarely
directions	A14, A140 towards Norwich. Right to A1120, through Debenham on B1077, right towards Bedingfield Street. Left at T-junc, then right. Right at church hall, cottage 300 yds on right.

Map 4 Entry 104

May Cottage may be small-scale – it's one half of a pair of Victorian farm cottages – but you won't feel oppressed. John and Judy have a cosy sitting room, with a door in one corner leading to steep and narrow stairs. You have the first floor to yourselves: a double bedroom, bright with crocheted counterpane, a little dressing room where wine, biscuits and morning tea tray wait invitingly, and a small but perfectly formed shower room. John and Judy are retired teachers, kind, thoughtful and full of quiet humour. Judy is chief gardener, while John cooks a terrific breakfast on the red Rayburn.

Abbey House

Mrs Sue Bagnall
Abbey House,
Monk Soham,
Framlingham,
Suffolk IP13 7EN

tel   01728 685225
email   sue@abbey-house.net
web   www.abbey-house.net

Fine old trees — oaks, limes, beeches and weeping willows — dignify the three acres of garden and seven of meadowland surrounding Sue's Victorian rectory on the site of an ancient abbey; evidence of her love of gardening — and her talent for it — is all around you. Early flowering yellow banksia climbs the front of the house, fighting for the limelight with the *Clematis montana* that tumbles around the door. The heated swimming pool (which you may use if you ask) lies enclosed in a sheltered suntrap surrounded by trellises of fragrant honeysuckle, jasmine and trachelospermum. Several passion flowers run riot and there's a gravel bed for hot- and dry-lovers: Japanese banana, agapanthus, verdant bamboo and interesting ornamental grasses. Plenty of new shrubs have gone in this year and the shrub walk also parades many mature plants including viburnum and rubus 'Benenden'. This is a thoroughly peaceful space to amble around and you can stay all day: sit and contemplate a game of croquet under the copper beech, admire the swans and ducks in the lovely pond lined with flag irises — best viewed from a picturesque arched wooden bridge. Then wander at will in the woodland with its early carpet of snowdrops and aconites; further afield you will find a small flock of sheep and assorted fowl.

rooms	3: 2 doubles; 1 twin with separate bath.
price	£60-£70. Singles £30-£35.
meals	Pub 5-minute drive.
closed	Christmas & New Year.
directions	From Earl Sohham A1120, to Monk Soham for approx. 2 miles. Right fork at top of hill, house 300 yds on left after bend and opp. Church Farm.

Map 4 Entry 105

A handsome, listed, Dutch-gabled house (1846) fronted by an impressive fishpond – the monks ate well here – upon which black swans glide. On land, the peacocks lord it over the chickens. Sue's welcome is warm and easy, her bedrooms simply and comfortably arranged, each with a couple of armchairs, garden or pond views. High ceilings and large windows make for a light, calm atmosphere. Settle down in front of the fire in the guest drawing room, or wander out through French windows to the shrub walk. Breakfast sausages and bacon are local; the eggs even more so.

Melton Hall

Mrs Lucinda de la Rue
Melton Hall,
Woodbridge,
Suffolk IP12 1PF

tel	01394 388138
mobile	07775 797075
email	cindy@meltonhall.co.uk
web	www.meltonhall.co.uk

There's more than a touch of theatre to this beautiful listed house. The dining room is opulent red; the drawing room, with its delicately carved mantelpiece and comfortable George Smith sofas, has French windows to the terrace. There's a four-poster in one bedroom, an antique French bed in another and masses of fresh flowers and books. The seven acres of garden include an orchid and wildflower meadow designated a County Wildlife Site. River walks, the Suffolk coast and Sutton Hoo – the Saxon burial site – are close by. Cindy, her three delightful children and their little dog, Snowball, welcome you warmly.

rooms	3: 1 double; 1 double, 1 single, sharing bath.
price	£90–£100. Singles from £41.
meals	Dinner £21–£29. BYO. Lunch & packed lunch available. Pub/restaurant across the road.
closed	Rarely.
directions	From A12 Woodbridge bypass, exit at r'bout for Melton. Follow for 1 mile to lights; there, right. Immediately on right.

Map 4 Entry 106

A curving drive past mature trees leads to rural peace in a town setting. Passers-by peep through the tall gates in spring to admire snowdrops, aconites and crocuses and later, daffodils. In summer, roses scramble up the porticoed façade of the de la Rue's elegant home set among lawns with an imposing flagpole, walled gardens and borders. A dozen box balls add a formal flourish to the sunny terrace. Within the Georgian walled area you'll find a formal paved rose garden with roses growing between flagstones. Walk through a rose-covered arch past a fruiting fig to the large kitchen garden with its immaculate little box hedges and paths. A complete change of mood comes at the far end of the main lawn: a superb sloping meadow and woodland. This is a Country Wildlife Site with southern marsh orchids and a profusion of wild flowers. More than 100 species have been recorded, from meadow saxifrage and cuckoo flowers to carpets of ladies' bedstraw and the purples and whites of knapweed and yarrow. A grass path follows the meadow's perimeter and goes through the adjoining woodland where birdlife flourishes. A garden that perfectly combines the formal and informal with the natural beauty of an all-too-rare plot of flower-filled grassland.

Shoelands House

Sarah Webster
Shoelands House,
Seale,
Farnham,
Surrey GU10 1HL

tel   01483 810213
fax   01483 813733
email   clive@clivewebster.co.uk

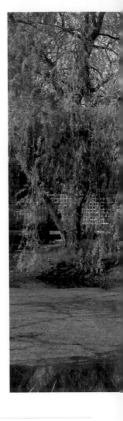

Behind the beautiful brickwork façade, history oozes from carved panel and creaking stair. The dining room, with its cross beams and stunning oak door, dates from 1616: Sarah and Clive know all the history. Ecclesiastical paintings, family photos, embroidered sofas, tapestry rugs; the décor is endearingly haphazard, nothing matches and the house feels loved. Bedrooms have white walls and beams, and big old radiators for heat; old-fashioned bathrooms are papered and carpeted. You are peacefully between Puttenham and Seale villages, just off the 'Hog's Back' – blissfully quiet. Readers love this place.

rooms	2 twins/doubles.
price	£80. Singles from £50.
meals	Occasional supper. Pub/restaurant 1 mile.
closed	Rarely.
directions	On Seale-Puttenham road, halfway between Guildford & Farnham, just south of the Hog's Back.

Map 3 Entry 107

The original front gardens were formal, as revealed by a painting from 1793. Sarah and Clive, having raised their family here, are now recreating this design to some extent, in four flower beds around a small terracotta urn. Over the years the common hardy geraniums have been replaced by more unusual plants – the garden is at its most colourful in late summer. The beds to the side of the path leading to the front door have been planted with David Austin roses and lavender, yellow species tulips and other peach-coloured flowers, then formally edged with box. The garden at the back – where a 16th-century dovecote once stood – is divided by a mellow brick wall, against which a contoured bed has been planted; the delphiniums are lovely in July. Further beds have been laid out in a goose-foot pattern, one grassy path leading to a willow, another to a bridge over the stream, a third to the end of the garden and an old box hedge. Small flowering trees and shrubs underplanted with perennials ensure colour much of the year. The medieval small lake – or big pond – has been revived in 1999, filled with water lilies and edged with bullrushes, while the original greenhouses have been allocated to the hens – the source of your breakfast eggs.

Nurscombe Farmhouse

Mrs Jane Fairbank
Nurscombe Farmhouse,
Snowdenham Lane,
Bramley,
Surrey GU5 0DB

tel	01483 892242
fax	01483 892242
email	fairbank@onetel.com
web	www.nurscombe.com

It is blissfully peaceful. You enter through an old archway, past irises and heavy wooden gates, to discover a farmhouse that goes back to the 15th century. Beautifully restored barns and stables are scattered around; sheep munch in the fields below. Though the original house has been added to many times, the old walls, ceilings and beams still remain. Simply furnished bedrooms have well-worn carpets, striped wallpaper and lots of character, with wonderful garden views. Frill-free bathrooms are in traditional working order. A proper farmhouse breakfast sets you up for super walks up the hill and onto the North Downs.

rooms	2: 1 double, 1 twin, each with bath & separate wc.
price	£70. Singles £40.
meals	Pub/restaurant 1 mile.
closed	Rarely.
directions	At roundabout in Bramley on A281, right up Snowdenham Lane. One mile uphill, house on right opposite white 5-bar gate.

Map 3 Entry 108

No fewer than 36 cypress trees had to be banished when Jane took over. Once they had gone, a garden, walled on three sides, was revealed. Since then she has worked steadily to achieve a true cottage-garden effect. Working on sandy soil, her aim is for it to look "casually cared for, not too formal". She has achieved this – brilliantly. A mixed herbaceous border behind the house has random repeat planting at either end. 'Iceberg' roses on a bargate wall provide a backdrop for a sloping border with a blue, pink and magenta colour scheme; at the back are *Crambe cordifolia*, *Malva moschata* and pretty cranesbill. In the vegetable garden, where there's a fine old wooden greenhouse, a tayberry flourishes against the back wall and herbs, root vegetables, beans, courgettes and sugar snaps grow. Fruit from the old apple and plum trees sometimes figures on the breakfast menu, along with wild mushrooms and nuts. The garden, set in 40 acres of gentle hills (bluebell woods, a trout-filled lake, a rowing boat), is visited by birds and the occasional hedgehog, fox or badger. None seem to help with the armies of slugs, which Jane tackles singlehandedly on damp evenings. A happier task is arranging tours to private Surrey gardens.

The Old Bothy

Willo & Tom Heesom
The Old Bothy,
Collendean Lane,
Norwood Hill,
Horley, Surrey RH6 0HP

tel	01293 862622
fax	01293 863185
email	willo@heesom.fsnet.co.uk
web	www.theoldbothy.co.uk

A fine house in a fabulous setting and much travelled people. Willo is a potter – her studio is in the garden – and Tom an old car enthusiast. From the barrel-vaulted living room, embellished with art from all over the world, are views to the North Downs on a clear day. The main guest room is downstairs, chic and compact. Pale blue walls with uplighting, an Art Deco bedhead painted with moon and stars, curtains of maroon shot silk; the ultra-modern bathroom has hand-made tiles in mottled aquamarine. Wonderful breakfasts too – and who would guess Gatwick was an eight-minute drive? *Older children welcome.*

rooms	2: 1 double; 1 single sharing bath (let to same party only).
price	From £70. Singles from £45.
meals	Pub/restaurant 400 yds.
closed	Occasionally.
directions	M23 onto A23. At Longbridge r'bout, A217 towards Reigate, left for Norwood Hill. 1 mile, left into Collendean Lane; house on right after 0.75 miles.

Map 3 Entry 109

A foliage fiesta! Green rather than flowery and fascinating for plantsmen, the garden was designed by Anthony Paul, renowned for his fondness for big-leafed plants. Tom is a keen gardener (a love inherited from a great aunt who had a nursery) and has labelled everything. As you turn into the drive there are great stands of interesting shrubs and mature trees underplanted with shrub roses and carex and it is lined with black walnut, amelanchier and *Viburnum rhytodiphyllum*. By the house is a dry bed with a wisteria; a *Sophora microphylla* leans close to the guest bedroom window. The house is well-covered by a Canadian concord vine, a *Magnolia grandiflora* and a jasmine – and around the side is the shady garden; ground cover plants include euphorbias, *Asarum europaeum*, *Ophiopogon japonica*, ferns and tightly packed Japanese anemones. A little path leads to a white bench with a sculptured back in the shape of a reclining, bikini-clad lady – she and the rest of the shady area are low lit at night so that they glow orange. As you emerge through to the back of the garden there are staggering views, a lawn with a night-lit weeping willow underplanted with snowdrops and aconites, and a colourfully clashing corner of mixed perennials. The decking is of diagonal wood planks and there's a shady clump of prolific fig trees beside a pebble garden which sports a Jane Norbury terracotta head. *RHS*.

Lordington House

Mr & Mrs John Hamilton
Lordington House,
Lordington,
Chichester,
Sussex PO18 9DX

tel   01243 375862
fax   01243 375862
email   audreyhamilton@onetel.com

On a sunny slope of the Ems valley, life ticks by peacefully as it has always done... apart from a touch of turbulence in the 16th century. The house is vast and impressive, with majestic views past clipped yew, pillared gates, box and walled garden to the AONB beyond. Inside is engagingly old-fashioned: Edwardian beds with firm mattresses and floral bedspreads, carpeted Sixties-style bathrooms, shepherdess wallpapers up and over wardrobe doors. Tea cosies and homemade marmalade at breakfast, big log fires and a panelled drawing room. *Children over five welcome.*

rooms	4: 1 double; 1 twin/double with separate bath/shower; 1 double, 1 single sharing bath/shower.
price	From £70. Singles from £35.
meals	Packed lunch from £5. Dinner £15–£25. Pubs 1 mile.
closed	Rarely.
directions	Lordington (marked on some road maps) west side of B2146, 6 miles south of South Harting, 0.5 miles south of Walderton. Enter thro' white railings by letterbox; fork right after bridge.

Map 3 Entry 110

Sheltered terraces and lawns give you every opportunity to take in the views over the Ems valley. This is an intriguing garden. Visiting 40 years ago, Sir Geoffrey Jellicoe described it as "a most interesting fragment of what once must have been a considerable 17th-century formal landscape". Old walls, pillared gateways, a bowling green, yew hedges and flights of steps still add character. It was John's father who first took on the Herculean task of bringing the place to heel. He maintained it almost single handedly for 40 years; the Hamiltons still have his notes. Since then, because of the drought, they have replaced the bedding plants in the long borders with low-growing aromatic shrubs, interspersed with pelargoniums, lilies, anemones and osteospermum. In the spring, the beds are bright with tulips and the drive is thickly bordered with spring flowers. Unusual trees are scattered throughout – a black mulberry, a paperbark maple, a fig grown from a cutting from Lambeth Palace, a newly planted liquidambar – and the walled kitchen garden produces vegetables and soft fruit. Overhead, buzzards wheel and mew; at dusk you may encounter rabbits, badger or deer.

73 Sheepdown Drive

Mrs Angela Azis
73 Sheepdown Drive,
Petworth,
Sussex GU28 0BX

tel   01798 342269
fax   01798 342269

A short walk from the centre of the historic town of
Petworth, number 73 lies in a quiet, 1970s cul-de-sac and
has glorious garden views. Once chairman of the National
Gardens Scheme, now a vice-president, Angela has a
background that will fascinate anyone who loves gardens
and, of course, she has a particular insight into the gardens
and nurseries of Sussex. Her conservatory overflows with
plants (so no room for breakfast!) but it's a real pleasure to
enjoy a coffee – and a gardening book – here in the sun,
and soak up that blissful view.

rooms	2 twins sharing bath & shower.
price	From £55. Singles from £35.
meals	Pub/restaurant 10-minute walk.
closed	Christmas & New Year.
directions	From Petworth on A283. Sheepdown Drive east of village centre.

Map 3 Entry 111

From the back of the house the view across the small valley to the South Downs is outstanding. Since taking on this sloping, 60-foot garden four years ago, Angela has transformed a tricky plot. Visible in its entirety from the windows above, the planting has been cleverly designed with many hidden corners. The area has been divided across the middle, with the view from the top end framed by the herbaceous borders that curve down either side. A central oval bed conceals an entrance through to the lower part of the garden and from here plants frame the view without obscuring it: a prunus gives height and shade to one side; azaleas, rhododendrons and weigela will be pruned as they grow to maintain a particular size. Owners of small gardens will delight to find one here with which they can comfortably identify. A gate at the bottom leads to a network of footpaths that lead you around much of the area without having to resort to the car. Walk round to the town – heaven for antiques-lovers – or down through the fields to the pub in Byworth for supper. *NGS Assistant County Organiser.*

Pindars

Jocelyne & Clive Newman
Pindars,
Lyminster,
Arundel,
Sussex BN17 7QF

tel   01903 882628
fax   01938 882628
email   pindars@btinternet.com
web   www.pindars.co.uk

A beaming welcome from Jocelyne sets the tone. She and Clive are excellent company and, now their children have flown, they are glad to share their home. The 1960s house is warm and stylish; it also feels well-loved and lived-in, with interesting furniture, books, magazines and some exceptional watercolours; two Burmese cats complete the happy picture. The road is busy but the guest sitting room faces the peaceful, beautiful gardens, as do two of the bedrooms (the other surveys Arundel Castle). Bedrooms are super, bathrooms white and pristine. Jocelyne's cooking is imaginative so breakfast and dinner will be delightful. *Minimum stay two nights preferred.*

rooms	3: 2 doubles; 1 twin with separate bathroom.
price	£65–£70. Singles £45.
meals	Dinner £20. Pub 0.5 miles.
closed	Rarely.
directions	1 mile south of A27 on A284. House on left after 1st sharp right-hand bend.

Map 3 Entry 112

The weeds towered above the children when Jocelyne and Clive bought the field nearly 40 years ago. Once the house was built, they had £5 left for creating the garden – from scratch! Over the years, they have softened and transformed the square lines of the field into a magical place of curves and corners, open vistas and secret places. Everything – terraces, swimming pool, flint wall with fountain – has been designed and built by them. They have also planted about 100 trees, including poplars, birches, eucalyptus, oaks and cherries, some of which are felled as necessary. Jocelyne's particular love is an *Acer platanoides*, fully grown and superb; another special tree is a big chestnut, reared from a conker and nursed back to life by Clive after it was split in half by the 1987 gale. The borders are a mix of shrubs and perennials with some summer bedding (though Jocelyne also fills pots with annuals, which she can then move around). She plants for foliage colour, shape and height in large, organically-shaped splodges. If plants seed themselves, they are often allowed to stay, giving a relaxed, unstudied effect. Swallows nest in the garage every year and green woodpeckers are frequent visitors.

Copyhold Hollow

Frances Druce
Copyhold Hollow,
Copyhold Lane,
Borde Hill,
Haywards Heath,
Sussex RH16 1XU

tel   01444 413265
email   bbgl@copyholdhollow.co.uk
web   www.copyholdhollow.co.uk

As pretty as a picture. Protected on one side by an ancient box hedge and fed by a natural spring, the garden is literally 'in' the hollow with the house. Frances has developed the whole thing herself over the last 13 years creating an acre of joy. Water lovers paddle happily around the stream's edge including flag irises, astilbes, unusual and prettily marked red and yellow mimulus, hostas and *Crocosmia lucifer*. There is an innovative green Giverny-like bridge, over which is fixed an arched sweet-chestnut tunnel now covered in wisteria, clematis, roses and jasmine. There's another arch further up the brick path, smothered in *Trachelospermum asiaticum*, roses and clematis. Walk through mixed borders to a patio — eating out here is fun — and feel protected from the weather: you are tucked in beneath a natural hanger of mature beech and oak trees and a giant redwood. Behind the house is a bank up to the tree line, with mown paths, camellias, rhododendrons and azaleas. The soil is acid and very heavy clay so not easy to work but it all looks perfect. Come at any time for something special; in the spring the garden is especially merry with wild daffodils, snowdrops, bluebells and wild orchids.

rooms	4: 2 doubles, 1 twin, 1 single. Extra bed available.
price	£70–£90. Singles £50–£55.
meals	Pub/restaurant 0.5 miles.
closed	Rarely.
directions	M23, exit junc.10a; B2036 for Cuckfield. There, over mini r'bout. At 2nd r'bout, left into Ardingly Rd; right at 3rd r'bout into Hanlye Lane; left at T-junc., 1st right for Ardingly; 0.5 miles on right.

Map 3 Entry 113

The delightful, 16th-century house hides behind a 1,000-year-old box hedge, its land delineated by an ancient field boundary. First a farm, then an ale house, Copyhold Hollow seems small from the outside, but opens into a quirky interior with many exposed timbers. Frances did the restoration herself, and coaxed the garden and woodland back to life: the results are charming. The guests' dining room and sitting room with inglenook fireplace are oak-beamed, uncluttered and cheerful; bedrooms have goosedown duvets and wonderful views. Your lively, independent hostess offers garden holidays and has masses of info on walks.

Shortgate Manor Farm

David & Ethel Walters
Shortgate Manor Farm,
Halland,
Lewes,
Sussex BN8 6PJ

tel	01825 840320
fax	01825 840320
email	david@shortgate.co.uk
web	www.shortgate.co.uk

The house is almost more flower-filled than the garden – not only with the fresh variety, but painted on porcelain (Ethel's expertise is astonishing), hand-crafted in sugar, and dried and hung in arrangements from the beams. Now fully tile-hung, the house was originally built in 1790 as a shepherd's cottage for the Earl of Chichester, and later extended. All the rooms are a generous size, one bedroom in particular, and delicious breakfasts are served in the bright dining hall. An excellent, relaxed place from which to explore some wonderful countryside.

rooms	3: 2 doubles, 1 twin.
price	£70–£80. Singles from £40, low season only.
meals	Pub within walking distance.
closed	Rarely.
directions	South on A22 to Halland; right at Halland Forge roundabout; Shortgate 0.5 miles on left.

Map 4 Entry 114

It's roses, roses, all the way up the poplar-lined drive to Shortgate Manor Farm.
More than 50 different varieties of white, pink and deep-red ramblers festoon
an avenue of poplars – and the Sussex barn at the end is simply smothered in
white 'Bobby James', 'Rambling Rector' and 'Seagull'. The Walters started with
the roses when they first began to create the garden, but gradually became so
smitten by the gardening bug that they have widened the scope of plants and
increased the number of beds over the years. Several pergolas frame rampant
clematis and honeysuckle – and yet more roses. Recent additions include a new
hot bed, and a wonderful collection of grasses which gives structure to the
garden during bare winter months. These exciting new schemes are fuelled
by Graham Gough's nearby nursery of unusual plants. Shortgate can now rightly
be called a plantsman's garden, and marks a radical change of direction in the
Walters' lives: pre-bed-and-breakfast days they used to breed thoroughbreds for
flat racing – although David does still travel in his capacity as an internationally
renowned judge of show horses. *NGS, HPS.*

Stone House

Peter & Jane Dunn
Stone House,
Rushlake Green,
Heathfield,
Sussex TN21 9QJ

tel   01435 830553
fax   01435 830726
web   www.stonehousesussex.co.uk

This part-Tudor, part-Georgian house has been in the family since 1432, its windows gazing over gardens and parkland that have been cherished for centuries. Peter and Jane are gentle and charming and the six bedrooms are period stunners: floral canopies and matching drapes, grand mirrors, family antiques. Delectable meals (game from the estate, vegetables, herbs and fruits from the gardens, wines from the cellars) are served at crisply dressed tables. Peter guides you to the gardens and castles of Sussex and Kent, Jane, a Master Chef, rustles up peerless picnics for Glyndebourne. *Children over eight welcome.*

rooms	6: 3 twins/doubles, 2 four-posters, 1 suite.
price	£115-£245. Singles £80-£115.
meals	Lunch & dinner £24.95.
closed	Christmas & New Year.
directions	From Heathfield, B2096, then 4th turning on right, signed Rushlake Green. 2 miles down hill and up into village. 1st left by village green to crossroads and house on far left, signed.

Map 4 Entry 115

Chatsworth in miniature. Five and a half acres of sweeping lawns, two lakes, 'hot' and 'cool' borders, an 18th-century rose garden to match the front of the house, a tunnel of apples and pears, an avenue of limes by falling pools and, perhaps most outstanding of all, a 1728 walled kitchen garden quartered by brick paths. Jane is a veg and herb guru, great-great-granddaughter of the designer who laid out some of Castle Howard and Kew, and modestly thrilled by her plot. One of her passions is colour, and she often plants in blocks for impact. The short border brims with yellows, whites and blues, the 100ft-long one with pinks, reds and golds, and the vegetable garden has a glorious palette: 'Red Rubine' brussel sprouts alongside grey-green 'Cavallo Nero', radicchio nudging yellow-green Chinese cabbage, marigolds cosying up to cornflowers, and dozens of unusual 'cut and come again' salads. Trees include a black poplar (rare for the south), a white mulberry and a magnificent Japanese maple. How does she achieve such abundance? Jane — supported by a delightful bunch of part-time gardeners — gives the thumbs up to comfrey manure, grit (tons of it) for a clay soil, mushroom compost to keep down weeds and a polytunnel for the veg.

Hailsham Grange

Mr Noel Thompson
Hailsham Grange,
Hailsham,
Sussex BN27 1DL

tel   01323 844248
email   noel-hgrange@amserve.com
web   www.hailshamgrange.co.uk

Since it was built at the start of the 18th century, this perfect house, set back from the road in a town where they still hold two cattle markets a week, has had few owners. No surprise there: it's the sort of place you'd want to hang on to. No standing on ceremony either, despite the décor: classic English touched with chinoiserie in perfect keeping with the house. Busts on pillars, swathes of delicious chintz, books galore and bedrooms a treat: a sunny double, a romantic four-poster, and two studio suites in the Coach House. Relaxed, friendly Noel serves summery breakfasts on the flagged terrace – in some style.

rooms	4: 1 double, 1 four-poster. Coach house: 1 double, 1 twin/double.
price	£85–£110. Singles from £60.
meals	Pubs/restaurants within walking distance.
closed	Rarely.
directions	From Hailsham High St, left into Vicarage Rd. House 200 yds on left. Park in coach yard.

Map 4 Entry 116

There is a quiet element of the unexpected in Noel's garden. Perhaps it's because of his upbringing in New Zealand, at a time when many gardens still clung to traditional English patterns but were enlivened by native exotics. Here, within a formal framework of box, yew and hornbeam hedging, Noel has created a whole series of gardens, yet within the formality he has mixed and juxtaposed his plants in an informal and original way. The effect is relaxed, romantic and subtly different. Separate areas are themed for colour – of foliage or flower – with plants chosen for scent and grouped in swathes so they blend into each other. All this has been achieved in the 18 years since Noel took over Hailsham Grange. When he arrived, he was presented with the challenge of a completely blank canvas and he is still constantly experimenting (the spring garden is where any that are doing badly are given their last chance – it's flourish or die!). There are several enticing spots to sit with an evening drink and contemplate all this beauty: a bench in the daffodil-filled spinney, a chair in the dell, and a seat in the enchanting gothic summerhouse.

Little Worge Barn

Susan & Stephen Moir
Little Worge Barn,
Willingford Lane,
Brightling,
Sussex TN32 5HN

tel   01424 838136
email   moirconsult@btinternet.com

Pootle down through Sugar Loaf Wood – where *Cold Comfort Farm* was filmed – to arrive at your own smart little cottage. Find a beamed, light-filled sitting room, a stylish bedroom and a tiny kitchen on full alert. Be brave and fend for yourselves, or arrange for delicious breakfasts and suppers to be brought to you. If you like, you can eat next door at Susan and Stephen's 17th-century barn (your hosts are great fun). So do your own thing – but make sure you walk these blessed hills and spot the six follies built by the local 1800s eccentric, Mad Jack Fuller.

rooms	Cottage with 1 twin/double, sitting room + kitchen.
price	£70-£90.
meals	Pub 1.5 miles.
closed	Christmas & New Year.
directions	Turn by church in Burwash down School Hill. After 3 miles, right at crossroads into Willingford Lane. Left after 100 yds onto concrete farm track; follow track to thatched barn at end, 0.75 miles.

Map 4 Entry 117

An exciting new garden. Stephen and Susan are garden designers and have left behind a 15-year-long, much-admired creation to paint a different picture here. The broad canvas is the achingly gorgeous sweep of valleys and hills that surround the barn; the challenge: to create a one-acre garden that doesn't detract from such splendour, *and* is practical to manage. To the east and south of the barn are two sunny terraces for sitting out; to the north, a sloped grassed area with views to the Wealden hills. The south-facing terrace is sunken and contains neat raised vegetable beds – a strong framework for wildly excitable lettuces and leaves; here pots add interest, and the warmth and shelter encourage salvias, euphorbias, penstemons, geraniums, cistus and hebe. There are plans brewing to terrace the hillside, create a vegetable and cutting garden and rustle up a hen run – not forgetting a device for water collection. Further afield are acres of mature woodland, ancient blackthorn hedgerows laden with honeysuckle, broom and holly; the windy conditions on the crest lead to stunted oaks and hawthorns. If all this makes you long to improve your own horticultural credentials you can walk from here to Sarah Raven's gardening school at The Cutting Garden.

Knellstone House

Linda & Stuart Harland
Knellstone House,
Udimore,
Rye,
Sussex TN31 6AR

tel   01797 222410
email   info@knellstonehouse.co.uk
web   www.knellstonehouse.co.uk

The Harlands have a beautiful old house, built as a hall in
1490, with sloping, uneven floors, mullioned windows and
rare dragon beams. Views reach across the Brede valley to
grazing sheep and then the sea. But there's no old world
inside: instead, a refreshingly modern and bright feel with
buttermilk walls, contemporary furniture, good lighting –
and an elegant collection of simple carved heads from all
over the world. Bedrooms are crisp, bathrooms are modern
with luxurious accessories. Breakfast is substantial and local;
lovely Rye is a short drive.

rooms	2: 1 double; 1 double with separate bath.
price	From £90.
meals	Pub 600 yds.
closed	Occasionally.
directions	Off B2089, eastwards through Udimore; 1.2 miles after Kings Head turn right; westwards from Rye, turn left, 0.3 miles past The Plough, up unmade-up drive.

Map 4 Entry 118

Just as the house is a mix of very old and deliciously modern, so is the garden. Although Linda and Stuart inherited some lovely old trees, a wood (once frequented by smugglers, apparently), a pond and a happy wisteria, they have already stamped their own personality on the garden and are continuing to do a lot more. The garden is in different sections: formal at the front, terraced and bowl-shaped at the rear with fabulous views to the sea. A parterre provides cut flowers and some fruit and vegetables, and an old barn is being converted into a greenhouse. Linda has a love of grasses, shaped beds and striking plants, many in dark reds, oranges and whites. Everything curves here – gateways, steps – to match the bowl shape. Then, for height, vertical railway sleepers, and a minimalist courtyard with reflection pool, steel girders and climbers. At the front, a formal garden with an emphasis on native plants is developing. Wildlife is abundant: kestrels lurk in the bowl, badgers bumble at night (and eat the Harlands' figs, mischievous things). The terrace around the house has good seating areas and there is a glass-covered veranda so in cooler weather you can still admire the views. Great Dixter, Sissinghurst and Pashley Manor are nearby, should you need further inspiration.

Shrewley Pools Farm

Cathy Dodd
Shrewley Pools Farm,
Haseley,
Warwick,
Warwickshire CV35 7HB

tel   01926 484315
mobile   07818 280681
web   www.shrewleypoolsfarm.co.uk

Everything is exuberant and down-to-earth about Cathy – and so is her garden. Originally planted by her mother-in-law in the 70s, the specimen trees and shrubs remain the same, with climbers and herbaceous perennials allowed to romp freely through the season. Cathy describes it as a fragrant, romantic garden: roses ramble through trees, scented wisteria and honeysuckle weave over the porch, and old-fashioned shrub roses perfume the borders. Great masses of hellebores herald the spring, and 30 different varieties of hostas are protected by the bantams who potter around gobbling up slugs. She enthusiastically reels off names, affectionately describing colours and habits ("There's this lovely little iris in the rockery called 'Mourning Widow' with almost-black flowers and fine leaves…"). Her busy bed-and-breakfast business makes her practical about maintenance: they work hard in the garden at the beginning and end of the season, but leave everything to perform by itself during the summer. And that it surely does. Shrewley Pools is a working farm smothered with flora; you'll see 'New Dawn' roses in the yard and clematis 'Perle d'Azur' romping over the stables. Bring your fishing rod; the four-and-a-half acre lake is stocked with 10,000 carp.

rooms	2: 1 family room (& cot); 1 twin with separate bath.
price	£55–£65. Singles from £40.
meals	Children's tea from £3. Pub 1 mile.
closed	Christmas & New Year.
directions	From M40 junc. 15, A46 for Coventry. Left onto A4177. 4.5 miles to Five Ways r'bout. 1st left, on for 0.75 miles; signed opp. Farm Gate Poultry: track on left.

Map 3 Entry 119

An early-17th-century beamed farmhouse on a mixed, arable-animal farm... breakfast couldn't be more farmhouse if it tried. There are Shrewley Pools' own bacon and bangers and organic eggs from next door. Log fires in the dining room, sitting room and hall, beams all over, charmingly irregular quarry-tiled floors, old family furniture and chintz. The twin is beamy, oak-floored and rugged. The family room has a generous king-size bed and a single bed, as well as a cot, and fat sheepskin rugs on a mahogany floor. This is a super place for families in summer – and children's teas and babysitting are easily arranged.

Salford Farm House

Jane & Richard Beach
Salford Farm House,
Salford Priors,
Evesham,
Warwickshire WR11 8XN

tel   01386 870000
email   salfordfarmhouse@aol.com
web   www.salfordfarmhouse.co.uk

An unusual garden, it is divided by a wing of the house; you pass under an open-sided brick and timber barn to cross from one side to the other, and the result is a wonderful shaded area for seating. It has been created over the last few years and has matured well thanks to the packed planting of roses, shrubs and herbaceous perennials: Jane has an artist's eye for colour, shape and groupings. Beautiful arrangements of plants in pots and a square, formal pond populated by water fowl show off her talent, clever curvy lawns as smooth as bowling greens, dotted with island beds, give the illusion of space. There is always another corner to peek around and plenty of height has been added: a pretty gazebo covered in clematis, weathered deer-fencing screens, and a large pergola the length of one wall. There are fun touches too with natural old log sculptures — one peers out between penstemons looking like the Loch Ness monster. Masses of tulips in spring, amazing interest and colour all summer and chrysanthemums and asters for the autumn: this is a garden worth visiting at any time. Richard is MD of Hillers, a mile down the road — a fruit farm, farm shop and display garden from which you can buy all the inspiration you need to take home with you. Have another look at Jane's colour groupings first — one could hardly do better.

rooms	2 twins/doubles.
price	£85. Singles £52.50.
meals	Dinner £25.
closed	Rarely.
directions	A46 from Evesham or Stratford; exit for Salford Priors. On entering village, right opp. church, for Dunnington. House on right, approx. 1 mile on, after 2nd sign on right for Dunnington.

Map 3 Entry 120

The house is beautiful within, solidly handsome without. Jane is a gifted interior decorator; the colours are splendid and all is in tip-top order. Jane and Richard are friendly, easy hosts; she was a ballet dancer, he has green fingers and the freshly picked produce from his fruit farm appears in pretty bowls on the breakfast table. The kitchen is engagingly beamed, warm and elegant. There are some fine pieces of furniture, sofas to sink into, a flagstoned hallway, ticking clocks, the smell of beeswax, and enough comfort to satisfy a pharaoh.

Blackwell Grange

Liz Vernon Miller
Blackwell Grange,
Blackwell,
Shipston-on-Stour,
Warwickshire CV36 4PF

tel   01608 682357
fax   01608 682856
email   sawdays@blackwellgrange.co.uk
web   www.blackwellgrange.co.uk

A former rickyard for the farm has been worked into a quarter acre of pretty English garden around the farmhouse. Old York stones with curved raised beds form grand steps up to the lawn; uninvited visitors – like tiny wild strawberries between the stones – have been allowed to stay where they pop up. There's a soft, relaxed feel to all the planting – no strict colour schemes or design-led rigidity – so that the rhythm from garden to countryside is fluent and delightful. Perfectly clipped hedges, neat lawns and careful planting around arches and pergolas show a more restrained side to the garden but somehow it all looks effortless anyway. Ancient barns have been used as scaffolding for the old roses, hops, jasmine and clematis which give colour on different levels, and a dear little summer house has splendid views over hills and woods. A circular stone seat hides behind a narrow walkway between the barns with more roses and clematis growing over it and hostas sit contentedly in old pots. A productive fruit and vegetable garden is neatly hidden behind the house; Liz's colourful show bantams roam here, checking for insects and laying tasty breakfast eggs. Lamb is reared too; if you want to take a whole one back for your freezer, just say the word.

rooms	3: 2 twins/doubles, 1 single.
price	From £70. Singles from £35.
meals	Pubs within 1.5 miles.
closed	Rarely.
directions	From Stratford-upon-Avon, A3400 for Oxford. After 5 miles, right by church in Newbold-on-Stour & follow signs to Blackwell. Fork right on entering Blackwell. Entrance beyond thatched barn.

Map 3 Entry 121

Admire the Wyandotte bantams strutting across the lawns – they are prize-winners. Outside: mellow stone, clipped hedges, broad paths, billowing plants and many varieties of hosta. Inside: flagstones, beams, creaking floorboards, mullioned windows and a huge inglenook. The sitting room comes with old books and polished furniture, and bedrooms with zip-and-link beds; two have sheep-dotted views through those deep-set stone windows. One ground-floor bedroom is ideal for wheelchair users and overlooks the garden. And there's homemade marmalade for breakfast.

The Old Manor House

Jane Pusey
The Old Manor House,
Halford,
Shipston-on-Stour,
Warwickshire CV36 5BT

tel   01789 740264
fax   01789 740609
email   info@oldmanor-halford.fsnet.co.uk
web   www.oldmanor-halford.co.uk

All garden lovers, but rosarians in particular, will adore the garden Jane and William have created over the past ten years. With a background of high mature trees and a sloping site, they have built a series of loosely, rather than formally, linked areas, adding beech and yew hedges vigorously and sympathetically to make a garden that sits well with their lovely old home. Old roses rule above all, climbing up walls, rambling over pergolas and arches, softening hard corners and, in a final flourish, scenting and colouring a rose avenue. There is a blend of the stiffer hybrid teas, which Jane inherited and can't find the heart to remove, and a riot of treasures from sources including Peter Beales. Jane is sending vigorous climbers like 'Kiftsgate' rocketing up the trees in the orchard – a gorgeous sight – but there is much, much more: cleverly planted borders, a delicious herb garden where sage, fennel, thyme and others rub shoulders, delightful colour-theming in flower beds bursting with good plants and so many details as well as a glorious overall feel to enjoy. William has strong ideas about design, Jane has strong ideas about plants and planting. Between them, they have made the very best of the lay of their three acres and their love of plants and garden design is infectious.

rooms	3: 1 double with separate bath; 1 twin, 1 single sharing bath (2nd room let to same party only).
price	From £80. Singles £50.
meals	Dinner from £25. Restaurant 2 miles.
closed	Rarely.
directions	From Stratford, A422 for 4 miles for Banbury. After 4 miles, right at r'bout onto A429 for Halford. There, 1st right. House with black & white timbers straight ahead.

Map 3 Entry 122

You'll be in your element if you fish or play tennis, for you can do both from the beautiful gardens that slope gently down to the river Stour. Jane, a Cordon Bleu cook, runs her 16th- and 17th-century house with energy and friendliness. A pretty blue twin bedroom and a single room are in a self-contained wing with its own large, elegant drawing and dining room; it's seductively easy to relax. The A-shaped double, with ancient beams and oak furniture, is in the main part of the house; it has a lovely bathroom and shares the drawing and dining rooms. A special walk goes through the village.

Marston House

Kim & John Mahon
Marston House,
Priors Marston,
Southam,
Warwickshire CV47 7RP

tel	01327 260297
fax	08703 835445
email	kim@mahonand.co.uk
web	www.ivabestbandb.co.uk

Kim has the sort of kitchen that city dwellers dream of: big and welcoming and it really is the hub of the house. She and John fizz with good humour and energy and take pride in those times when family and guests feel easy together. You will be offered tea on arrival, homemade jams for breakfast, Cordon Bleu meals... perhaps even a guided walk round the fascinating, historic village. The house is large with a wonderful garden, tennis court, terrace and croquet lawn. The rooms are big, soft and supremely comfortable; you will be spoiled within an inch of your lives.

rooms	3: 1 double, 1 twin/double, each with separate bath; 1 twin/double with separate shower.
price	From £85. Singles from £60.
meals	Supper £22. Dinner £28 (min. 4). Pub 5-minute walk.
closed	Rarely.
directions	M40 exit 11. From Banbury, A361 north for 7 miles; at Byfield village sign, left into Twistle Lane; on to Priors Marston; 5th on left with cattle grid, after S-bend (3 miles from A361).

Map 3 Entry 123

Three quarters of an acre laid to lawn with terraces, curved herbaceous borders, beech hedging and a field with an ancient carp pond. Kim claims to be a cheat who doesn't know the Latin names for anything but she inherited this garden some 15 years ago when it had nothing except a scratchy old lawn. Since then she has "begged and borrowed" plants and transformed it into a gorgeous space for people and wildlife. Kim is conservation conscious, nothing is sprayed and she hates garish colours so all is soft and gentle, from the south-facing old stone terrace to the open countryside ahead. Many old trees festooned with rambling roses give height and the autumn favourites of maples and acer add vibrant colour. A second big herbacous border lies at the bottom of the garden brimming with gentle colour and backed by a curved beech hedge. Then there is just rolling countryside – a great place for doggie people. There is a relaxed, humorous atmosphere around Kim and her garden – you just know that if your child bounded around boisterously she wouldn't mind and if you didn't know the name of a plant she wouldn't think less of you. A gorgeous place to stay.

The Old Rectory

John & Maril Eldred
The Old Rectory,
Luckington,
Chippenham,
Wiltshire SN14 6PH

tel   01666 840556
fax   01666 840989
email   b&b@the-eldreds.co.uk

An architectural oddity – the house has an 1830s façade, yet parts are 14th century. Enjoy the lovely garden in summer, log fires in winter, and the smell of coffee wafting from the kitchen at breakfast time. Maril has made some bold choices of colour in the main rooms – the strong blue of the dining room has real impact. Bedrooms are big and light with pretty fabrics and softer colours; bathrooms are smart and new. Do visit the church; it's a step away, through the gate in the 12th-century wall.

rooms	2: 1 double, 1 twin.
price	£85. Singles £50.
meals	Pub in village 0.25 miles.
closed	Occasionally.
directions	From M4 junc. 17, north for Malmesbury. 2nd left for 5 miles. At Sherston, left onto B4040 for Luckington. 1.5 miles on, leaving Brook End on left, house on left 0.25 miles before Luckington centre.

Map 3 Entry 124

Undiluted Cotswold charm so perfect that scenes for *Pride and Prejudice* were filmed close by. Sweeping down the drive, past stables and round to the front of the house gives you an idea of what has been achieved here: wide lawns and lavender borders, thrusting young trees and walled herbaceousness. Sturdy old-timers, like the three larches en route to the church, look on and wisteria drapes over the façade, framing the breakfast room window. John and Maril will tell you about their future plans; it's a somewhat tricky garden as it slopes down to a finger tributary of the Avon. John's in charge of trees and has planted a woodland of largely indigenous specimens. The yew hedge that borders the East lawn will be kept to a strict six-foot height and be balanced by a thick hornbeam hedge. Maril is embarking on an RHS course and her wide, sheltered border is due for replanting in pinks, blues and whites. She also loves to grow flowers for the house and food for the table; her vegetable garden is sheltered by plum and damson trees, with a mixed beech hedge beyond. In winter good structure and contrasting dogwood stems mean the garden is never dull.

Ridleys Cheer

Sue & Antony Young
Ridleys Cheer,
Mountain Bower,
Chippenham,
Wiltshire SN14 7AJ

tel   01225 891204
fax   01225 891139
email   sueyoung@ridleyscheer.co.uk

Ridleys Cheer, in a quiet rural hamlet but just nine miles from the splendour of Bath, was originally a small 18th-century cottage but enlarged in 1989 by the architect, William Bertram. One addition was the large conservatory where summer guests can breakfast amid plumbago and jasmine. There's a beautiful drawing room with log fires for winter, and charming bedrooms, beautifully light – one with pretty French fabric, another with a bedspread embroidered by Sue's grandmother. From here, the eye is ceaselessly drawn to the glories of the garden below. Sue is an experienced Cordon Bleu chef and her dinners are divine.

rooms	3: 1 double; 1 double, 1 twin, sharing bath.
price	From £80. Singles £40.
meals	Lunch £15. Dinner with wine, £30. Packed lunch £8.
closed	Occasionally.
directions	M4 junc. 17. At Chippenham, A420 for Bristol; 9 miles, right at x-roads in hamlet, The Shoe; 2nd left; 1st right into Mountain Bower (no sign). Last house on left; park on drive opposite.

Map 2 Entry 125

What a garden! Plantsmen traditionally sacrifice design on the altar of collecting, but Antony and Sue combine both in a breathtaking, informal, 14-acre garden packed with rare shrubs and trees. Born gardeners, the Youngs began here modestly 38 years ago. A defining moment came when Antony abandoned industry for garden design. He now works on commissions, including large private gardens in this country and in France. In the lower and upper gardens, lawns sweep through displays including 120 different shrub and species roses, daphnes, tulip trees and 15 different magnolias. A two-acre arboretum containing a wide range of rare and interesting trees – beech, planes, hollies, manna ash, zelkova, over 30 different oaks – has been planted over the past 15 years, with radiating broad mown rides and groups of acers in small glades. Serbian spruce were selected to attract goldcrests, which now nest here. Beyond, a three-acre wildflower meadow with 40 species of native limestone flora, a magnet for butterflies in June and July. By the house are witty touches of formality with a potager and box garden, but the overall mood is of profuse informality with glorious details and a ravishing collection of plants. Antony wears his knowledge with engaging lightness. Ridleys Cheer opens for the NGS and private groups, and you can buy plants propagated from the garden. *NGS, Good Gardens Guide**.

St James's Grange

Carolyn & David Adams
St James's Grange,
West Littleton,
Chippenham,
Wiltshire SN14 8JE

tel   01225 891100
email   dandcadams@stjamesgrange.com
web   www.stjamesgrange.com

Hard to believe this barn conversion, in a peaceful, South Cotswold hamlet, is under 20 years old; it is a serenely comfortable home with good furniture and interesting art finds. Carolyn puts you at ease with tea in the open-fired, French-windowed guest 'snug', where reclaimed wooden flooring shows off the rugs. Upstairs the bright, larger double room has passion-flower curtains framing a garden view; the smaller, minty-fresh double and twin — both with garden views — share a family-style bathroom, with separate shower. The Adams are keen to introduce people to this rich AONB area. *Children over six welcome.*

rooms	3: 1 twin/double; 1 double, 1 twin sharing bath & shower.
price	£55–£65. Singles £40.
meals	Pubs 2 miles.
closed	Christmas & occasionally.
directions	From A46 towards Bath for West Littleton. House on right just after red phone box at top of village green.

Map 2 Entry 126

A thoroughly pleasing mix of garden influences which include French and English-cottage, with the odd touch of Elizabethan-style formality. Carolyn says she's still learning through trial, error and ever-evolving ideas – and it all takes place in approximately an acre of what was, not so long ago, a flat field. David has made a grand job of the dry stone walling that borders the terrace (perfect for summer breakfasts) and the small croquet lawn edged with pleached limes and lavender. There's a thriving walled kitchen garden tucked in by fruit trees and a copse effect of indigenous trees; these act as a windbreak beyond the trim beech hedging that encircles the sun dial. A recently-created courtyard area to the south of the house is sheltered by dry stone walls up which roses, clematis and honeysuckle are making their way; tones of white, silver, pinks, blues and purples are planted in the new curving raised beds and already look well-established. The house walls are dressed in the rambling rose 'Phyllis Bide" and wisteria, terracotta pots tumble with geraniums and herbs, water gently drops onto an old millstone in the centre. Hot yellows, oranges and reds have been woven into the re-worked border at the front of the house; so peaceful is it that partridges nest in the wild garden areas and tiny chicks can sometimes be seen following mum across the lawn. *NGS*.

The Coach House

Helga & David Venables
The Coach House,
Upper Wraxall,
Chippenham,
Wiltshire SN14 7AG

tel   01225 891026
email   david@dvenables6.wanadoo.co.uk
web   www.upperwraxallcoachhouse.co.uk

The elegant two-acre landscaped garden was created from pastureland over 20 years ago. The grounds are 600 feet above sea level, where winter winds whip across the surrounding landscape. Shelter is all-important to protect the more tender plants and the solution has been to design a garden that is a splendid blend of open lawns, well-planted borders and masses of well-placed young trees which create large areas of dappled green. Closely-planted shaped banks and a natural rockery give further protection and winter interest. The overall mood is one of a private park with both open and intimate areas and plenty of colour. The main lawn is beautifully tended and becomes an excellent croquet lawn in milder weather. Helga is the flower person, David the tree and lawn specialist; they make an excellent team, having brought together a good collection of unusual herbaceous plants and many varieties of shrubs. Helga loves colour theming, and her planting includes a clever mixture of yellows and bronzes in one herbaceous border. Favourite plants include her groups of euphorbias and hostas. There's a delightful ornamental kitchen garden to one side of the house; like the rest of the garden, it has been carefully planned for low maintenance but maximum interest.

rooms	2: 1 double with separate bath/shower; 1 twin/double let to same party only.
price	£60–£70. Singles £35–£40.
meals	Dinner with wine, £18. Pub 2 miles.
closed	Rarely.
directions	From M4 junc. 17, A429 for Chippenham. A420 to Bristol (East) & Castle Combe. After 6.3 miles, right into Upper Wraxall. Sharp left opp. village green; at end of drive.

Map 2 Entry 127

In an ancient hamlet a few miles north of Bath, an impeccable conversion of an early 19th-century barn. Bedrooms are fresh and cosy with sloping ceilings; the drawing room is elegant with porcelain and chintz, its pale walls the perfect background for striking displays of flowers. Sliding glass doors lead to a south-facing patio, then to a well-groomed croquet lawn bordered by flowers, with vegetable garden, tennis court, woodland and paddock beyond. Helga and David, generous and kind, tell you all you need to know about the region, from Bath just below to the golf courses so nearby. Dinners are excellent value.

Great Chalfield Manor

Patsy Floyd
Great Chalfield Manor,
Melksham,
Wiltshire SN12 8NJ

tel   01225 782239
email   patsy@greatchalfield.co.uk

A National Trust house – a rare example of the English
medieval manor complete with 14th-century church – and
a family home where you will be treated as a guest not
a visitor. Flagstones, a Great Hall with Flemish tapestries,
perfect panelling, fine oak furniture and ancient elegance
inspire awe – but Patsy dispels all formality with a gorgeous
smile. Proper four-posters in the stone-walled bedrooms are
swathed in the softest greens and pinks, the bathrooms are
deeply old-fashioned and the only sound is bird ballad.
Kitchen suppers follow large drinks in the prettiest panelled
sitting room. *Special two-night stays with local gardens tour.*

rooms	2 four-posters, each with separate bath.
price	£100. Singles £80.
meals	Supper £25. Pub/restaurant 1 mile.
closed	Occasionally.
directions	From Melksham B3107 to Bradford on Avon. 1st right to Broughton Gifford, through village, first left signed Great Chalfield, 1 mile drive.

Map 3 Entry 128

Stand in the middle of the lawn, close your eyes and imagine that Titania and Oberon have just fluttered past – open your eyes and they have. A structure of neatly clipped yew houses, upper and lower moats, herbaceous borders, huge lawns and an orchard have been immaculately tended and then enchanced by Patsy's love of soft colour and roses. The south-facing rose terrace brims over with scented pink roses that bloom all summer long, ramblers scrabble over anything with height, including old stone walls and the fruit trees in the orchard – and they are not alone; there is honeysuckle in abundance too, rambling hither and thither to waft its gorgeous English smell. Lavender and nepeta – the gentlest of hues – even the 'red border' is soft with smudgy colour, never garish. Water weaves through the grass in little streams which feed the serene, lily-laden moats and there is a magical woodland walk bursting with snowdrops in February. Patsy learned about gardening by "doing it" and gains ideas and inspiration from the tours she organises for 'The Garden Party' – but she has very firm ideas of her own especially when it comes to design and colour. There is a hazy, bloom-filled dreaminess about Great Chalfield. Perhaps Puck really does sprinkle something into your eyes as you go up the long, grassy drive...
NGS, Good Gardens Guide.

Broomsgrove Lodge

Mr & Mrs Peter Robertson
Broomsgrove Lodge,
New Mill,
Pewsey,
Wiltshire SN9 5LE

tel   01672 810515
fax   01672 810286
email   diana@broomsgrovelodge.co.uk

It is a pleasure to stay here, in a pretty thatched house with an owner who has a talent for both gardening and interior design. The sitting room, decorated in terracotta and pale green, leads to a lovely, big conservatory with fine views of garden and hills. Diana serves breakfast here – eggs from the chickens that strut in the field, and freshly-squeezed orange juice. Fresh, pretty bedrooms, polished bathrooms, plates from Sicily and Portugal on the walls and pictures bought during their time in Hong Kong. Walks along the lush Avon & Kennet Canal are a step away.

rooms	3: 1 twin; 1 twin with separate bath; 1 extra single available.
price	From £70. Single £40.
meals	Pub/restaurant 1.5 miles.
closed	Christmas & New Year.
directions	From Hungerford A338 Burbage r'bout B3087 to Pewsey. Right in Milton Lilbourne to New Mill; under bridge, through village, over canal; lodge on left at entrance to farm.

Map 3 Entry 129

Some people just seem to have the knack for creating exciting surroundings outside as well as in. Diana moved to Broomsgrove Lodge in 1996 after six months in Hong Kong, and is extremely happy tending home, guests and garden. She and Peter found themselves with a picture-book setting: the thatched house gazes over serene and open countryside, with a pretty conservatory that has wonderful long views. From the slope outside, they have created a sunken terrace: a mass of pots planted with colourful annuals and bulbs, all grown on site. And the pots continue up the steps leading onto the lawn. Their grandchildren love the camomile seat cut into the terrace retaining wall; a lovers' seat encircles the trunk of the oak tree up on the lawn, the perfect spot from which to gaze on the gravel garden and herbaceous border. Diana's pride and joy is her flourishing vegetable garden that supplies a whole range of vegetables for family and friends.

Idover House

Christopher & Caroline Jerram
Idover House,
Dauntsey,
Malmesbury,
Wiltshire SN15 4HW

tel	01249 720340
mobile	07968 216573
fax	01249 720340
email	christopher.jerram@humberts.co.uk

A large, mature country-house garden which Christopher and Caroline have carefully restored to complement their long, elegant house (18th century and originally the Home Farm for Dauntsey Park). The stables are a reminder of its days as a hunting box for the Duke of Beaufort's hunt. There are glorious lawns, rose-covered dry stone walls and an open, sunny atmosphere. The mature trees are very handsome and include a perfectly shaped decorative sycamore and two lofty Wellingtonia. Rose-lovers will be delighted with the restored 1920s rose garden, its symmetrically shaped beds planted in delicate shades of pink and white; the design was drawn for them by the rosarian Peter Beales. The grounds are a fascinating mix of formal, informal and wild, with plenty of colour from a series of borders replanted under the direction of Sylvia Morris, including a deep herbaceous border. Hedges of yew, beech and lime give structure and form, and a copse of decorative trees gives shade, good leaf form and colour. Kitchen garden enthusiasts will be envious of the Jerrams' beautifully tended plot, reached via the duck pond surrounded by flag iris, and the yew hedge walk. On sunny days, linger by the pool garden with its summer house. In spring, enjoy the bulbs in the woodland. A charming family garden. *NGS, RHS.*

rooms	3 twins.
price	£80. Singles £50.
meals	Dinner £27.50.
closed	Christmas & New Year.
directions	From Malmesbury, B4042 for Wotton Bassett. 2.5 miles on, fork right to Little Somerford. At bottom of hill, right for Gt. Somerford. At x-roads, left to Dauntsey. House 1.25 miles on left at bend.

Map 3 Entry 130

Grand and friendly, all at once. You can settle down by the huge fireplace in the handsome panelled drawing room with its log fires in winter, and breakfast or dine in the pink, low-ceilinged dining room with its lovely views of the garden. Caroline's a Cordon Bleu cook and naturally the scrumptious food includes produce from their wonderful vegetable garden. The guest rooms are light and elegant, the bathrooms pristine. Very much a lived-in family home, with no shortage of horsey pictures and a rogues' gallery of family portraits upstairs. *Children over eight welcome.*

Luggers Hall

Mrs K G Haslam
Luggers Hall,
Springfield Lane,
Broadway,
Worcestershire WR12 7BT

tel	01386 852040
fax	01386 859103
email	luggershall@hotmail.com
web	www.luggershall.com

This handsome home was built by the Victorian Royal
Academy garden artist, Sir Alfred Parsons. Red and Kay have
renovated and remodelled both the house, which is listed,
and garden. You are given a key to your own wing; staying
here is a luxurious experience with swagged curtains and
cushions piled high on beds. The sound of gently cascading
water drifts up through the window of one room; the other
looks over the garden to the hills beyond. Edwardian origins
are enhanced by William Morris-style materials, richly
coloured décor and old prints and photographs of Broadway.
Minimum stay two nights at weekends. Self-catering available.

rooms	2 doubles.
price	£65–£95.
meals	Restaurants in village within walking distance.
closed	Rarely.
directions	Off Broadway High Street. Turn off at Swan Inn. Luggers Hall on Springfield Lane.

Map 3 Entry 131

Not many glamorous career air hostesses are prepared to seize a knapsack-sprayer to tackle the first stage of reclaiming a garden. This is how Kay began at Luggers Hall, and reinvented herself as a passionate gardener and knowledgeable plantswoman. With husband Red's help, Alfred Parsons's two-and-a-half-acre Edwardian garden has been recreated, using old aerial photographs, prints and Parsons's own paintings as guides to his original layout. Kay, also a trained artist, has an eye for shape, colour and texture, her personal stamp fusing with that of the original owner. Garden rooms surround the central lawn, and clever use of architectural plants with big leaves such as rheums and *Paulownia tomentosa* disguise the flatness of the site. In the walled garden with its central fountain, the richly planted borders lead the eye round carefully blended colours of the spectrum. There are two stunningly planted rose gardens, one with mounds of white roses and white lavender with pale blue salvia, the other with pink roses edged with lavender and in-filled with nepeta and penstemon. Through the castellated yew hedge is a secluded koi pool garden, where it's bliss to curl up by the summer house with a book. The pretty potager below the guest bedrooms leads into Kay's mini-nursery – she has a passion for propagating. Red's tearoom caters for visitors on charity open days. B&B guests, of course, can enjoy the delights of the garden at any time. *NGS, Good Gardens Guide.*

Millgate House

Austin Lynch & Tim Culkin
Millgate House,
Richmond,
Yorkshire DL10 4JN

tel   01748 823571
mobile   07738 298721
email   oztim@millgatehouse.demon.co.uk
web   www.millgatehouse.com

Prepare to be amazed. In every room of the house and in every corner of the garden, the marriage of natural beauty and sophistication exists in a state of bliss. The four Doric columns at the entrance draw you through the hall into the dining room and to views of the Swale Valley. Beds from Heals, period furniture, cast-iron baths, myriad prints and paintings and one double bed so high you wonder how to get onto it. Tim and Austin, both ex-English teachers, have created something special, and breakfasts are superb.

rooms	3: 1 double, 1 twin; 1 double with separate bath/shower.
price	£85-£95. Singles £65.
meals	Restaurant 5-minute walk.
closed	Never.
directions	Next door to Halifax Building Society in the centre, opp. Barclays at bottom of Market Place. Green front door with small brass plaque.

Map 6 Entry 132

Nothing about the elegant façade of Austin and Tim's home hints at the treasures which lie behind. Wandering into the drawing room you are drawn, magnet-like, to the veranda to discover the full impact of the garden below. A stay at Millgate House without exploring it would be an unforgivable omission; no wonder that when Austin and Tim entered the Royal Horticultural Society's 1995 National Garden Competition they romped away with first prize. This famous walled town garden deserves every last bouquet and adulatory article it has received. A narrow shady lane to one side of the house, adorned with immaculate hostas, introduces the main garden. Here the long terraced grounds, sloping steeply down towards the river and overlooked by the great Norman castle, are divided into a rhythmic series of lush compartments. All is green, with cascades of foliage breaking out into small, sunny open areas before you dive beneath yet more foliage to explore further secret areas. Plantsmanship, a passion for old roses, hostas, clematis, ferns and small trees and a love of many different leaf forms come together triumphantly. As William Blake said: "Exuberance is beauty". If you just want to explore the garden you can phone Austin and Tim to arrange a visit. *NGS, Good Gardens Guide, RHS Associate Garden.*

Cold Cotes

Ed Loft
Cold Cotes,
Felliscliffe,
Harrogate,
Yorkshire HG3 2LW

tel	01423 770937
fax	01423 779284
email	info@coldcotes.com
web	www.coldcotes.com

What was a five-acre field, facing a dominant westerly, has been shaken up
royally! It is now a series of dazzling 'zones' starting next to the house with
a stone-flagged terrace with clumps of thrift, miniature geraniums, euphorbias
and pots of blue agapanthus. In front is a red bed made up of oriental poppies,
dahlias, tulips and penstemon, then stone steps down to a formal garden.
Golden hops scrabble over an obelisk, a pond is surrounded by sunny herb beds
and hedging breaks it up into sections. Another hot bed is around the corner,
a woodland walk is planted with cherry, sorbus, beech, alders and oak and there
are some impressive sweeping borders inspired by the designer Piet Oudolf and
containing his beloved prairie plants and grasses. A cobblestone walk (Penny
Lane) ambles along a stream with a little bridge, planted around with gunnera,
periwinkle, ivy and comfrey, leading to a thriving pond. A fruit and veg garden
provides abundant produce; a little lawned area is surrounded by cherry trees
and has a perfect seating area with old wooden furniture. A new garden focusing
on shade lovers in a woodland setting is in its first exciting season; a circular
wooded walk with naturalistic planting is in preparation. A garden for quiet
contemplation, filled with birdsong. *Open to the public 2 September & by appointment.*

rooms	5: 3 doubles, 2 twins/doubles (2 with own sitting rooms).
price	From £65. Singles £55.
meals	Light bites & supper by arrangement. Pub/restaurant 2.5 miles.
closed	20 December–1 January.
directions	A59 from Harrogate for 7 miles towards Skipton. Right after Black Bull pub, signed RAF Menwith, onto Cold Cotes Road. Third on right, 500 yards from A59.

Map 6 Entry 134

Ed and Penny have meticulously restored this 1890s farmhouse on the edge of the Yorkshire Dales. A sitting room with polished boards, creamy walls, squashy sofas, roaring fire and loads of books is covered in Ed's paintings (his studio is upstairs). The light, long dining room with its three full-length windows faces the garden and has a sprung floor should you need to dance. Bedrooms are purpose-designed for B&B with pale walls and carpets, brass beds, fine thick fabrics, roomy bathrooms and some long garden views. Homemade cakes for tea, local bacon and sausages for breakfast, local and home-grown produce for evening meals.

Fountains House

Clive and Gill King
Fountains House,
Burton Leonard,
Harrogate,
Yorkshire HG3 3RU

tel   01765 677537
email   info@fountainshouse.co.uk
web   www.fountainshouse.co.uk

Warm stone under a terracotta roof, Fountains is a house
full of sunshine at the edge of the village, with kind,
unflappable owners. The fresh, pretty bedrooms promise
a good sleep (in spite of a dash of road noise in the double
at the front) and the bathrooms are terrific. Fat sofas and
charmingly grouped pictures make the sitting room most
inviting and there are free-range eggs, local bacon and
homemade bread for breakfast. If you become addicted
to Gill's homemade jams and marmalades, you can always
buy a jar to take home.

rooms	2: 1 double, 1 twin.
price	From £70–£75.
meals	Supper, 3 courses, £18.50. Pubs 3-minute walk.
closed	Rarely.
directions	From A61 Harrogate Ripon road, turning for Burton Leonard at garage. Enter village, house on right, 500 yds. From A1 exit at junc. 48. Signed for Burton Leonard. Through village, past green, house 200 yds on left.

Map 6 Entry 135

An old lady used to live here and the garden had become horribly overgrown. Ivy rampaged and sombre firs blotted out the wide country views. When Clive and Gill took over in 2004, they sacrificed all but one of the firs but kept the two large Corsican pines (the cones make fabulous firelighters). Clearing the choked herbaceous borders, they planted foxgloves, delphiniums and roses among the shrubs, with exochorda and variegated philadelphus peeping out from the jumbled, cottage-garden mix. It's pretty and unpretentious: a smooth lawn for croquet, roses on the walls, lavender and herbs by the kitchen door, lilac and laburnum, almond and cherry trees. The country-cottage feel is enhanced by a generous scattering of honeysuckle, lilies and peonies. Beyond an old low stone wall, an expanse of cornfield stretches into the distance. Unsurprisingly, pheasants and partridge are frequent visitors, as well as blackbirds and thrushes, wrens and wagtails, all keeping a weather eye out for the Kings' elderly tabby cat. A sheltered terrace makes a delightful place for tea or a sundowner before dinner – Gill's a generous, eclectic cook; the vegetables come from Clive's allotment.

Shallowdale House

Anton van der Horst & Phillip Gill
Shallowdale House,
West End,
Ampleforth,
Yorkshire YO62 4DY

tel   01439 788325
fax   01439 788885
email   stay@shallowdalehouse.co.uk
web   www.shallowdalehouse.co.uk

Each window frames an outstanding view – this spot, on the edge of the North York Moors National Park, was chosen for them, and the house arranged to soak up the scenery, from the Pennines to the Wolds. This is a stylish, elegant and large modern house with a huge mature hillside garden. The spacious bedrooms and bathrooms are coordinated and comfortable; the drawing room has an open fire in winter. Phillip and Anton love what they are doing, so you will be treated like angels and served freshly cooked dinners of outstanding quality. *Children over 12 welcome.*

rooms	3: 2 twins/doubles; 1 double with separate bath/shower.
price	£85–£105. Singles £67.50–£77.50.
meals	Dinner, 4 courses, £32.50. Pub/restaurant 3 miles.
closed	Christmas & New Year.
directions	From Thirsk, A19 south, then 'caravan route' via Coxwold & Byland Abbey. 1st house on left, just before Ampleforth.

Map 6 Entry 136

Keep climbing and by the time you get to the top of the garden you will feel
you've had a hearty country walk; sit on a bench and breathe that Yorkshire air.
The many specimen trees planted when the house was built 40-odd years ago
are now grown up: weeping birch, cypress, cherry, maple, acer and copper
beech hover over swathes of grass underplanted with thousands of bulbs, a
double rockery groans with scented shrubs like viburnum, rosemary and choisya
– while cistus, hardy geraniums, ceanothus, fuchsias and potentilla are popped
in for colour. Lose yourself in the landscape – a lovely park-like atmosphere
prevails – and sit and drink in the peace. Nearer the house there are more
formal beds, a mini-orchard, a sunny terrace with tinkling water feature and
clematis and roses that march over the arches. Mixed planting everywhere but
in such good taste. Hard work for just the two of them but Anton never goes
up, or down, the hill without an armful of dead-heads and flotsam; their
gorgeous dog gambols around while they discuss projects to tackle next.

Riverside Farm

Bill & Jane Baldwin
Riverside Farm,
Sinnington,
Pickering,
Yorkshire YO62 6RY

tel   01751 431764
fax   01751 431764
email   wnbaldwin@yahoo.co.uk

A charming long, low Georgian farmhouse that overlooks
the river and the village green. Gleaming old family
furniture, Bill's family photographs up the stairs, and two
handsome bedrooms facing south over the scented cottage
garden. There's pretty Colefax & Fowler sweet pea
wallpaper in the twin, and Osborne & Little topiary trees
in its bathroom. Breakfast is deliciously traditional – this is
still a working farm – and there's an excellent pub for
supper a short walk from the house. Elegant surroundings,
excellent value and Jane a practical and generous hostess
who will look after you well. Special indeed.
Minimum stay two nights.

rooms	4: 1 double; 1 twin with separate bath; 2 singles with separate or shared bath.
price	From £60. Singles £40.
meals	Pub/restaurant 5-minute walk.
closed	November-March.
directions	From Pickering A170; 4 miles to Sinnington. Into village, cross river; right into lane for Riverside Farm.

Map 6 Entry 137

Not only have Jane and Bill created a two-acre garden over the last 20-odd years, but Jane is also the National Gardens Scheme organiser for North Yorkshire. Her knowledge of every garden and its owner on her patch means she can arrange private visits – but there is plenty at Riverside Farm, too, to interest the plantsman. As you open the little gate that leads to the front door, two big old stone troughs overflowing with helichrysum and geraniums introduce you to a cottage garden paradise. Jane was inspired by Rosemary Verey's circular lawn with four beds at Barnsley; she keeps a close eye on the colour scheme, preferring to keep pink plants to a minimum, and has a light touch when controlling the self-seeding. The overall effect is beautifully natural and uncontrived – a truly difficult task, as any gardener will tell you. Pretty pink shrub roses have been given special permission to romp in the long, deep herbaceous bed that is, again, artfully natural. This runs parallel to the River Severn which flows down the garden's eastern border. A 'Kiftsgate' rose amply covers a 30-foot barn, and from the garden behind there's a lovely vista through the huge rose arch of 'Félicite et Perpetue' – inviting you to explore the gorgeous wild area, with its pond and mown paths meandering towards young woodland. *NGS.*

The Wold Cottage

Mrs Katrina Gray
The Wold Cottage,
Wold Newton,
Driffield,
Yorkshire YO25 3HL

tel	01262 470696
email	katrina@woldcottage.com
web	www.woldcottage.com

Drive down through mature trees, a proper entrance with signs (and the occasional seasonal caravan) to an attractive, well-proportioned house set in mature trees. Rooms in the main house are sumptuous, light and comfortable, with thickly-lined curtains and spotless bathrooms; two in the annexe are larger and neat as a pin. The light and cheerful guest sitting room has thick carpets and plenty of sofas; loll here with a glass of Derek's locally-brewed beer while you look forward to a locally-sourced dinner. Discover the unspoilt Wolds on foot, fuelled by a fabulously generous Yorkshire breakfast, or pop to the coast.

rooms	5: 2 doubles, 2 twins, 1 family room.
price	£70–£100. Singles £45–£55.
meals	Supper £18.50. Wine £10.
closed	Never.
directions	A64 onto B1249. Through Foxholes to Wold Newton. In village, take road between pond & pub; signed on right.

Map 6 Entry 138

The heart of this spreading, two-acre garden is the west-facing lawn, with its generous, curving mixed beds and new pond, while the views are to mown fields, clusters of trees and the hedgerows that mark the boundary of the 200-acre farm. Ten thousand native trees have been planted in 18 years, many to fend off the prevailing westerly winds. To the back and side lies a small orchard (apples, plums, figs), a large kitchen garden edged with wooden uprights (Katrina's father-in-law manages the veg), a young yew walk and a quiet lawned corner with a bench. A brick arbour with an 18th-century garden inscription makes another peaceful resting place. Steps leading to this area are bounded by classic flowering shrubs and interesting perennials, while an established knot garden, edged with box and filled with lavender buzzing with bees, softens the landscaping near the self-catering cottages. Pots of jolly petunias abound: Katrina aims for colour 52 weeks a year. She and Derek, who find gardening therapeutic and happily share the tasks – including the mowing! – recommend you visit the wonderful plant nursery up the road. Failing that, they are typically generous with cuttings. Owls are regular visitors and 71 varieties of bird were spotted last spring.

Scotland

Newtonmill House

Mr & Mrs Rickman
Newtonmill House,
By Brechin,
Angus DD9 7PZ

tel   01356 622533
fax   01356 622533
email   rrickman@srickman.co.uk

The house and grounds are in apple-pie order; the owners are charming and unobtrusive. This is a little-known part of Scotland; come to explore the glens, find deserted beaches and traditional fishing villages, or play a round or two of golf on one of the many good courses nearby. Return to a cup of tea in the elegant sitting room, then a proper supper of seasonal, local and homegrown produce. Later find crisp sheets, soft blankets, feather pillows, fresh flowers, homemade fruit cake and sparkling, warm bathrooms with thick towels; you will be deeply comfortable here. *Children over ten welcome.*

rooms	2: 1 twin; 1 double with separate bath.
price	£80-£96. Singles £50-£58.
meals	Dinner £16-£26. BYO. Packed lunch £10. Pub 3 miles.
closed	Christmas.
directions	From Aberdeen/Dundee A90, take B966 towards Edzell. On for 1 mile, driveway/entrance marked by pillars and gatelodge; signed.

Map 9 Entry 139

Stephen and Rose have been enlarging and enhancing these lovely gardens for 23 years. Borders, beds, lawns, woodland and pastures are bounded by old walls, hedges and burns. At the heart of it all is the walled garden that faces the gracious laird's house, its 'entrance' an iron gate in the shape of a mill wheel, its grass walk bounded by herbaceous borders. Formal box hedges edge rectangular beds where fruit, vegetables and flowers grow in glorious profusion — one full of irises, another of peonies. Another contains a croquet lawn, perfect with a revolving summer house and an arbour of honeysuckle and clematis. Espaliered and fan-trained apples, pears and plums clothe the walls, roses clamber and fall in a delicious harmony of scents and hues, a group of Japanese maples shades *Podophyllum hexandrum* and, in a corner, an 18th-century 'doocot' stands, home to happy doves. The heavy soil has been improved over the years with horse and sheep manure; most of the crops are grown with organic principles in mind, and much surplus is given away. Twenty varieties of potato are grown, the raspberries do famously and, in the woodland areas, primroses, bluebells, narcissi and martagon lilies thrive.

Glecknabae

Iain & Margaret Gimblett
Glecknabae,
Rothesay,
Argyll & Bute PA20 0QX

tel   01700 505655
fax   01700 505655
email   gimblettsmill@aol.com
web   www.isleofbuteholidays.co.uk

The wonderful view is a fabulous surprise as you walk in through the front door to the dining hall: the windows opposite look down over the front garden to a 180° panorama of the sea and islands. Tapestries on walls, an Aubusson-style rug on a polished ash floor, and a log fire in the sitting room. Everywhere is light and bright: two of the guests' pretty little bedrooms are at one end of the house, with comb ceilings and velux windows. The third is on the ground floor with French windows leading onto the paved courtyard garden. The Gimbletts treat guests as friends, and if you eat in it will be by the Aga.

rooms	3: 1 double, 1 twin; 1 twin/double with bath.
price	£60-£70.
meals	Occasional dinner from £12.50. Pub/restaurant 7 miles.
closed	Rarely.
directions	Follow shore Road to Port Bannatyne. At A844 sign, left at Kames Castle Gate Lodge towards Ettrick Bay; bear right, cross bridge & follow track to end of tarmac; right, cross cattle grid, up drive to house.

In the house the Gimbletts recycle almost everything, from bottles to clothes. In the garden nothing is wasted; bricks and stones from old buildings are used to create new raised beds and dry stone dykes while old roof timbers are converted to smart decking and vegetable waste is composted in three rotated heaps. A wind turbine may follow.

Map 8 Entry 140

The usual exclamation from visitors to Glecknabae is "Magic!", but the Gimbletts had the foresight and imagination to realise that when they bought the place derelict in 1993, brambles, nettles, warts and all. Within two years, having reconstructed the house, they won an award for their courtyard garden: since then they have created a series of small gardens all around the house, divided by hedges and trees. Deliberately avoiding the usual Scottish theme of rhododendrons and azaleas, they have planted a garden for all seasons: snowdrops in January, a natural area of trees and shrubs, a bog garden stashed with primulas and irises. Alpine plants take every advantage of the naturally stony environment, popping up through cracks in smooth rock and clustering in raised beds in the gravel garden. From seats in sheltered spots you can gaze at the unsurpassable views down Bute, over to mainland Argyll and across to the islands of Arran and Inchmarnock. It's three minutes' walk down to the shore and the wildlife is abundant: you can see deer and otters, or basking shark and porpoises if it's warm, and the place is full of birds, from buzzards and the occasional golden eagle, to tiny goldfinches. Magic indeed. *SGS, HPS.*

Barnhay Country B & B

Stuart & Jenny Baker
Barnhay Country B & B,
Barnhay,
Kinaldy Meadows,
St Andrews,
Fife KY16 8NA

tel   01334 477791
email   barnhay@btinternet.com
web   www.barnhay.com

Stuart and Jenny shed their old lives to concentrate on their passion for gardening here in this isolated country spot, five minutes from St Andrews. Part of a spacious development of modern bungalows with wooden fences, the house is airy and light, and the furnishings and paintings in the sitting room comfortable and contemporary. Modern bedrooms – one black and white, the other Rennie Mackintosh style – have firm beds and good towels. Breakfast is a full-blown affair, mostly local or organic and with homemade jam from their own fruits.

rooms	2 doubles.
price	From £68.
meals	Dinner £25. Pub 3.5 miles.
closed	January; one week in May; mid-September.
directions	A915 from St Andrews towards Largo. After 4 miles, turn left towards Stravithie. After 1 mile, Kinaldy Meadows on right.

Map 9 Entry 141

Hard to believe that just five years ago this was a four-and-a-half-acre field with drainage problems. Stuart and Jenny have created an enchanting series of zones which start formally near the house with a spiral herbaceous border encircling a pergola up which 'Rambling Rector' and golden hop are creeping. The hugely productive vegetable and fruit plots are well fenced to keep out the stiff westerlies, a stone dyke edges the rear garden, ha-ha like, as the ground slopes down to the long pond bursting with wildlife, crossed by a rickety bridge. Admire it all from the decking with an evening drink and plenty of birdsong. Other interest around the house includes a mosaic pillar and two water features. Further away, walk along mown paths through a wildflower meadow to the newly-planted trees, mostly alders; when they have created more shelter, ornamentals like *Prunus serula* will be added. There are some charming and quirky features like the little hill they have built to view the whole effect, and a mini amphitheatre so the grandchildren can perform. Jenny and Stuart have great fun working together – he the muscle and mower, she the merry planter and grower from seed; both pitch in for weeding. Future plans are constant and evolving; they are still experimenting and loving it. A garden to visit again and again.

Cambo House

Mr & Mrs Peter Erskine
Cambo House,
Kingsbarns,
St Andrews,
Fife KY16 8QD

tel	01333 450054
fax	01333 450987
email	cambo@camboestate.com
web	www.camboestate.com

This is a Victorian mansion in the grand style, with staff. Magnificent, luxurious bedrooms; the four-poster room was once used for servicing the dining room, which is more of a banqueting hall. You are welcome to view this, and also the first-floor billiard room and drawing room. There is a delightful sitting room for your use on the ground floor overlooking the fountain, and you have breakfast in the smaller dining room. If you B&B in the studio apartment for two, with its dear little sitting area in a turret, you may come and go as you please during the day. *Tennis court available.*

rooms	3: 1 four-poster, 1 studio for 2; 1 twin/double with separate bath/shower.
price	£90-£126. Singles £45-£63.
meals	Dinner from £42.50. Pub 1 mile.
closed	Christmas & New Year.
directions	A917 to Crail, through Kingsbarns. Follow signs for Cambo Gardens, follow drive to house.

Map 9 Entry 142

A garden of renown, stunningly romantic all year round. There is a spectacular carpet of snowdrops, snowflakes and aconites in the 70 acres of woodland following the Cambo burn down to the sea; bulbs, including many specialist varieties, are available by mail order. A woodland garden is in a continuing state of development, and, in May, the lilac walk through 26 varieties is a glorious, delicious-smelling display. The Cambo burn carves its way across the two-acre walled garden: here, a huge range of herbaceous perennials and roses fill the borders with colour through summer. A willow weeps artfully between a decorative bridge and a Chinese-style summerhouse looking as though it has stepped out of a willow-pattern plate. The potager created in 2001 has matured brilliantly, the hot red and yellow annuals among the vegetables and the herbaceous perennials carrying colour through August – as does the inventively-planted annual border with its castor oil plants, grasses and *Verbena bonariensis*: no Victorian bedding plants here. In September the colchicum meadow is at its best, and an autumn border has been developed using late herbaceous perennials mixed with grasses. There's always something new at Cambo, and it's on a high with the buzz of success about it. *SGS, Good Gardens Guide.*

Inwood

Lindsay Morrison
Inwood,
Carberry,
Musselburgh,
Midlothian EH21 8PZ

tel   0131 665 4550
email   lindsay@inwoodgarden.com
web   www.inwoodgarden.com

Lindsay and Irvine built this modern bungalow in 1983; you are minutes from the city centre but surrounded by deep countryside within the Carberry Tower estate. Both guest bedrooms have a light, modern feel with laminated wood flooring in the bathrooms, cream and white linen and towels, good lighting and comfortable chairs by the windows for a garden view. The guest sitting room is filled with books and videos, and computer access is here for those who really cannot get away from it all. And there's a pretty conservatory that opens to the garden.

rooms	2: 1 double, 1 twin.
price	£80.
meals	Pub 1 mile.
closed	Mid-January–mid-March.
directions	From A1 Edinburgh to Berwick, A6124 to Dalkeith. Follow signs to Carberry, left at A M Morrison sign; left at Inwood Garden sign.

Map 9 Entry 143

A year after they had finished the house, the Morrisons started on the garden; it is maturing beautifully, although they confess to having made a few mistakes over the years! Just over an acre surrounding the house was cleared and made ready for 110 tons of top soil, then seeded; the huge flower beds were cut out later. Rabbits and deer were a problem so fencing was required; now you don't see them, under their overcoat of climbing roses and clematis. About 20 large beds are cut into the immaculate lawns and filled with a mixture of structural plants, large shrubs and some unusual foliage. The natural backdrop of woodland provides the inspiration for the hard landscaping and there's no trace of those 'mistakes'; the grass paths swoop convincingly, the bog garden boggles, the pond has obediently filled with frogs, toads and newts, the greenhouses are immaculate and an arbour is the perfect place to sit and admire it all. Lindsay takes the planting seriously and hands out monthly leaflets about what is flowering to visitors. There isn't a dull season; rambling roses in early summer, hydrangeas and some rare exotics like *Musa basjoo* and *Ensete ventricosum 'Maurelii'* later on. In autumn, colchicums and tricyrtis put in an appearance among the changing leaf tints; in spring, the woodland bursts with snowdrops, wood anemones, trilliums and others. A proper plantsman's garden; you can also buy cuttings. *SGS, RHS, Good Gardens Guide.*

Kirknewton House

Tinkie & Charles Welwood
Kirknewton House,
Kirknewton,
Midlothian EH27 8DA

tel	01506 881235
fax	01506 882237
email	cwelwood@kirknewtonestate.co.uk
web	www.kirknewtonestate.co.uk

Rooms are lovely and large, having once been part of a
more extensive house dating from the 17th century. Since
the complete reorganisation of the ground floor in the
1980s, modern comforts have been added to compliment
the history. A fine, polished oak staircase, fresh flowers in
the hall, rugs on the floor; the large double bedroom has a
four-poster bed with a white canopy and a view over the
rose garden and its little fountain. Lots of fruit for breakfast
– feast upon it in a stately manner in the dining room, or
snug up to the Aga in the kitchen.

rooms	2: 1 double, 1 four-poster, each with separate bath.
price	£100. Singles £50.
meals	Dinner £22-£50. Pub/restaurant 4 miles.
closed	Christmas-February.
directions	From either A70 or A71 take B7031. 0.25 miles from Kirknewton going south, drive on left opposite small cottage.

Map 9 Entry 144

You get the best of two worlds at Kirknewton: a large, comfortable house in peaceful landscaped woodland gardens – and Edinburgh, 30 minutes by car or train. The Welwoods have farmed here since they took over the family home in 1981; both are keen gardeners, so they set to maximizing the potential of the garden the moment they arrived. There are azaleas and rhododendrons in brilliant abundance in spring, and primulas and meconopsis scattered throughout; and, to lengthen the season, a long herbaceous border was created in a walled garden – wonderful in summer. A single long wall remains from an old part of the house that was demolished after the war: it faces south, sheltering the garden from the prevailing wind, and is covered in a glorious array of climbing roses such as 'Alchemist', 'Maigold', 'Schoolgirl' and 'New Dawn'. A stream flows down by the spring border into a pond in front of the house, and here rodgersia and stately gunnera flourish. You are close to Malleny Garden, and as Tinkie is a county organiser for Scotland's Gardens Scheme, she knows all about private gardens in the area. *SGS*.

Inverugie

Lucy Mackenzie
Inverugie,
Hopeman,
Moray IV30 5YB

tel   01343 830253
fax   01343 831300
email   machadodorp@compuserve.com
web   www.inverugiehouse.co.uk

The garden is imbued with family history – Lucy's family has been here for 70 years. During the Second World War, the entire walled garden – one and a half acres, double-tiered and reached via a bluebelled woodland walk – was dug up by soldiers who planted potatoes for the war. Lucy's grandmother later rescued it with the help of one of the gardeners who helped to create the BBC Beechgrove garden in Aberdeen. Now the top third is a resplendent fruit and vegetable garden with heavenly views. Below, lawns, shrubs and trees, and a wide stone path weaving its way around box hedges, bee pond (happy bees!) and curved rose and herbaceous borders. The bottom section of the garden has a 'yellow' garden and another gorgeous rose garden; many of the roses were bred up here with creative input from Lucy's grandmother. Although her garden areas are distinct, Lucy has allowed scope for spontaneity and whim: euphorbia, hosta, alchemolis and meconopsis are dotted throughout… and the little garden house brings on jasmine and pelagoniums in spring that are transferred to the house in early summer. Inverugie is surrounded by 30 stunning acres: rolling fields, ancient protected woodland and a cup and ring standing stone dating from 3000BC. No wonder Lucy is passionate about it all.

rooms	2: 1 twin; 1 double with separate bath.
price	£50–£70. Singles £35.
meals	Dinner £25. Pub/restaurant 3 miles.
closed	Christmas & New Year.
directions	To Forres on A96, through Kinloss on B9089 to College of Roseisle village & over B9013. Veer right (for Duffus) & 1.3 miles on, left to Keam Farm. Past farm, house at end of road through stone pillars.

Map 12 Entry 145

An unusually squat Georgian house but handsome, with its lofty porticos, generous bays, tall windows and impressive drive. The feel is solid and traditional inside: velvet sofas in sage-green and rose, floral curtains at pelmetted windows, touches of Art Deco… toile de Jouy in the double, cream padded headboards in the twin. The large dining and drawing rooms look over ancient woodland, pasture land and grazing sheep; beyond, beaches, castles, standing stones and rivers rich with salmon and trout. Lucy is a dynamo – finding time for riding, fieldsports, a small knitwear business, three young children and you.

Nether Swanshiel

Dr Sylvia Auld
Nether Swanshiel,
Hobkirk,
Bonchester Bridge,
Roxburghshire TD9 8JU

tel   01450 860636
fax   01450 860636
email   aulds@swanshiel.wanadoo.co.uk
web   www.netherswanshiel.fsnet.co.uk

Shiel (or shieling) means 'summer grazing', a name still apt in this fertile and deeply rural area. Originally built around 1760, Nether Swanshiel is one of four houses in the tiny hamlet of Hobkirk. When the Aulds arrived in 1996 their one-acre garden was a wilderness, but they set to, cutting back undergrowth and thinning trees, and opening up the views towards Bonchester Hill and down the river to the church. Gradually the original structure re-emerged; this now forms the basis for their own creation. The garden and house talk to each other through the new terrace, and a herbaceous border around the retaining wall supplies the house with the fresh flowers that Sylvia loves to have in the rooms. The Aulds are keen members of the Henry Doubleday Research Association, and their organic methods are reaping rewards: the garden is alive with birds and an ever-increasing population of bees and butterflies. Old-fashioned yellow azaleas scent the spring, wild orchids flourish under the fruit trees in the wild corner, and martagon lilies pop up in unexpected places. This is a tranquil place for both wildlife and visitors: a recently acquired paddock has meant the addition of pygmy goats, Jacob sheep, hens and two geese. *HDRA, Friend of Royal Botanic Garden, Edinburgh.*

rooms	3: 2 twins, each with separate bathroom; 1 single (let to same party only).
price	£70. Single £35.
meals	Dinner £20 (if staying min. 2 nights). Village pub 1 mile.
closed	November–February.
directions	B6357 or B6088 to Bonchester Bridge. Turn opp. pub (Horse & Hound). Beyond church 1st lane to right. Set back off road.

Map 9 Entry 146

In gorgeous, unspoilt border country this historic, Grade II-listed Georgian manse is handy for all points north and an easy drive away from Edinburgh. Sylvia is a thoughtful hostess and excellent cook: Aga-baked scones or gingerbread for tea, organic produce (whenever possible) for dinner, and a choice of good things such as kippers, proper porridge, corn fritters, compotes and homemade bread for breakfast. You eat by the big Victorian bay window overlooking the terrace in the cosy guest sitting room with a log fire. Sleep deeply in your very private rooms, simply and softly furnished, with good beds.

Wales

Rhydlewis House

Judith Russill
Rhydlewis House,
Rhydlewis,
Llandysul,
Ceredigion SA44 5PE

tel   01239 851748
fax   01239 851748
email   judithrussill@aol.com
web   www.rhydlewis-house.co.uk

An 18th-century house in a friendly village with a wealth
of nurseries — perfect for gardeners. This ex-drovers'
trading post stylishly mixes traditional with new: modern
furniture by students of John Makepeace, exposed stone
walls, rugs on polished wooden floors. The dining room
has quarry tiles, an inglenook and Welsh oak cottage-style
chairs. A sunny double room with checked fabrics
overlooks the garden; warm reds, oranges and creams are
the colours of the twin. Judith is a terrific cook who uses
mostly local produce (Welsh cheeses, an excellent smokery
in the village). Single visitors are particularly welcome.

rooms	3: 1 double, 1 twin; 1 double with separate bath.
price	From £50–£54. Singles £25–£27.
meals	Dinner £17. BYO.
closed	Christmas.
directions	North on A487. Right at north side of Sarnau, signed 'Rhydlewis'. T-junc. right to B4334. In Rhydlewis at sharp right bend, left. 40 yards on left.

Map 2 Entry 147

Judith can look out on her acre of garden with pride: the planting, apart from a few mature trees and some crocosmia, is entirely her own. There are several seats from which to admire the fruits of Judith's labours, and the garden, begun in the spring of 2000, has matured well. The upper level of two main areas of lawn has an arbour tucked into an angle of the old workshop building, from where you can gaze back up at the house. On the lower lawn white-flowering shrubs form a backdrop against a wall to the gravel garden; rest on a bench and admire the hot reds, oranges and yellows of crocosmia in the herbaceous border opposite. Walk through the honeysuckle arch and discover a wide mixture of flowering shrubs: evergreens (protection from the wind), weigela, berberis and hydrangeas for season-long colour, and an under-planting of primroses, violets and *Anemone blanda*. From yet another seat you can watch all the village comings and goings. No modern garden is complete without a deck and Judith's makes an ideal spot for tea or an evening drink; as you sip, admire her pots of hostas, fuchsias and begonias.

Broniwan

Carole & Allen Jacobs
Broniwan,
Rhydlewis,
Llandysul,
Ceredigion SA44 5PF

tel   01239 851261
fax   01239 851261
email   broniwan@btinternet.com
web   www.broniwan.com

Carole and Allen's committment to the environment and passionate interest in wildlife are what makes this garden special, and a Tir Gofal Educational Access farm surrounds it. Carole designed the formal parts around the house, extending and replanting the original beds. There's a small lawned area on the upper level bordered by deep beds of hydrangea, aquilegia, agapanthus and rosemary with a little wrought-iron fence covered in clematis at the front. The narrow pathways, built with bricks from an old pig-sty and with Victorian tiled edging, lead to a large shrub border of camellias and rhododendrons, bamboo, ceanothus, irises, broom and bright pieris; then more lawns and a rose bed. Further on is a border of eucalyptus trees and the fruit and vegetable garden. A mown path through the grasses meanders to the meadow; meticulous records are kept of all the animals, birds, wild flowers and trees. Broadleaf woodlands, waterside and wetland areas, hedgerow restoration and maintenance, parkland, pond areas and grassland meadows mean Broniwan is teeming with birds (including the elusive red kite), butterflies, rare wild flowers and even otters. Allen is happy to take guests on farm walks; Carole loves the garden and will chat easily about her plans.

rooms	2: 1 double; 1 double with separate bath.
price	From £60. Singles £30.
meals	Supper £11.50. Dinner £20. Packed lunch available.
closed	Rarely.
directions	From Aberaeron, A487 for 6 miles for Brynhoffnant. Left at B4334 to Rhydlewis; left at Post Office & shop, 1st lane on right, then 1st track on right.

The Jacob's follow an eco-friendly system of managing farm, animals, gardens and home. On the organic farm (accredited by the Soil Association), Aberdeen Angus cattle provide natural fertilizer for the fruit and vegetable garden, and footloose hens donate your breakfast egg. In the house the wood burner is fuelled by storm-felled trees, and only bio-degradable products are used.

Map 2 Entry 148

Carole and Allen have created a model organic farm, and it shows. They are happy, the cows are happy and the kitchen garden is the neatest in Wales. With huge warmth and a tray of Welsh cakes they invite you into their ivy-clad home, cosy and inviting with its warm natural colours and the odd vibrant flourish of local art. Another passion is literature (call to arrange a literary weekend). Tree-creepers, wrens and redstarts nest in the garden, there are views to the Preseli hills, the National Botanic Garden of Wales and Aberglasney are nearby, and the unspoilt coast is a ten-minute drive.

The Yat

Krystyna Zaremba
The Yat,
Glascwm,
Llandrindod Wells,
Powys LD1 5SE

tel   01982 570339
fax   01982 551032
email   krystyna.zaremba@ntlworld.com

Come for stunning scenery, a characterful household and an engaging hostess. The listed house, once the home of the wicked squire of Bevan, has hung on to ancient flags and beams; the feel, thanks to cultured, charming Krystyna, is of a Polish country house bright with music, books and bouncy dog. Bedrooms are quaint, bathrooms plain with special touches (white robes, good soaps) and there's space to roam: a sitting room, a conservatory, a snug library with games. At breakfast expect cooked Welsh at its best and three types of organic bread, yours to toast. Dinners sound equally scrumptious.

rooms	2: 1 double, 1 twin.
price	£60.
meals	Dinner, 3 courses, £25 (incl. glass of wine, coffee & biscuits).
closed	Rarely.
directions	Directions from Hundred House village: road to Glascwm, signed at crossroads; at next T-junc., left over hump-backed bridge; left at next junction; 1st house on right.

Map 2 Entry 149

In a supreme setting of rolling hills studded with sheep is the Yat: a listed house dating from the 15th century, with logs piled in the porch and swallows dipping in and out. The sloping terraces around the house are thought to date from Elizabethan times; the remains of flagstone paths can be detected still. Seventeen years ago Krystyna and Derek fell in love with these eight acres, where nature predominates and the only sounds you hear are birdsong and the whispering wind. The first thing they did was plant trees on the steep slopes to the sides. Now there are 1,000 – mostly deciduous, some coniferous – providing shelter for plants and a wonderful haven for wildlife. The ancient terraces were extended in the south-facing part of the garden, retained by ivy-straggled stone walls and reached by stone steps. The garden, an on-going project, is a mixture of formal and wild: of blackcurrant bushes and wild strawberry plants that have merrily self-seeded, of tiered organic vegetable gardens and topiary. Pass the overgrown pond down the lane to the ruins of a baptistry and a tiny patch of burial ground. Or sit by the fountain that trickles over the little cast-iron boy with swans, and hear the doves coo. There's a sense of timelessness to this place: in Krystyna's words, "a unity of mind, man and nature".

Birds in your garden

The decline in numbers of our native bird species is a worry, particularly of the migratory variety (54% of the 121 long-distance migratory birds have suffered plummeting numbers since the 1970s) while house sparrows have fallen in numbers by 60% over the last 30 years. The exact cause of this decline is a mystery, but climate change is thought to be a major culprit.

Yet many of the owners in this book have gardens that are bursting with birds. What's their secret? With a little bit of extra thought we can attract birds to our gardens that wouldn't otherwise come – so here's a month by month guide to help you.

January
When the weather is very cold, woodland birds like woodpeckers, fieldfares and redwings will boldly venture into urban gardens looking for berries or fruits to eat. Welcome them with well-stocked feeders, tables and scattered scraps. Fallen apples are a good food source still so leave them where they are and maybe add some sliced fruit that you might otherwise compost. Leave last year's vegetation, fallen leaves and twigs where they fall so that ground feeders can ferret through them for insects.

February
The days are starting to lengthen now and you'll notice an increase in birdsong. The males start to stake out their territory for mating and nesting. Keep stocking up the feeders, if there is snow on your lawn clear a little space for insect hunting and don't forget to check for ice forming on water supplies. Birds need a drink too!

March
A flurry of nest-building gets underway and you will see common birds like blackbirds, robins and wrens darting about with twigs and bits of plant. Why not help them out by leaving little nest presents near their feeders (bits of straw, hair from your hairbrush and dried moss are most welcome usually).

April
Tempting as it is to tidy up now spring is promised, the birds will be out looking for food to feed their young, so keep feeders well stocked with seeds and nuts and try to leave some undisturbed patches if you have enough space. Fledglings love the grubs and insects found in these places.

May
Spring has truly sprung now and swallows, swifts and martins arrive. Supplies of berries and nuts are naturally dwindling, but mild weather will generate a fresh food

supply of grubs and insects. If you live near woodland you might spot a flycatcher or a bullfinch attracted by the buds on your fruit trees.

June

Adult birds continue to collect food for fledglings until late into the evening. Exhausting work, so make sure the feeders and tables are well stocked for them. If you get aphids on your plants it's best to avoid spraying as this can kill ladybirds and other useful insects – a vital summer food source for baby birds.

July

The competition for food hots up in this month, and it often coincides with people going away and not replenishing a food supply for the garden birds. Remember to stock up before you go, or ask a neighbour to do it for you – your birds may be relying on you!

August

Don't forget much-needed drinking and bathing water when the weather is very dry. By mid-August swifts have already left for warmer climates, and swallows and martins will start to gather together – presumably they need longer to plan their journey.

September

Birds now start to prepare for the winter to come. Resident birds

Photo Russell Wilkinson

become quieter and are no longer fighting over territory. Encourage visitors by leaving seed heads on thistles, teasels and sunflowers. Don't tidy up too much!

October

Berries, seeds and nuts are in abundance now and the beady-eyed jay may be spotted looking for somewhere to hide his hazelnuts and acorns. Let your lawn grow a bit longer and avoid spraying it – insect-hunting birds will use it as an all-round feeder.

November

Birds will continue to feast on berries this month – fattening up for the cold weather. Song thrushes and blackbirds look for worms and fallen fruit, groups of finches can be a common sight on feeders.

December

The fiercely territorial robin will start to mark out his territory this month in preparation for next year's breeding. This is a good time for bird watching as the bare winter branches make it easier to spot them.

Garden organisations

You should find your hosts well-informed about gardens and nurseries in their areas. However, the details of the following organisations and publications may be of help when planning a trip. Publications are in italics.

The National Trust (NT)
Britain's premier conservation charity looks after the largest and most important collection of historic gardens and cultivated plants in the world. Over 200 gardens and landscape parks encompassing over 400 years of history are open to the public throughout England, Wales and Northern Ireland. They employ more than 450 skilled gardeners and thousands more volunteers.

The National Trust Gardens Handbook, and *The National Trust Handbook 2005*, listing all Trust properties open to the public, are available at £7.99 each from the Trust's own shops, good bookshops and from the National Trust.

PO Box 39, Warrington,
Cheshire WA5 7WD
Tel: 0870 458 4000
www.nationaltrust.org.uk
enquiries@thenationaltrust.org.uk

The National Trust for Scotland (NTS)
The conservation charity that protects and promotes Scotland's natural and cultural heritage for present and future generations to enjoy. *The National Trust for Scotland Guide 2005* features more than 128 properties in its care, and costs around £5.

Wemyss House, 28 Charlotte Square,
Edinburgh EH2 4ET
Tel: 0131 243 9300
Fax: 0131 243 9301
www.nts.org.uk
information@nts.org.uk

National Gardens Scheme (NGS)
The famous '*Yellow Book*'. A guide to over 3,500 gardens in England and Wales, the majority of which are not normally open to the public. Divided by county, this invaluable book briefly describes the gardens and lists the days on which they open for charity.

photo Billy Bolton

The National Gardens Scheme Charitable Trust, Hatchlands Park, East Clandon, Surrey GU4 7RT
Tel: 01483 211535
Fax: 01483 211537
www.ngs.org.uk
ngs@ngs.org.uk

Scotland's Gardens Scheme (SGS) Scotland's own *'Yellow Book'* features around 350 private gardens north of the border that are not normally open to the public but which open their gates for charity on certain dates. *Gardens of Scotland 2005* will be available from mid-February, and full details of the gardens will also appear on the web site.

42a Castle Street,
Edinburgh EH2 3BN
Tel: 0131 226 3714
www.gardensofscotland.org
sgsgardens@btconnect.com

The Royal Horticultural Society (RHS) Since its foundation in 1804, the Royal Horticultural Society has grown to be the UK's leading garden charity. It promotes gardens and good gardening practices through its inspirational flower shows, and over 1,000 lectures and demonstrations. Its four flagship gardens are Wisley in Surrey, Rosemoor in Devon, Hyde Hall in Essex, and Harlow Carr in North Yorkshire. The Society has also joined forces with over 120 partner gardens in the UK and Europe that offer free access to its members. Among the RHS's many publications, the following are very useful:

The RHS Garden Finder by Charles Quest-Ritson and *The RHS Plant Finder*, both published by Dorling Kindersley at £12.99.

80 Vincent Square,
London SW1P 2PE
Tel: 0845 260 5000
www.rhs.org.uk
info@rhs.org.uk

National Council for the Conservation of Plants and Gardens (NCCPG)
The NCCPG seeks to conserve, document, promote and make available Britain and Ireland's great

photo John Coe

biodiversity of garden plants for the benefit of horticulture, education and science. An independent charity, it has 40 local groups supporting its aims through their membership and their propagation and plant sales. These efforts, together with the dedication and enthusiasm of National Plant Collection™ Holders, enable the NCCPG to fulfil its mission to conserve the vast gene pool of plants cultivated within the British Isles. *The National Plant Collections Directory 2007* listing over 650 National Plant Collections will be available from March (£6.50 inc. p&tp).

The Stable Courtyard,
Wisley Gardens, Woking,
Surrey GU23 6QP
Tel: 01483 211465
Fax: 01483 212404
www.nccpg.com info@nccpg.org.uk

Henry Doubleday Research Association (HDRA)
The HDRA is Europe's largest organic membership organisation dedicated to researching and promoting organic gardening, farming and food. The Association has three organic display gardens open to the public, at Ryton near Coventry, Yalding near Maidstone in Kent, and Audley End near Saffron Walden in Suffolk. On two weekends a year, some HDRA members open their gardens to the public. For details, see the web site.

Ryton Organic Gardens,
Coventry CV8 3LG
Tel: 024 7630 3517
Fax: 024 7663 9229
www.hdra.org.uk
enquiry@hdra.org.uk

Hardy Plant Society (HPS)
The Hardy Plant Society was formed to foster interest in hardy herbaceous plants. With 12,000 members and over 40 groups in England, Scotland and Wales, the Society aims to provide information about the wealth of both well- and lesser-known plants, and to ensure that all worthy plants remain in cultivation and have the widest possible distribution. The Society's show garden at Pershore College in the Cotswolds is open 10am-4.30pm daily (entrance free). The HPS organises study days and residential weekends, and publishes

photo left Quentin Craven
photo right britainonview.com

an annual seed list offering over 2,500 varieties, many unobtainable commercially.

Pam Adams, The Administrator, Little Orchard, Great Comberton, Pershore, Worcestershire WR10 3DP
Tel: 01386 710317
Fax: 01386 710117
www.hardy-plant.org.uk
admin@hardy-plant.org.uk

Cottage Garden Society (CGS)
The CGS was founded in 1982 when many 'old-fashioned' plants were becoming unavailable commercially. Now there are 35 groups, and 9,000 members worldwide, and cottage garden flowers have become more

photo Tom Germain

readily available. The CGS continues to help its members find plants that are only produced in a few specialist nurseries, and gives them the opportunity to find 'treasures' through its annual Seed Exchange.

Clive Lane, Administrator, 'Brandon', Ravenshall, Betley, Cheshire CW3 9BH
Tel: 01270 820940
www.thecgs.org.uk
clive_lane_cgs@hotmail.com

Alpine Garden Society (AGS)
With 14,000 members, the AGS is one of the largest specialist garden societies in the world. Founded in 1929, it promotes interest in alpine and rock garden plants, including small plants and hardy perennials, many bulbs and ferns, hardy orchids, and dwarf trees and shrubs, encouraging their cultivation in rock gardens and conservation in the wild. The AGS has a show garden at Pershore, and organises worldwide tours to see plants in their natural habitats.

AGS Centre, Avon Bank, Pershore, Worcestershire WR10 3JP
Tel: 01386 554790
Fax: 01386 554801
www.alpinegardensociety.net
ags@alpinegardensociety.net

Herb Society
The UK's leading society for increasing the understanding,

use and appreciation of herbs and their benefits to health. It has its headquarters at the delightful and historic Sulgrave Manor, which dates from 1539, and was once the home of George Washington's ancestors. The Society has created two herb gardens there, one of which received an RHS Silver Medal award at Chelsea.

Sulgrave Manor, Sulgrave,
Nr Banbury, Oxfordshire OX17 2SD
Tel: 01295 768899
Fax: 01295 768069
www.herbsociety.co.uk
email@herbsociety.org.uk

Plantlife International
Britain's only membership charity dedicated exclusively to conserving all forms of plant life in its natural habitat.

14 Rollestone Street, Salisbury,
Wiltshire SP1 1DX
Tel: 01722 342730
Fax: 01722 329035
www.plantlife.org.uk
enquiries@plantlife.org.uk

Garden History Society
The Society's threefold aims are firstly to promote the study of the history of gardening, landscape gardening and horticulture; secondly to promote the protection and conservation of historic parks, gardens and designed landscapes,

and to advise on their restoration; and thirdly, to promote the creation of new parks, gardens and designed landscapes.

70 Cowcross Street,
London EC1M 6EJ
Tel: 020 7608 2409
Fax: 020 7490 2974
www.gardenhistorysociety.org
enquiries@gardenhistorysociety.org

The Association of Gardens Trusts
This national organisation represents the growing number of County Garden Trusts whose main aim is to assist in the protection,

photo www.paulgroom.com

conservation, restoration or creation of garden land in the UK for the education and enjoyment of the public.

70 Cowcross Street, London EC1M 6EJ Tel/fax: 020 7251 2610
www.gardenstrusts.org.uk
agt@gardenstrusts.org.uk

The Historic Gardens Foundation
A non-profit-making organisation set up in 1995 to create links between everyone concerned with

the preservation, restoration and management of historic parks and gardens. Its Historic Gardens Review is published twice a year and offers lively and authoritative coverage of historic gardens worldwide. Members also receive three newsletters annually.

34 River Court, Upper Ground, London SE1 9PE
Tel: 020 7633 9165
Fax: 020 7401 7072
www.historicgardens.org
office@historicgardens.org

Further visiting

Museum of Garden History
The world's first Museum of Garden History was founded in 1977 at the restored church of St Mary-at-Lambeth next to Lambeth Palace, the London residence of the Archbishop of Canterbury, just across the Thames from the Houses of Parliament. The Museum's unique collection tells the story of the history of gardening and the work of celebrated gardeners. Special focus is given to the Tradescant family who were gardeners to Charles I and Charles II. Plants first introduced to Britain by the Tradescants in the 17th century feature in the Museum's garden, as does the Tradescant family tomb. Open daily 10.30am-5pm, but closed for two weeks over Christmas

Lambeth Palace Road,
London SE1 7LB
Tel: 020 7401 8865
Fax. 020 7401 8869
www.museumgardenhistory.org
info@museumgardenhistory.org

Border Lines
Border Lines takes select groups
to outstanding private gardens in
the UK, including many that are not
open to the general public. Three
gardens are visited on each day

tour, and the party is shown around
by the owner, designer or head
gardener. Refreshments include a
two course lunch with wine, and
there is also an opportunity to buy
plants. A gorgeous day out.

Cary Goode, Rhodds Farm,
Lyonshall, Herefordshire HR5 3LW
Tel: 01544 340120
Fax: 01544 340129
www.border-lines.co.uk
info@border-lines.co.uk

photo Russell Wilkinson

Garden fashion – a brief history

Out with the fence and in with the ha-ha – so-named because the ditch that allows a "through-view... makes one cry 'Ah! Ah!'" In the 18th century the English landscape garden – the clumps of trees, the meandering paths, the temples, grottos, lakes and hills (seemingly so random yet so carefully composed) came to the fore. Horace Walpole championed the new romantics, William Kent, Capability Brown and Humphrey Repton, "who leaped the fence and saw that all nature was a garden". The new irregularity was seen as the direct result of admirable British liberalism while scorn was poured on the illiberal French. Versailles' gardens, trumpeted Walpole, were "the gardens of a great child". Le jardin anglais became all the rage.

The fashion for landscape among the landowning classes reached its pinnacle in the early 19th century. And in the process most of the elaborate, early 17th-century gardens of England (though not of more conservative Italy and France) were swept away.

Little by little the characteristics of the traditional garden have given way to a modern eclecticism, while increased accessibility of unusual plants has led to new takes on old fashions. A flood of rhododendron introductions began in the 19th century when botanists started foraging in the Himalayas; willows followed from Japan and roses from China. Today's gardens are an anthology of garden styles, from ornamental to wild. At the same time the fascination with plantmanship has resulted in a flowering of plant nurseries and an interest in 'water-wise' exotics.

Fashions come and go, from the rock garden craze of the Thirties to the Percy Thrower 'colour my garden' approach of the Sixties to our modern penchant for succulents like aeoniums... while 'wild' drifts of alliums and grasses are the very essence of garden chic.

Jo Boissevain

photo left Roberto Caucino; Dreamstime.com
photo right John Coe

Garden books

Vita Sackville-West's Garden Book
(Michael Joseph, 1968)
A year in Vita's garden at Sissinghurst in Kent. On daffodils: "If you want exhibition blooms, you will plant them in bare beds; but if you want a drift looking right and happy, you will fling a handful over a stretch of grass and plant them where they fall and roll." A small book rich in garden tips generously shared.

Henry Mitchell on Gardening
(First Mariner Books, 1999)
Witty essayist and columnist on The Washington Post in the seventies, Mitchell was one of the few garden writers to admit that misery is a major operating principle in the life of the

gardener... which is "one of unexpected failures and sorrows, somewhat redeemed by unexpected and utterly accidental triumphs."

Green Thoughts: A Writer in the Garden by Eleanor Perenyi
(Modern Library, 1981)
In essays that range in length from a paragraph to several pages, the writer (married to author E B White) is as enchanting and informative about worms in her Connecticut garden as she is about the horticultural exploration of the Spanish Conquistadors.

Pan Garden Plants Series: Roses
(Pan, 1988)
1,400 perfectly photographed roses, from damask mosses to floribundas, accompanied by descriptions of each rose's origin and parentage. Also in the series: *Shrubs*, *Bulbs*, *Perennials*, *Kitchen Garden Plants*, *Indoor Plants* and *Annuals*. A treat.

Dear Friend and Gardener
by Beth Chatto & Christopher Lloyd
(Frances Lincoln, 1998)
An engaging exchange of letters between Beth Chatto, who wrested her garden from wilderness in East Anglia, and the late Christopher Lloyd, whose Great Dixter remains a place of pilgrimage. It's all here, from battles with hailstorms in June to matted Biddy-Biddy, "so tiresome in your socks" in February.

The Plant Hunters
by Toby Musgrave, Chris Gardner
and Will Musgrave
(Ward Lock, 1999)
"Even in a century as eclectic as the
18th, with its full complement of
eccentrics and geniuses, there was
no one quite like Sir Joseph Banks".
(He discovered 7,000 new species,
gave Botany Bay its name and
created Kew.) Beautiful pictures
illustrate fascinating stories.

The Potting Shed Papers
by Charles Elliott
(Frances Lincoln, 2002)
In a crop of quotable, funny and
charming essays, the writer, an
American living and gardening on
the borders of Wales, casts a

perceptive eye over numerous
garden-related subjects, from his
fear of growing tree peonies to 'sex
and the single strawberry' (modern
strawberries are hermaphrodite).

*The HDRA Encyclopaedia of Organic
Gardening*
(Dorling Kindersley, 2005)
Easy but informative, pitched at
serious gardeners without alarming
the novice. The photography and
design are all you'd expect of DK,
there's an excellent chronological
A-Z of vegetable and salad crops
and a troubleshooting section of
common plant problems.

The Greenhouse Gardener
by Anne Swithinbank
(Frances Lincoln, 2006)
A beautiful and informative book on
growing flowers and vegetables
under glass, accompanied by big,
bold pictures.

The Great Vegetable Plot
by Sarah Raven
(BBC Books, 2006)
Vegetable gardening is on a roll!
This colourful manual places
the emphasis on old and new
cultivars including many lesser
known varieties that look and
taste stunning. Recipes scattered
throughout are the cherry on
the cake.

Jo Boissevain

Good gardens

We would like to have included all the gardens we know of in this section, and nurseries too, but we lack the space, so listed here is a selection of gardens from *The Good Gardens Guide*: their 2* gardens. If you want to make the most of any garden visits this is an invaluable guide, as is the NGS '*Yellow Book*' (www.ngs.org).

Buckinghamshire
Ascott
Wing, Leighton Buzzard
www.ascottestate.co.uk
The National Trust

The Manor House
Church Road, Stevington, Bedford
www.kathybrownsgarden.homestead.com
Kathy Brown

Cliveden
Taplow, Maidenhead
01628 605069
The National Trust

Stowe Landscape Gardens
Buckingham
01280 822850
The National Trust

Waddesdon Manor
Waddesdon, Aylesbury
www.waddesdon.org.uk
The National Trust

West Wycombe Park
West Wycombe
01628 488675
The National Trust

Cambridgeshire
Anglesey Abbey Gardens
Lode, Cambridge
01223 811200
The National Trust

Christ's College
St Andrew's Street, Cambridge
01223 334900

University Botanic Garden
Cambridge
01223 336265
University of Cambridge

Cheshire
Ness Botanic Gardens
Ness, Wirral
www.merseyworld.com/nessgardens

Tatton Park
Knutsford   01625 534400
Cheshire County Council
The National Trust

photo Julia Richardson

Cornwall
Caerhays Castle Garden
Caerhays, St Austell
www.caerhays.co.uk
Mr F J Williams

Chyverton
Zelah, Truro
01872 540324
Mr N Holman

Heligan
St Austell
www.heligan.com
The Lost Gardens of Heligan

Trebah
Falmouth
www.trebah-garden.co.uk
Mr & Mrs J A Hibbert
Trebah Garden Trust

Tresco Abbey
Tresco, Isles of Scilly
01720 424105
Mr R A Dorrien-Smith

Trewithen
Truro   01726 883647
Mr & Mrs A M J Galsworthy

Cumbria
Holker Hall
Cark-in-Cartmel, Grange-over-Sands
www.holker-hall.co.uk
Lord & Lady Cavendish

Levens Hall
Kendal

www.levenshall.co.uk
Mr C H Bagot

Derbyshire
Chatsworth
Bakewell
www.chatsworth.org
The Duke & Duchess of Devonshire

Devon
Castle Drogo
Drewsteignton
01647 433306
The National Trust

Knightshayes
Bolham, Tiverton
01884 254665
The National Trust

Good gardens

Marwood Hill
Marwood, Barnstaple
01271 342528
Dr J A Smart

RHS Garden Rosemoor
Great Torrington
01805 624067
The Royal Horticultural Society

Dorset
Abbotsbury Sub-Tropical Gardens
Abbotsbury, Weymouth
www.abbotsbury-tourism.co.uk
Ilchester Estates

Cranborne Manor Garden
Cranborne, Wimborne, Minster
www.cranborne.co.uk
Viscount & Viscountess Cranborne

photo britainonview.com

Forde Abbey
Chard, Somerset
www.fordeabbey.co.uk
Mr M Roper

Mapperton
Beaminster
www.mapperton.com
The Earl & Countess of Sandwich

Essex
The Beth Chatto Gardens
Elmstead Market, Colchester
www.bethchatto.co.uk
Mrs Beth Chatto

Gloucestershire
Barnsley House
Barnsley, Nr Cirencester
www.opengarden.co.uk
Mr & Mrs Charles Verey

Hidcote Manor Garden
Hidcote Bartrim, Chipping Camden
01386 438333 The National Trust

Kiftsgate Court
Chipping Camden
www.kiftsgate.co.uk
Mr & Mrs J G Chambers
The National Arboretum

Westonbirt
Westonbirt, Tetbury 01666 880220
The Forestry Commission

Sezincote
Moreton-in-Marsh
Mr & Mrs D Peake

Hampshire and the Isle of Wight
Exbury Gardens
Exbury, Southampton
www.exbury.co.uk
Mr E L de Rothschild

Mottisfont Abbey Garden
Mottisfont, Romsey
01794 340757
The National Trust

The Sir Harold Hillier Gardens &
Arboretum
Jermyns Lane, Ampfield, Romsey
www.hillier.hants.gov.uk
Hampshire County Council

West Green House Garden
West Green, Hartley
Wintney, Hook
01252 844611
Miss Marylyn Abbott

Hertfordshire
Benington Lordship
Benington, Stevenage
www.beningtonlordship.co.uk
Mr & Mrs C H A Bott

Hatfield House, Park & Gardens
Hatfield
www.hatfield-house.co.uk
The Marquess of Salisbury

Kent
Goodnestone Park
Goodnestone, Nr Wingham,
Canterbury 01304 840107
Lady FitzWalter

photo britainonview.com

Hever Castle & Gardens
Hever, Edenbridge
www.hevercastle.co.uk
Broadlands Properties Ltd

Sissinghurst Castle Garden
Sissinghurst, Cranbrook
01580 710701
The National Trust

Lancashire
Gresgarth Hall
Caton
www.arabellalennoxboyd.com
Sir Mark & Lady Lennox-Boyd

London area
Chiswick House
Burlington Lane, Chiswick, London
020 8995 0508
London Borough of Hounslow &
English Heritage

Good gardens

Hampton Court Palace
East Molesey, Surrey
www.hrp.org.uk
Historic Royal Palaces Trust

Royal Botanic Gardens
Kew, Richmond, Surrey
www.kew.org
Trustees

Norfolk
East Ruston Old Vicarage
East Ruston, Norwich
www.e-ruston-oldvicaragegardens.co.uk
Graham Robeson & Alan Gray

Northamptonshire
Coton Manor Gardens
Guilsborough, Northampton
www.cotonmanor.co.uk
Mr & Mrs Ian Pasley-Tyler

Cottesbrooke Hall
Cottesbrooke, Northampton
www.cottesbrookehall.co.uk
Capt & Mrs J Macdonald-Buchanan

Northumberland
Belsay Hall, Castle & Gardens
Belsay, Newcastle-upon-Tyne
01661 881636
English Heritage

Oxfordshire
Blenheim Palace
Woodstock, Oxford
01993 811091
The Duke of Marlborough

Oxford Botanic Garden
Rose Lane, Oxford
01865 286690
University of Oxford

Rousham House
Nr Steeple Aston, Bicester
www.rousham.org
Charles Cottrell-Dormer

Westwell Manor
Burford OX18 4JT
Mr & Mrs T H Gibson

Shropshire
Hodnet Hall
Hodnet, Market Drayton
01630 685202
Mr A E H & The Hon Mrs Heber-Percy

Wollerton Old Hall
Wollerton, Hodnet, Market Drayton

photo britainonview.com

01630 685760
John & Lesley Jenkins

Somerset
Cothay Manor
Greenham, Wellington
01823 672283
Mr & Mrs Alastair Robb

Greencombe
Porlock
01643 862363
Greencombe Garden Trust

Hadspen Garden & Nursery
Castle Cary
01749 813707
Mr N A Hobhouse & N & S Pope

Staffordshire
Biddulph Grange Garden
Grange Road, Biddulph,
Stoke-on-Trent
01782 517999
The National Trust

Suffolk
Helmingham Hall Gardens
Stowmarket
www.helmingham.com
Lord Tollemache

Somerleyton Hall & Gardens
Somerleyton, Lowestoft
www.somerleyton.co.uk
Lord & Lady Somerleyton

Surrey
Painshill Landscape Garden

Portsmouth Road, Cobham
www.painshill.co.uk
Painshill Park Trust

RHS Garden Wisley
Wisley, Woking
www.rhs.org.uk
Royal Horticultural Society

The Savill Garden
(Windsor Great Park)
Wick Lane, Englefield Green
01753 847518
Crown Estate Commissioners

Sutton Place
Guildford
01483 504455
Sutton Place Foundation

Good gardens

Nymans
Handcross, Haywards Heath
01444 400321
The National Trust

Wakehurst Place Garden &
Millennium Seed Bank
Ardingly, Haywards Heath
www.kew.org
The Royal Botanic Gardens, Kew

Wiltshire
Iford Manor
Bradford-on-Avon 01225 863146
Mrs Cartwright-Hignett

Stourhead
Stourton, Warminster
www.nationaltrust.org.uk

The Valley Gardens
(Windsor Great Park)
Wick Road, Englefield Green
01753 860222
Crown Estate Commissioners

Yorkshire
Castle Howard
York
www.castlehoward.co.uk
Castle Howard Estates Ltd

Sussex
Great Dixter
Dixter Road, Northiam, Rye
www.greatdixter.co.uk
Christopher Lloyd & Olivia Eller

Newby Hall & Gardens
Ripon 01423 322583
R Compton

Sheffield Park Garden
Sheffield Park
01825 790231
The National Trust

Studley Royal & Fountains Abbey
www.fountainsabbey.org,uk
The National Trust

West Sussex
Leonardslee Gardens
Lower Beeding, Horsham
www.leonardslee.com
The Loder family

Scotland
Aberdeenshire
Crathes Castle Garden
Banchory, 01330 844525
The National Trust for Scotland.

photo britainonview.com

Angus
House of Pitmuies
Guthrie, By Forfar,
01241 828245
Mrs Farquhar Ogilvie

Argyll & Bute
Arduaine Garden
Oban   01852 200366
The National Trust for Scotland

Benmore Botanic Garden
Dunoon, Argyll   01369 706261
Royal Botanic Garden Edinburgh

Crarae Garden
Minard, Inveraray,
01546 886614/886388
Crarae Gardens Charitable Trust

Mount Stuart
Rothesay, Isle of Bute,
01700 503877
Mount Stuart Trust

Ayrshire
Culzean Castle & Country Park
Maybole
01655 884400
The National Trust for Scotland

Dumfries & Galloway
Castle Kennedy & Lochinch Gardens
Stranraer, Wigtownshire
01776 702024
The Earl & Countess of Stair

Logan Botanic Garden
Port Logan, Stranraer, Wigtownshire

photo Tom Germain

www.nbge.org.uk
Royal Botanic Garden Edinburgh

Edinburgh
Royal Botanic Garden Edinburgh
Inverleith Row
0131 552 7171

Glasgow
Inverewe Garden
Poolewe, Ross & Cromarty
01445 781200
The National Trust for Scotland

Lanarkshire
Little Sparta
Dunsyre, Lanark,
South Lanarkshire
Dr Ian Hamilton Finlay

Perth & Kinross
Drummond Castle Gardens
Muthill, Crieff
01764 681257
Grimsthorpe & Drummond Castle
Trust Ltd

Good gardens

Scottish Borders
Manderston
Duns, Scottish Borders
www.manderston.co.uk
Lord Palmer

Wales
Conwy
Bodnant Garden
Tal-y-Cafn, Colwyn Bay
www.oxalis.co.uk/bodnant
The National Trust

Powys
Powis Castle & Garden
Welshpool 01938 554338
The National Trust

Ireland
Co. Down
Mount Stewart
Greyabbey, Newtownards
028 4278 8387
The National Trust

Rowallane
Saintfield, Ballynahinch
028 9751 0131
The National Trust

Dublin
Dillon Garden
45 Sandford Road, Ranelagh
Dublin 6
Helen & Val Dillon

Co. Waterford
Mount Congreve
Kilmeaden 51 384115
Mr Ambrose Congreve

Co. Wicklow
Mount Usher
Ashford 404 40116/40205

France
Normandy
Château de Brécy
14480 St Gabriel-Brecy 231 801148

Château de Canon
14270 Mezidon 231 200507

Parc Floral des Moutiers
76119 Varengeille-sur-Mer
235 040233

Le Vasterival
76119 Ste-Marguerite-sur-Mer
235 851205

photo left Julia Richardson
photo right britainonview.com

2007 is a special year in the history of *The Good Gardens Guide*, which has been published annually since 1990. For the first time, it is lavishly illustrated with full-colour photographs and maps, and thanks to generous sponsorship from Saga Insurance Ltd, is also linked to a dedicated website, giving garden lovers another outlet to browse for places to target as they plan their excursions.

Over 1,250 gardens and public spaces are described by an independent team of dedicated enthusiasts, and the entries include all the up-to-date information needed for a successful visit. This year there are 60 outstanding gardens – historic and contemporary, rural and modern – making their first appearance in the Guide, plus an indispensable listing of nurseries where plants for sale may be seen growing in attractive adjoining gardens.

'*The most consistently reliable guide there is*' Tim Richardson
'*You can never go wrong by buying the latest edition*' Stephen Anderton
'*The classic yearly*' Robin Lane Fox

Published by Frances Lincoln Ltd
4 Torriano Mews, Torriano Avenue, London NW5 2RZ
www.franceslincoln.com
ISBN 978-0-71122-697-5

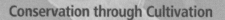

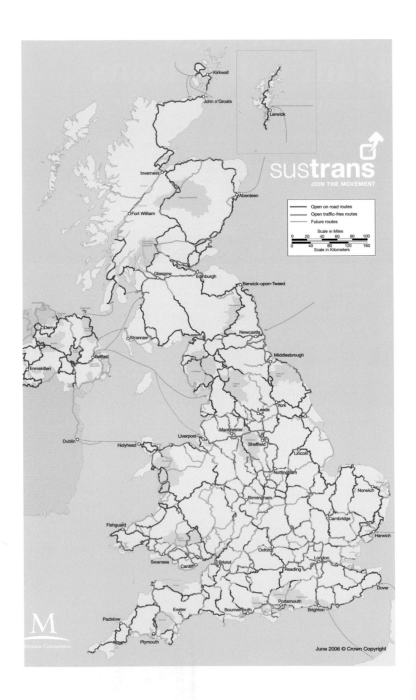

Houses near the National Cycle Network

We have teamed up with Sustrans this year; their flagship project, the National Cycle Network, has over 0,000 miles of safe and attractive cycle and walking routes around the UK. The map shows the routes in red; cross-reference to our maps at the front of the book to plan your trip. We have listed the B&Bs within two miles of the Network so you could plan an entire trip cycling your way between our special places.

Sustrans is a charity working on practical projects to encourage people to walk, cycle and use public transport, in order to reduce motor traffic and its adverse effects. In 2003, the Network carried 126 million trips by cyclists, walkers and other users including people with wheelchairs or pushchairs.

Contacts

For more information on the National Cycle Network and Sustrans and a copy of their free information pack, please call 0845 113 0065 or fax 0117 915 0124. Their user-friendly web site www.sustrans.org.uk allows you to search by town or postcode to find the nearest route to your B&B. They can also help you choose where to visit and plan your journey by train, ferry or bike.
Do email the Sustrans team at info@sustrans.org.uk

Photo David Hughes, Dreamstime.com

These Special Places are within two miles of the National Cycle Network.

Fine Breakfast scheme

By accepting their pledge, we are relying on owners' integrity and honesty to keep to the points listed below. It's not a perfect scheme but the message is right – that it is important to choose food carefully and support local economies. Over 100 owners have signed the pledge. Please understand that those who have not signed the pledge have done so for a variety of reasons and this does not mean they do not provide delicious breakfasts too.

Fine Breakfast Scheme – Pledge

1. I promise always to serve breakfasts of only the best available ingredients – whether organic or locally sourced.

2. Any certified organic ingredients will be named as such. (Note that the word 'organic' is a legal term. Any uncertified 'organic' ingredients cannot be described as organic.) Where there is a choice of organic certifier I will prefer the Soil Association if possible, recognising that their standards are generally the most demanding.

3. All other ingredients will be, whenever reasonably possible, sourced locally from people and institutions that I know personally and have good reason to believe provide food of the best quality.

4. Where I have grown food myself, I will say so.

5. I will do my best to avoid shopping in supermarkets if good alternatives exist within a reasonable distance.

6. I will display the Fine Breakfast cards in the breakfast room or, if I prefer, in the bedrooms. (We accept that some of you may not want to use the cards.)

7. I know that the scheme is an imperfect instrument but accept its principles.

Wheelchair accessible
Full and approved
wheelchair facilities

Limited mobility
Need a ground-floor
bedroom and bathroom?

All day
You can stay all day at
these places if you wish

Budget
You have a double room for
£70 or under

No car?
This property is within 10 miles of a coach/train station and the owner can arrange collection

Singles
There is a single room OR a double room is charged at half rate, or less

Quick reference indices

Cuttings
You can buy cuttings from the owner

Horse
Stabling for guests' horses

The Trust team

A couple of years ago Alastair set up a company charitable fund and asked volunteers among his staff to distribute the money. The Trust Team was born. Our brief is to avoid 'sticking-plaster' charities and look to the long-term, with at least half of the money going to local projects. We debate and wrangle, but are united in enthusiasm for the charities we've chosen to support, and we have a new goal: to match the company's donation through our own fundraising. Like many of our owners, we want to help others and be a part of our community.

We hope to build genuine, long-term relationships with the charities we support. At present we are working with:

Hartcliffe Health and Environmental Action Group, Bristol
www.sustainweb.org/sauce/resources_case_hart.asp
HHEAG runs allotments where local people learn to grow and cook their own vegetables. Their market gardens supply their co-operative store – providing local people with fresh, organic food at low prices.

Kingsweston School, Bristol, and Muakwe village, Cameroon
Kingsweston has been working to improve the school in Muakwe village and has formed close links with the community. Our recent charity gig raised money to provide solar panels for the local teacher training college.

Salt of the Earth (SCAD) www.salt-of-the-earth.org.uk
SCAD work in southern India to improve the living standards and autonomy of the very poorest local communities. A new tree-planting scheme will be part of our carbon offsetting and provide local job opportunities.

Tibet Eyecare Programme tibet.volcanostudio.com or www.rokpauk.org
High altitude, bright sunlight and widespread poverty cause visual problems for many Tibetans – usually solved by a pair of spectacles. The ROKPA project has helped to provide free medical, optical and dental care to the poor.

Cardiostart www.cardiostart.org
Cardiostart send cardiac surgeons, nurses, equipment and supplies to developing countries. They visit a place several times, training local people and building up equipment until their support is no longer needed.

Giving money is satisfying, but we also realise that we are in a brilliant position to raise awareness through our books. On the opposite page are a few UK projects we've chosen.

Kate Shepherd & Allys Williams
On behalf of the Trust Team (email: trust@sawdays.co.uk)

Special UK charities

Gardens can be about more than just beauty – education, repose and healing are important too

With that in mind, we approached the owners in *British Bed & Breakfast for Garden Lovers* looking for garden projects we could promote and support. Everyone who wrote to us was passionate about their chosen cause. We've selected just a few schemes: ones that we believe really make a difference to individuals and the local community. We hope you like our choices.

"Seed to Sheep": Interactive gardens at Richmondshire Museum

Suggested by Austin Lynch & Tim Culkin from Millgate House in Yorkshire, entry 132

Sally Reckert is creating two gardens to teach children, teenagers and adults about the agricultural and horticultural history of Swaledale. She aims to get people involved in hands-on organic gardening, encourage a sustainable approach to the land and bring a widely dispersed rural community together.

Bridewell Organic Gardens

Suggested by Helen Stevenson from Manor Farmhouse in Oxfordshire, entry 83

It was a derelict walled garden on the Wilcote House estate until a group of volunteers, promoting the organic principles of horticulture, took it on. The gardens, ornamental and productive, now provide a refreshing haven for visitors while those with mental health problems give the garden its life with their hard work and inspirational ideas. (www.bridewellorganicgardens.co.uk)

Gardening for the Disabled Trust

Suggested by Richard & Patricia Stileman from Boyton Court in Kent, entry 60

The trust supplies grants to residential homes, hospices and individuals around the UK and, with the aid of volunteers, adapts gardens to meet the needs of the disabled. Soil is brought to a height that suits, and the correct tools are supplied so that, despite advancing age, illness or disability, gardeners may continue to enjoy their pastime. (www.gardeningfordisabledtrust.org.uk)

Beautiful as they were, our old offices leaked heat, used electricity to heat water and space, flooded whole rooms with light to illuminate one person, and were not ours to alter. We failed our eco-audit in spite of using recycled cooking oil in one car and gas in another, recycling everything we could and gently promoting 'greenery' in our travel books. (Our Fragile Earth series takes a harder line.)

After two eco-audits we leaped at the chance to buy some old barns closer to Bristol, to create our own eco-offices and start again. Our accountants thought we were mad and there was no time for proper budgeting. The back of every envelope bore the signs of frenzied calculations, and then I shook hands and went off on holiday.
Two years later we moved in.

As I write, swallows are nesting in our wood-pellet store, the fountain plays in the pond, the grasses bend

Photos above Quentin Craven

before a gentle breeze and the solar panels heat water too hot to touch. We have, to our delight, created an inspiring and serene place.

The roof was lifted to allow us to fix thick insulation panels beneath the tiles. More panels were fitted between the rafters and as a separate wall inside the old ones, and laid under the underfloor heating pipes. We are insulated for the Arctic, and almost totally air-tight. Ventilation is natural, and we open windows. An Austrian boiler sucks wood-pellets in from an outside store and slowly consumes them, cleanly and – of course – without using any fossil fuels. Rain-water is channelled to a 6,000-litre underground tank, filtered, and then flushes loos and fills basins. Sun-pipes funnel the daylight into dark corners and double-glazed Velux windows, most facing north, pour it into every office.

We built a small green oak barn between two old barns, and this has become the heart of the offices, warm, light and beautiful. Wood plays a major role: our simple oak desks were made by a local carpenter, my office floor is of oak, and there is oak panelling. Even the carpet tiles tell a story; they are made from the wool of Herdwick sheep from the Lake District.

Our electricity consumption is extraordinarily low. We set out not to flood the buildings with light, but to provide attractive, low background lighting and individual 'task' lights to be used only as needed. Materials, too, have been a focus: we used non-toxic paints and finishes.

Events blew our budgets apart, but we have a building of which we are proud and which has helped us win two national awards this year. Architects and designers are fascinated and we are all working with a renewed commitment. Best of all, we are now in a better position to encourage our owners and readers to take 'sustainability' more seriously.

I end by answering an important question: our office carbon emissions will be reduced by about 75%. We await our bills, but they will be low and, as time goes by, relatively lower – and lower. It has been worth every penny and every ounce of effort.

Alastair Sawday

Photo above Paul Groom
Photo below Tom Germain

Special Escapes

Cosy cottages • Sumptuous castles • City apartments
• Hilltop bothies • Tipis and more

A whole week self-catering in Britain with your friends or family is precious, and you dare not get it wrong. To whom do you turn for advice and who on earth do you trust when the web is awash with advice from strangers? We launched Special Escapes to satisfy an obvious need for impartial and trustworthy help – and that is what it provides. The criteria for inclusion are the same as for our books: we have to like the place and the owners. It has, quite simply, to be 'special'. The site, our first online-only publication, is featured on www.thegoodwebguide.com and is growing fast.

www.special-escapes.co.uk

Where on the web?

The World Wide Web is big – very big. So big, in fact, that it can be a fruitless search if you don't know where to find reliable, trustworthy, up-to-date information about fantastic places to stay in Europe, India, Morocco and beyond....

Fortunately, there's www.specialplacestostay.com, where you can dip into all of our guides, find special offers from owners, catch up on news about the series and tell us about the special places you've been to.

www.specialplacestostay.com

The Little Food Book   Edition 1, £6.99

By Craig Sams, Chairman of the Soil Association

An explosive account of the food we eat today. Never have we been at such risk – from our food. This book will help clarify what's at stake.

The Little Money Book   Edition 1, £6.99

By David Boyle, an associate of the New Economics Foundation

This pithy, wry little guide will tell you where money comes from, what it means, what it's doing to the planet and what we might be able to do about it.

www.fragile-earth.com

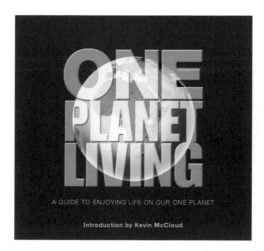

One Planet Living is a practical guide providing us with easy, affordable and attractive alternatives for achieving a higher quality of life while using our fair share of the planet's capacity. Two environmental organisations, BioRegional and WWF, have come together to promote a simple set of principles to make sustainable living achievable.

- Zero carbon – how to reduce our dependence on fossil fuels by supporting renewables
- Natural habitats and wildlife – how to reconnect with the natural world around us
- Local and sustainable food – temper our desire for strawberries in January and go for local, organic and seasonal instead
- Sustainable water – simple ways of cutting back on water consumption because every drop counts
- Sustainable transport – shifting our reliance on planes and car journeys and suggesting enjoyable alternatives
- Culture and heritage – how a sense of identity contributes towards our legacy
- Zero waste – reduce, repair, re-use, recycle and buy recycled
- Equity and fair trade – supporting local development and decent prices for all traders
- Sustainable materials – how buying recycled or sustainable products can protect and enhance our natural world
- Health and happiness – go for the simple things in life and feel better for it

This inspiring little book with an foreword by Kevin McCloud, takes each of these principles and shows the reader how to embrace and apply them to their everyday lives.

£4.99 – small change for big change

Order form

All these books are available in major bookshops or you may order them direct.
Post and packaging are FREE within the UK.

British Hotels, Inns & Other Places	£14.99
British Bed & Breakfast	£14.99
British Bed & Breakfast for Garden Lovers	£14.99
Croatia	£11.99
French Bed & Breakfast	£15.99
French Holiday Homes	£12.99
French Hotels, Châteaux & Other Places	£14.99
Greece	£11.99
Green Places to Stay	£13.99
India	£11.99
Ireland	£12.99
Italy	£14.99
London	£9.99
Morocco	£11.99
Mountains of Europe	£9.99
Paris Hotels	£10.99
Portugal	£10.99
Pubs & Inns of England & Wales	£13.99
Spain	£14.99
Turkey	£11.99
One Planet Living	**£4.99**
The Little Food Book	£6.99
The Little Money Book	£6.99
Six Days	£12.99

Please make cheques payable to Alastair Sawday Publishing   Total £

Please send cheques to: Alastair Sawday Publishing, The Old Farmyard, Yanley
Lane, Long Ashton, Bristol BS41 9LR. For credit card orders call 01275 395431
or order directly from our web site www.specialplacestostay.com

Title   First name   Surname

Address

Postcode   Tel

GBB4

If you do not wish to receive mail from other like-minded companies, please tick here n
If you would prefer not to receive information about special offers on our books, please tick here n

Report form

If you have any comments on entries in this guide, please let us have them.
If you have a favourite house, hotel, inn or other new discovery, please let us
know about it. You can return this form, email info@sawdays.co.uk, or visit
www.specialplacestostay.com and click on 'contact'.

Existing entry

Property name:_____

Entry number:_____ Date of visit: ___ / ___ / ___

New recommendation

Property name:_____

Address: _____

_____

Tel: _____

Your comments

What did you like (or dislike) about this place? Were the people friendly?
What was the location like? What sort of food did they serve?

_____

_____

_____

_____

_____

_____

_____

_____

Your details

Name: _____

Address: _____

Postcode: _____ Tel: _____

Index by surname

Index by surname

Index by place name

Index by place name

Photo Billy Bolton

[0, 2, 3]

(2) Horsleygate Hall

(1) Derbyshire

Robert & Margaret Ford
Horsleygate Hall,
Horsleygate Lane,
Holmesfield,
Derbyshire S18 7WD

tel   0114 289 0333
fax   0114 289 0333

(3) Margaret and Robert are dedicated, skilful, knowledgeable gardeners and their talents are abundantly clear from the moment you arrive. Margaret is a true plantsman who knows and loves her plants; Robert is the garden architect. He has added delightful touches, including a pergola fashioned from the iron pipes of the old greenhouse heating system, a breeze house thatched in Yorkshire heather and fences made from holly poles. Exploring the garden is enormous fun – there are so many surprises. The sloping site includes a woodland garden with gazebo, hot sun terrace, rockeries, pools, a fern area, a jungle garden, mixed borders and an exquisite ornamental kitchen garden. The Fords are keen on evergreen shrubs and have an interest in euphorbias. They have a particularly unusual collection of herbaceous perennials and are always on the lookout for fresh treasures to add to their collection. Quirky statuary peeps out at you from unusual places and all around the garden are strategically placed seats where you can soak up the varied displays. The overall theme is one of informality, with walls, terraces, paths and well-planted troughs hidden from each other. Lovely in spring, gorgeous in the full flower of summer, and good for autumn colour and winter interest, too. NGS

rooms	3: 1 double; 1 family room, 1 twin sharing bath.
price	£80–£70. Singles from £40.
meals	Pub/restaurant 1 mile.
closed	23 December–4 January.
directions	M1 exit 29; A617 to Chesterfield; B6051 to Millthorpe; Horsleygate Lane 1 mile on, on right.

Map 6 Entry 19

(4) Wake up to the sounds of hens, ponies and doves as they cluck, strut and coo in a charming old stableyard outside. The house was built in 1783 as a farmhouse and substantially extended in 1856; the garden was once home to the hounds of the local hunt. The house has a warm, timeless, harmonious feel, with worn kilims on stone flags, striped and floral wallpapers, deep sofas and pools of light. Breakfast is served in the old schoolroom and is a feast of organic eggs, honey, homemade jams and fruit from Margaret's superbly maintained kitchen garden. Glorious setting... and place. *Children over five welcome.*

(5) rooms	3: 1 double; 1 family room, 1 twin sharing bath.
(6) price	£60–£70. Singles from £40.
(7) meals	Pub/restaurant 1 mile.
(8) closed	23 December–4 January.
(9) directions	M1 exit 29; A617 to Chesterfield; B6051 to Millthorpe; Horsleygate Lane 1 mile on, on right.

(11)

(10) Map 6 Entry 19